BOUND

BOUND

Living in the Globalized World

Scott Sernau

KUMARIAN
PRESS

Bound: Living in the Globalized World

Published 2000 in the United States of America by Kumarian Press, Inc.,
1294 Blue Hills Avenue, Bloomfield, Connecticut 06002 USA.

Production and design by Nick Kosar, Richmond, Virginia.
The text of this book is set in Sabon 10/13.2.
Proofread by Jody El-Assadi.
Index by Robert Swanson.

Printed in Canada on acid-free paper by
Transcontinental Printing and Graphics, Inc.
Text printed with vegetable oil-based ink.

∞ The paper used in this publication meets the minimum requirements
of the American National Standard for Information Sciences—Permanence of
Paper for Printed Library Materials, ANSI Z39.48–1984.

Library of Congress Cataloging-in-Publication Data
Bound, living in the globalized world / Scott Sernau.
    p.   cm.
Includes bibliographical references and index.
    ISBN 1–56549–112–2 (pbk: alk. paper). — ISBN 1–56549–113–0 (cloth : alk.
paper)
    1. Globalization.   2. International relations and culture.   3. Civilization,
Modern—21st century. I. Title: Living in the globalized world. II. Title.
HM841 .S47 2000
303.48'2—dc21   00–042828

09 08 07 06 05   10 9 8 7 6 5 4 3 2

Second Printing 2005

Contents

To my students in
International Inequalities and Development
and in World Societies and Cultures
for thinking deeply and for caring deeply.

1

THE CALL OF THE WORLD

Origins of the Global System

> When the courts are decked in splendor
> weeds choke the fields
> and the granaries are bare.
> —Lao Tzu, sixth century B.C.

AT THE CLOSE OF THE twentieth century, few people who were not well versed in international economics could even identify the World Bank and the International Monetary Fund (IMF)—although they have been in existence since the end of World War II—let alone identify the recently created World Trade Organization (WTO). At the beginning of the twenty-first century, Seattle has been rocked by mass protests and violent confrontations over a meeting of the WTO. Weeks later, the streets of Washington, D.C., were filled with local police, the FBI, the Secret Service, and even the National Guard as protests and demonstrations disrupted meetings of the IMF and the World Bank. In both cities, delegates from around the world were shuttled through clouds of tear gas and showers of bottles into closed door meetings on global economic policy. Out in the streets, speeches by labor leaders were applauded by demonstrators in whale costumes, and young people with monikers like "Star-flower" joined hands in songs of protest with seventy-year-old self-proclaimed "raging grannies." What has happened to the world we thought we knew?

Globalization has become the descriptor of the turn of the century. At the turn of the last century, theorists looking at the world saw industrialization. Industry was changing the planet, the steam engine was changing the face of the planet, the steam train was bringing us together, and everyone had better get on board. Now those places first on board are experiencing "deindustrialization" and are described as post-industrial. By the middle of the twentieth century, theorists looking at the world saw "modernization." Products were modern, buildings were modern, people were modern, ideas were modern, and if they weren't, they needed to catch up. Modernization is no longer much in vogue either. A whole new school of thought describes everything from architecture to theory as "postmodern." The word of the hour is globalization. Production is global, styles are global, and we are called on to think globally. To economists, globalization refers to a particular pattern of transnational production and free trade. For most, however, the term has come to mean something more than that. It is the descriptor of our age—a time when the world is at our door. Just how new is this new state of affairs and what created it? Before stepping forward into this brave new world it may be helpful to take a quick glance back over our shoulder.

Robbing the Cradle of Civilization

Where did civilization begin? What made the modern world? My elementary school textbooks left me, and probably many others, with the impression that civilization began in Egypt, then moved west to Greece, then west again to Rome, then staggered through a few centuries of plague, darkness, and crusades, before following Richard the Lion-hearted back to England. From England it was transplanted to the United States, where it has been centered ever since. I supposed it was called Western Civilization because it kept moving westward until it finally reached California, where it either flourished or disintegrated, depending on one's point of view.

As superficial as that elementary school understanding may be, it has sparked debates (not always that much more sophisticated) across many U.S. campuses. My elementary school texts were steeped in an idea that goes back to eighteenth-century Europe. The idea is that the finest in civilized thought first emerged in ancient Greece and Rome, hence these are "classical" civilizations. These insights were lost for long while, hence "the Dark Ages," then Europe experienced a rebirth, "Renaissance," and in rediscovering the classics, Europe came out of the dark and experienced the "Enlightenment." Since this was a process ultimately fixed in Western Europe (where these thinkers resided), this was Western Civilization. As colonists took these ideas on to the United States, Canada, and Australia, they too became "Western." Scholars in this line of thought contend that if Americans are to understand their foundations they must steep themselves in the classics (Greece and Rome) and the great works of the European Renaissance and Enlightenment, as well as the British and French enlightenment thought that influenced the nation's founders, or often "founding fathers."

Challenges to this line of thought are many. Feminists wonder what happened to the founding mothers. Native American revisionists point to the influence of the League of the Iroquois as a model for American government more immediate than the Magna Carta. A particularly strong challenge has come from so-called Afrocentric scholars (see Asante 1987 for a strong statement of the idea; Early 1995 for a balanced critique). In his controversial *Black Athena*, Martin Bernal (1981) attempts to topple what he sees as the myth of Western Civilization by stressing the importance of Afro-Egyptian thought to the founding of Greece and Rome. A campus Afrocentric book sale includes posters of black Egyptian Pharaohs and pictures of Cleopatra looking more like Whitney Houston than Elizabeth Taylor (Cleopatra was, in fact, an olive-skinned Macedonian). Titles speak of Greek philosophy as "stolen" Egyptian philosophy. Spain is a backward western outpost until reached by the Moors, who are portrayed as black Africans (they were a multiethnic mix of Arabs and Berbers). Once Moorish civilization departs, Spain "grovels in darkness." Other accounts report new evidence of a host of global innovations having their roots in ancient African civilizations.

The debate between Afrocentric proponents and the proponents of Classicism and Western Civilization gets more interesting as new faces are added to the American campus. Middle Eastern students point out that the "dark ages" was a time of great flourishing in Baghdad and the Arab world, and suggest Europe's renaissance came from Islamic influences. Asian students point to the wealth of innovations first implemented in China. Anthropologists point to the genius of Native America, our "native roots" and the debt in foods, medicines, and more that we owe to "Indian givers" (Weatherford 1988).

The debate is invigorating in that it has added fresh voices and fresh ideas to a campus curriculum core that was fixed centuries ago. It is also at times a bit disconcerting as each partisan group brings out its own set of heroes and villains. Where is the real cradle of civilization and who are the impostors? Afrocentrism has delightfully reversed many of the older Eurocentric assumptions, but are the new contentions any more accurate? Why would any one place, east or west, north or south, be the source of all things bright and beautiful? Just exactly what is "stolen philosophy" in a world filled with exchanging ideas?

Those staking their reputations on this debate do so with such vigor because they realize that this is not just about history, but about our future. To understand what in the world is happening and where it is going, we must understand where it has been. To know where you stand it helps to know where you've been and where you've been headed. It also helps to have a sense of the big picture. I will contend throughout this book that this big picture does not lead to either Eurocentrism or Afrocentrism, but to a thorough-going geocentrism. Such a perspective forces us to relinquish a view of any one set of ideas and ideals, whether Western Civilization or American culture, as the ultimate savior or sinner; humanity itself is the problem and the solution.

The genius of humanity has always been born of the interchange of people and ideas. Many have been eager to claim their land or heritage as holding the cradle of great ideas, or of that elusive idea of civilization itself, but we have found that the world is filled with such cradles. Further, the most fertile marriages of ideas have been interracial and cross-cultural. Some have been love matches, others have looked more like capture and rape, yet it is from this passionate embrace of peoples that the world we know is born. The longing to explore, to meet, and to reach beyond is as old as the first human footprints striding out of Africa. What is new is the frequency and intensity of the embrace of peoples, and the way it regularly refashions the planet within our lifetimes.

Exchange: Highways of History

Innovation has been born foremost of the intense regional interchange among centers of power and between these centers and their hinterland, and secondly born of the seed of far-flung ideas carried by more intrepid travelers.

Long before the days of expanding empires and royal-sponsored expeditions people interacted over considerable distances. The North Trail along the Front Range of the Rocky Mountains extends for thousands of miles between Canada and Wyoming (Stark 1997). Some think it may have been part of a network that ultimately connected northern Canada and the great civilizations of ancient Mexico in the original North American Free Trade Zone. This prehistoric NAFTA was certainly not a superhighway of commerce, yet it may have formed a thread in a web that bound the continent. It carried refugees: The Navaho and the Apache, those quintessential southwestern tribes, have their origins in northern Canada. It carried innovations: the bow and arrow was invented by hunters in the forest country of Canada and gradually diffused all the way to Mexico, while growing corn diffused north from central Mexico all the way to New England. It carried products: shell jewelry from the Pacific has been found buried in the Great Plains, obsidian from Yellowstone has been unearthed in the cache of a Hopewell chieftain on the banks of the Ohio. It carried social interchange: the ball game of ancient Mexico became various forms of lacrosse, played in inter-village rivalries across North America. Far to the south, the one large domesticated animal of the Americas, the llama and its cousins, was used to haul cargos over the incredible slopes of the Andes. Villages isolated by colossal mountain peaks were soon linked in networks of trade that would become the great Inca empire.

The glimpses we get of ancient Europe, Asia, and Africa repeat this pattern. Archeologists were thrilled at the discovery of the Austrian "ice man," a man preserved in Alpine ice from the day he fell to his death over seven thousand years ago. What was this man doing with his straw-stuffed boots, striding over snowfields in the Austrian alps? He presumably was not on a ski trip. Evidence suggests he was carrying bronze-age goods between villages in the valleys of what is now Switzerland to the north and the Italian valleys to the south—a traveling salesman so motivated he was not going to be stopped even by the Alps themselves.

The creation of urban centers added new impetus to this interchange. In ancient Mesopotamia, gatherers harvested the wild grasses of the hill country, hunters sought the wild auroch, and fishers clustered along the river bottomlands. Over the course of centuries, out of the interchange of these growing populations came the domestication of the grasses (which we know as wheat, rye, barley, and oats), the taming of the beast we now know as cattle, and the harnessing of this now domestic ox to pull plows through the irrigated bottomlands that soon flourished in grains. The production was plentiful enough to support privileged classes who did not farm themselves, but clustered in growing cities with a taste for the finer things in life. To acquire both the prerogatives of power—fabrics and dyes for fine clothing and jewelry for adornment—and the means of maintaining power—such as metals for armaments—they looked ever further afield. The cities of Mesopotamia required a large hinterland of farmers, herders, and traders to bring them the best of their known world. This concentration of materials and human energy in turn created an explosion of innovation that moved far beyond their immediate region.

A similar pattern was followed on the opposite edge of the great Asian continent. As varieties of rice were cultivated in the plentiful water of southeastern China, a new civilization was born, one which in time would be even more populous and creative. In colder, drier northern China wheat was the preferred crop, and became the staple of yet another great society. North and south China would trade and interact for centuries before finally merging into a single dynasty, a society that is even today still divided by differences in dialect and custom. While China grew along the Yellow (Hwang Ho) and Yangtze Rivers, and Mesopotamia grew along the Tigris and Euphrates, elements of both centers found their way to the Indus valley, where a dynamic civilization incorporated elements of both in an explosion of creative energy.

To the southwest of Mesopotamia, across the desert and hill country of the Middle East, whose harsh expanses nonetheless bustled with herders, traders, nomads, and raiders, the fertile strip of the Nile attracted a larger, more settled population. Egyptian attempts to domesticate their wildlife, such as the zebra and the gazelle, met with limited success, but they soon borrowed the ox and the granary. The horse came with uninvited invaders. The Egyptian civilizations of the Nile combined the Mesopotamian innovations with those of their southern neighbors in the higher reaches of the Nile as far as the hills of Ethiopia, into new and fabulous forms. As better vessels were developed that could manage the unpredictable waters of the Mediterranean, this sea, whose name means "between the worlds," became a lake of commerce and interchange. Phoenician sailors traded and settled the varied coasts and islands, maybe even circling the African continent and beginning an exchange of cultures that continued for centuries. We remember the great cities who each for a period of centuries sat at the nexus of this Mediterranean trade: Athens, Alexandria, Carthage, Rome, Constantinople, Venice. Each was proud of its glorious achievements—some insufferably so, but from the broader lens of time and space, the great achievement was this semi-sheltered trading ground afforded by the Great Sea between the worlds: a Mediterranean cradle of culture and society.

The Greeks claimed they sprung from the Greek soil but linguists trace their origins to the great early movements of Indo-European people that spanned from Ireland to India. For a brief moment, Alexander the Great united the eastern half of this expanse, eager to spread Greek culture as he went. Yet this culture was already an amalgam of hundreds of European and Asian influences. One of the cities that bore his name, Alexandria, Egypt, flourished with a great library that collected this immense reserve of human learning, and museum-laboratories that built upon this learning with constant innovation. An Alexandrian librarian, Eratosthenes, used basic trigonometry to accurately measure the circumference of the world, while a female mathematician, Hypatia, laid the foundations of modern algebra. Were these people Greeks, Africans, Egyptians, Carthaginians, Phoenicians, or something else? In truth, it is hard to know because Alexandria flourished as a multiracial, multicultural nexus of innovation that burst with ideas from across the traveled world. The library came to be ignored by powerful and suspicious rulers, fell into decline, and was burned. The organizational genius had since shifted westward to Rome and Carthage. To modern geography, one was "European" and one was "African," but they both grew as they incorporated the ideas and the products of an interconnected Mediterranean world.

At the peak of its growth, Rome was heavily dependent on the granaries of north Africa from the regions of Carthage all the way to Egypt, still growing those Mesopotamian grains. The Romans encountered the Chinese empire as Chinese trade officials established links in the second century B.C. This link, the fabled Silk Road, was always tenuous, however, for the road traveled through the central Asian steppe country controlled by Persia and its successors, who played centuries-long roles as trading middlemen. The two widely separated agrarian civilizations, the Roman Mediterranean and the Chinese empire, had to be content with the handful of products and rumors of one another that were relayed across the vast reaches of open steppe country. Yet these "empty lands" were hardly empty. They were traversed by nomadic herding peoples who also created a link between these world empires (Weatherford 1994). When scattered across the steppe, the settled civilizations despised these people as the barbarians. These were the Tartars, from the Greek Tartarus, literally the people of Hell to their settled neighbors. When a powerful and persuasive tribal leader decided to have a word with his haughty farm-bound neighbors about these designations and organized these people on the move—as did Attila with his Huns or Genghis Khan with his Mongols—settled people in both East and West trembled. But with either their short-lived empires or with their centuries of quieter wandering between moments of blood and glory, the herders of the steppe linked East and West.

The Chinese, like their Western counterparts, were sure that they were at the center of the world with all the answers worth knowing. Their Mongol conquerors held no such pretensions—perhaps they had seen too much in their travels. Genghis Khan's grandson, Kublai, was more than willing to host that famous assemblage of traveling salesmen, Marco Polo and his uncles. The Polos could travel across great expanses in relative safety with passes provided by the Mongol emperor, and returned home with stories and ideas that would both anger and fascinate their Venetian countrymen. Some herders founded civilizations of their own. Inspired by Muhammad, nomadic Arabs founded an Islamic civilization that spread west across the southern Mediterranean, and east through the Persian hill country. They were later succeeded by the Turks, another herding people, originally pressed from central Asia. In fact, much of the history of Europe and Asia is the struggle between nomadic people of the dry center of the continent with their great herds and the settled farmers along its fringes.

The struggle between mounted herders and settled farmers continued through the centuries of what we have come to call the Middle Ages, until a Chinese innovation reached a divided and worn-torn Europe where it flourished: the mixing of gunpowder and the casting of cannon. With gunpowder, the Chinese could expel their Mongol conquerors. With refinements on gunpowder weapons, the Europeans were ready to become global conquerors.

Empire: Have Gun, Will Travel

The world of 1500 was divided into clusters of power linked only loosely by more intrepid travelers. China had built great ships to trade with, and dominate, the southwestern Pacific, but was more eager to build a cohesive land empire strong enough to resist any future invasions from the steppe country. India was a cluster of principalities in the south, but was dominated by Muslim rulers in the north—invaders from the steppe country who combined ancient Indian tradition with Islamic and central Asian organization, and created such monuments as the Taj Mahal. Africa was largely a village-based rather than a city-based network of cultures. A few grand kingdoms and sultanates held power over sub-Saharan regions, but were isolated from the Mediterranean by Saharan sands. Great caravans crossed the desert through trading centers such as Timbuktu, maintaining a constant but fragile link between the Mediterranean and the African interior.

The Americas held two great centers of power. While Romans watched for northern "barbarians," the great cities of the Valley of Mexico had fought with each other, and each in turn had fallen to northern invaders from the desert country, peoples hardened and desperate like their Asian steppe counterparts, sometimes with borrowed technology such as the bow and arrow. In 1500, the latest of these barbarian invaders, the Mexica, people we know as the Aztec, ruled an expansive empire. In South America, dominance of a long stretch of coast and highland had recently fallen to the people who would be called the Inca. The great Mayan cities of Central America had already succumbed to wars, both foreign and civil, and returned to fiercely independent rainforest villages, yet these still provided a link between more powerful neighbors north and south.

Western and central Europe in 1500 was united, though not for long, by Roman Catholic Christianity, and divided by geography and politics into a host of competing kingdoms, duchies and principalities, independent city-states, and contested hinterland. The old dream of a revitalized Roman empire was not enough to politically bind together this divided land. The only counterpart Marco Polo could offer to the great Chinese-Mongol emperor was the Pope, who held prestige, but was always dependent on friendly kings and princes to wield power. As a great land empire was not attainable, it was apparent to a growing number of the powerful that power must again come from control of the sea. Venice had grown rich controlling Mediterranean sea lanes and trading with wealthy Constantinople, but mighty Constantinople had fallen to the Turks, recast as Istanbul, and Venice was in decline, literally as well as figuratively sinking into the sea.

Spain had culturally flourished as Islamic invaders from across the Mediterranean had added their culture to this historic crossroads. Ferdinand of Aragon and Isabella of Castile were less than appreciative of their continuing contributions, however, and had eagerly pushed them out across the Mediterranean or into it. Finally in control of a semi-united Spain, they sought to establish their Christian kingdom, expelling all remaining Moslems and Jews. Yet trade was power, and Moslem Turks controlled the trade routes, so they listened eagerly to the ideas of an itinerant Genoan sailor who went by the name of Columbus. Columbus, a remarkably adept sailor and completely inept geographer, assured them by his calculations that he could get to China and the Spice Islands by sailing around a remarkably small world. Eratosthenes had measured the real circumference of the globe, but Ferdinand and Isabella did not have much of a classical education and so they financed a voyage.

A poor strip of rugged land that had maintained its independence from slowly united Spain was Portugal. Its monarch, Prince Henry, knew that the only way Portugal could gain power was to look to the sea, no longer the Mediterranean but now the open Atlantic. First their voyages took them to the Canary and Azores Islands, some of the first European colonies. They continued south, bypassing the Saharan caravan routes to coastal West Africa. Once around Africa's southern tip they had the prized access to the Indian Ocean.

These longer voyages and ventures into open ocean required ever bigger and better ships and better navigation. Empires that sought to control the seas had always faced a problem: how to fight effectively from aboard a ship. The ancient Greeks destroyed Persian fleets in close quarters with rams, the Romans defeated Carthage with hooks and boarding planks, the Constantinople-based Byzantine empire perfected incendiary "Greek fire" for short distances. Each method was limited to close quarters and was most effective in narrow confines. As European powers competed to build bigger and better cannon, they faced the problem of moving large numbers of heavy cannon through muddy fields and over bad roads. Yet the two extensions of power complemented one another perfectly. Large, stable ships could transport cannon, lots of them, and cannon could allow ship-board commanders to attack ports, coasts, and other vessels with great power. Larger ships could also carry horses and guns to extremely distant points. Gunboat diplomacy was born and unleashed on the world with a vengeance.

First to feel its effects were the Americas. The two great landmasses of the world—Eurasia-Africa, "the old world," and the Americas, "the new world" (terms obviously coined by Europeans and not native Americans)—had been largely separate realms since the glaciers of the last age retreated. Speculation has abounded about contacts with Phoenician, Chinese, or even West African sailors. If they existed, they were not enduring. Norse sailors reached the Canadian coast via Iceland and Greenland. They, however, arrived in a sense too early. They had good ships and steel weapons, but no horses and above all no guns. They faced a native population proficient in the use of the bow and gave up in despair. They had the navigational knowledge to establish contact, but not the force to establish control. As seekers of land rather than trade, they turned elsewhere.

Columbus arrived seeking spices and silks and found an exotic land filled with new products—in time new world cotton would be far more important than Chinese silk, and new world foods would change the diet of Europe far more than Indonesian spices. The Spanish sea of boundless opportunity was now no longer the Mediterranean but the Caribbean. The Spanish tentatively explored the mainland coast encountering, like their Norse predecessors, considerable local opposition, especially among the independent and battle-seasoned Maya. Yet the inhabitants of the lands between north and south America, "Mesoamerica," had two profound misfortunes.

One is that contact between peoples can spread disease as well as ideas and products. The deadliest weapon that the steppe people ever unleashed on Europe was not the Mongolian bow but the Bubonic plague. In this Europe's misfortune became its fortune in the New World. Eurasians had been in close contact with one another, and with rodents, ever since the Mesopotamians started growing and storing grain. The depredations of the diseases that went with this contact probably kept rising populations in check for many centuries. At the same time, the close proximity to animals that came with their domestication brought other diseases, most notably influenza and the "poxes." Chicken pox really is related to a disease of fowl, and the far deadlier smallpox was related to a disease of livestock known as "cow pox." Farmers, herders, and travelers in Europe, Asia, and to a certain extent Africa, had shared these diseases with one other for centuries, acquiring partial immunities by a process of deadly selection—the survivors were the ones most resistant. The Americas, in contrast, were much freer of infectious disease. A smaller land area with more dispersed people who were less in contact with rodents, livestock, and their fleas had fewer plagues—until the Europeans arrived. The native population was decimated, later to be replaced by European settlers and African laborers.

The other great disadvantage was that the Mesoamericans and South Americans were proficient workers of gold and silver and not of steel and lead. New world precious metals—scattered veins of gold and an incredible abundance of silver—turned every poor kid in Seville and Granada into a would-be explorer, adventurer, and conquistador. With horses covered in armor, swords of Toledo steel, and an array of firearms, accompanied by allies resentful of the still-new "barbarian" empires, and preceded by an army of plagues and poxes, the New World quickly fell to the old. What was often taught in elementary school as a story of discovery is really a story of contact and conquest, but also a story of exchange.

The native American empires were always on a precarious footing because they lacked a reliable food supply large enough to feed great cities. They had corn, which under their cultivation became one of the most resilient and adaptable plants anywhere in the world. They combined corn with beans, which together make a complete protein source for humans, and with many varieties of squash, which adds needed vitamins. In South America, they had the potato, another remarkable source of starch and vitamins. They were very well suited to feed a village, but not a city. They had no plows. The problem was not that they were not clever enough to invent one, but that they had no way to pull it. Likewise, it has been said that they never invented the wheel. In fact, they used wheels as symbols and toys, but had nothing to pull a wagon. Horses and camels first developed in the Americas but had long since fallen to extinction from changing climates and prehistoric hunters (probably human). The only beast of burden in South America was the lama, a member of the camel family, and like its old-world cousin, better suited to carrying than to pulling. In Mexico they had turkeys and small dogs. They understood a great deal about cultivation but no one was going to get a turkey to pull a plow.

With the Spanish came plow agriculture. They brought donkeys, mules, and oxen. They brought herd animals, sheep, and goats. And of course they brought the horse. This animal facilitated farming in Mexico while freeing other groups from the farm. Native farmers in the southwest and the fringes of the plains hunted buffalo when available, but depended on their gardens of corn, squash, and beans to survive. With the horse, they could now match the speed and range of the bison and again become primary hunters. This was not a step "back" as was sometimes suggested, for they were not "simple" hunters, but sophisticated herders of horses and, increasingly, raiders, traders, and warriors. The Apache, those northern hunters who had never much taken to bean farming, were the first to capture and tame the feral horses. Others soon envied, or feared, their new lifestyle and followed suit. An American plains culture flourished momentarily, before further European encounters would crush it.

While we are well schooled in how the Europeans changed America, we often know much less about the profound changes in Europe that came with American contacts. Most significant were the incredible plant resources. With fewer domestic animal resources, the Americans had been extraordinary cultivators of plants—more foods and medicines come from the plants of the new world than from the much larger land area of the old world. Corn, what most of the world calls maize, circled the globe as a hardy and drought and disease-resistant staple in Europe, Asia, and Africa. Potatoes remade whole societies in northern and eastern Europe. Producing far more calories per acre, withstanding harsh climates, and hidden underground when marauding armies swept over, they became the peasant's salvation. Haitians call their many potato varieties "the poor man's friend" and the poor of Ireland, Germany, Poland, and Russia all agree. American cotton, longer and more suited to mechanized cloth production, helped usher in the first phase of the European industrial revolution. American gold and silver flowed in to make money abundant enough to finance it all. The greatest exchange since the Ice Age utterly remade both "worlds."

Not all explorers came west. Once the Portuguese had turned the corner on the tip of Africa at the Cape of Good Hope, they could now envelop the Indian Ocean. Portuguese cannon-wielding ships quickly brushed aside the Egyptian fleet and Arab traders to dominate markets in Africa and India, and in time, the Indies and Japan. There are riches in exchange, and the well-poised middleman can claim the greatest portion in profits. Tiny Portugal could not dream of an old-style land empire that would encompass the millions of Africa and Asia, but they now had something better—a trade network, an economic empire. Local powers could enforce order in the interior and the Portuguese galleons could be left to maintain a profitable order on the seas.

Profits always bring rivalries, and the two Iberian powers, Spain and Portugal, now not only breathed down on one another on their common neck of the European continent, but met halfway around the globe in their race to encircle its markets. Spain had pushed across the Pacific expanses to the Philippines, and their ships plied three oceans in a trade that linked Madrid, Mexico, and Manila. To avoid what might have been the first world war between these two Roman Catholic European powers, the Pope simply divided the world. One half belonged to Spain, the other to Portugal. No one else need be consulted.

We can only imagine what the Chinese emperor thought of such vanity. We know what the newly Protestant northern Europeans thought. Undisputed power no longer came from the Pope but from the gun port. The tiny Netherlands, newly independent from Spanish masters and Spanish Catholicism, and busily building dikes to keep from sinking into the sea, had, like the tiny swamp of Venice before it, no option for power, prestige, and privilege but to turn to the sea. With slightly better ships and much better bankers, by the 1600s the Dutch came to dominate the seas and the trade routes. Only a few ports were needed to anchor their ships and a vast commercial empire: Cape Town in South Africa, Malacca in what became the Dutch East Indies, and later a few outposts in remote islands and coast lands such as Guyana, Aruba, and Manhattan. In time, the British built still better ships and still bigger banks, and by the 1800s the British empire came to eclipse all others.

This was not, however, exactly like the empires of old. The imperial idea was as old as the ancient empires of the Middle East, but the goal of the British was not to control the land but the terms of trade. British products needed markets and the homeland needed materials to make yet more. Ideally, exchange between the colony and any other rivals, most notably France, was to be curtailed. This required some delicacy: this policy too brazenly imposed in the American colonies led to a revolt, not surprisingly aided by the French. The British learned carefully from this experience, finding better ways to control the governments and the guns, and maintained an empire that endured through the second world war. The decades following World War II saw the dismantling of the old empires and the creation of a new world economic order, yet one with the centers of wealth and information still concentrated in the imperial centers and the former colonial world struggling to overcome persistent poverty.

Dynamics of a Global System

What is the key to the modern world? What made the West rich and the rest poor? The postwar years brought two competing explanations to these questions. Modernization theory—in fact not a single theory but a collection of ideas dominant in the capitalist West—contended we should blame traditionalism. In time worldwide industrial capitalism would bring modern attitudes (such as risk-taking, investment, and achievement orientation), modern technology, and modern institutions (educational, financial, and political). The road from traditionalism was long but once established these three would bring prosperity (Rostow 1960).

A counter argument, and in fact a pointed critique, emerged in Latin America (Prebisch 1950; Frank 1967; Cardoso and Faletto 1979) and became known as dependency theory. It contended we should blame colonial imperialism. Worldwide industrial capitalism in fact brings exploitation, domination (both political and economic), and distortion (both political and economic).

In his many critiques of industrial capitalism, Marx stressed internal domination and exploitation by a ruling capitalist class and a distortion of the labor process he termed alienation. A series of subsequent thinkers extended this approach to the international level. The British economist Hobson saw in the scramble to colonize Africa a grim capitalist determination for new markets and materials. This thinking was articulated in Russia by Lenin (1948) in his call for world revolution. It was not enough to decry the exploitation of the British worker by British capitalism; one must also understand the role of British capitalism in the impoverishment of the Indian worker. This focus on external forces laid the foundation for dependency thinking and much neo-Marxism.

The collection of ideas described under the rubric of dependency and neo-Marxism were most systematically incorporated into a single theory in the work of Immanuel Wallerstein (1974). Wallerstein's approach, termed world systems theory, is one of the most influential and comprehensive attempts to understand the modern world economy and its politics. Wallerstein contends that the world has been dominated by a series of world economies focused around earlier empires but that in the sixteenth century a true single world economy was created by European capitalist expansion. That world system has a core of wealthy, powerful countries who control the patterns and terms of trade, a semi-periphery of middlemen and intermediaries in the process, and a periphery of poor nations who bear the brunt of the brutal demands of global capitalism. Wallerstein contends this world system has had only three world masters since its founding, each standing at the "core of the core": the United Provinces (Netherlands), the United Kingdom (Great Britain), and the United States. The center of the core may shift, and some countries may move between periphery and semi-periphery, or core and semi-periphery, but the world system itself is extremely stable and enduring, and in fact can only be overturned by a worldwide socialist movement. The world system is too powerful for any single country to escape or change and the system can only be brought down as whole.

The world systems approach has generated an enormous amount of research and analysis. Within academic circles at least it is no longer the alternative approach but the dominant explanation of global inequalities. As an explanation of current global entanglements, however, it is lacking in several ways. First, while the focus is on the world system, the actors and the units of analysis are still individual nations: those of the core, periphery, and semi-periphery. Increasingly, these descriptors no longer follow national lines. In New York and Washington, one can walk from a political and economic core through semi-peripheries into the neighborhoods of a desperate periphery within an hour.

Second, Wallerstein focuses strongly on the uniqueness of the sixteenth century and its capitalism. A careful examination of the history, and prehistory, of our planet suggests more that we're merely playing a new verse in a very old song. Nothing we are experiencing is utterly new and without precedent, except for the unprecedented intensity and rapidity of the changes. In a three-volume study of civilization and capitalism, historian Fernand Braudel examines the emergence and expansion of European capitalism. Braudel is less insistent that the sixteenth century marked a distinctly new period in economic history, but rather "that capitalism has been potentially visible since the dawn of history, and that it has developed and perpetuated itself down the ages" (Braudel 1984, 620). Despite their differences, Wallerstein and Braudel, like Marx himself, provide powerful reminders of the role of the economic system—the means of production and exchange—in shaping the history of societies and the globe.

Others give less weight to capitalism as a fundamental explanation, rooting economic arguments in their broader social and environmental context. Gerhard Lenski (1966) proposes an ecological-evolutionary theory that focuses on the "socio-techno heritage" of societies. The changes in basic subsistence technology from hunter-gatherers to horticulturalists and herders, agrarian and maritime societies, and ultimately to industrial society create new potentials, demand new social organization, and create new concentrations of power. The broad vision of Lenski's approach is a powerful reminder to look beyond the struggles of our "recent" Western European dominated history to the very foundations of human society. Even Andre Gunder Frank, one of the founders of dependency thinking, has begun to look back not just to the five hundred years of European dominance but to five thousand years of empire building (Frank and Gills 1993). The roots of the modern world system, and miseries of underdevelopment, may have come with the first agrarian empires.

In his Pulitzer-prize winning account of the sweep of human experience, Jared Diamond (1997) steps back for the wide angle view of humans in their environment and suggests that ultimately the course of history is rooted in geography and environmental variation, although the exact results of this are hard to determine since they are mediated by complex historical struggles. Yet human ability, genius, and capability are evenly distributed among humanity (rejecting racist theories to the contrary), so variation in experience must be rooted in natural variation: differing climates, differing resources, differing natural options for domestication and production.

Marx is the real originator of the idea, if not the slogan, that "it's the economy, stupid." Marx's historical materialism contends that all political and social relations are rooted in the relations of production. Lenski stresses that the economy is rooted in the technology of subsistence (Marx called this the forces of production). Diamond contends that the technology of production is rooted in environmental possibilities afforded by geography.

Debates about the nature of the modern world center around three powerful forces:

1. *Capitalism* is the profit-driven system of private accumulation and reinvestment that drives the world economy. In this scenario, the fundamental shift is toward new ways of doing business centered around the acceptance of money and private profit. The stagnant monopolies of the national monarchies are broken, and a new burst of productive energy is unleashed. Capitalism eventually penetrates all world markets and societies, transforming them and bringing them, for better or worse, into the world economy.

2. *Industrialism* is the fundamental shift in the basis of society, founded on harnessing non-animal energy sources to drive productive machinery. In this scenario, the fundamental shift is the industrial revolution, beginning in Britain in the early 1700s. The subsequent diffusion of industrial production leads to the rise of industrial society with rapid population growth, urbanization, a growing industrial proletariat, and industrialized agriculture. Eventually the entire world enters the era of mass production and mass consumption.

3. *Imperialism* is the process of international domination and empire building. In this scenario, the key event is the rise of global imperialism based on military conquest and European firepower. Old trade systems are disrupted and replaced by one controlled by the great European powers, who become great by the very nature of this system, which allows for appropriation and control of the world's wealth. Imperialism proceeds in two great waves, the first beginning in the sixteenth century with the formation of the Spanish, Portuguese, British, French, Dutch, and Russian

empires. This is an older form of mercantile ("get the gold") imperialism. It is replaced in the nineteenth century by a new wave of industrial ("get the materials and markets") imperialism. To the list of old imperialists are added other newly industrial nations: Germany, Italy, Belgium, the United States, and Japan. The competition between these industrial powers eventually sparks the great world wars of the twentieth century.

The weight given to these three forces shifts in differing views of the making of the modern world. Modernization theory and current free market approaches have typically focused on the combination of capital and industry. The economic rationality and competitive efficiency of capitalism, coupled with the productive power of industrialism, made the rich nations rich, and still provides the best hope for poor nations. Dependency and world systems theories focus on the combination of capitalism and imperialism. The profit imperative of capitalism drives the capitalists to seek and capture ever larger resource bases and markets, destroying local economies, and creating a poor periphery in an ever more integrated world system.

The contending approaches each offer their set of clashing explanations on why the poor are poor. To the first camp, China is poor because traditional, inward-looking rulers failed to adopt new technologies and ways of doing business, holding all these ideas suspect, and keeping their nation in a state of suspended development while European innovation sped ahead. To the second camp, China was held hostage not so much by its own government as by a wolf-pack of militaristic nations—European as well as Japan and the United States—that demanded economic concessions and political acquiescence to gross exploitation.

Similarly, one finds two theories on why Latin America is poor. In scenario one, Latin America had the misfortune of belonging to the wrong empire. Unlike Canada and the United States, its culture and society was Spanish rather than British, dominated by agrarian rather than industrial organization and values, by a crown monopoly rather than capitalist commercial interests. In scenario two, Latin America had the misfortune of being "ripped off" twice: first by Spanish and Portuguese mercantilists, then by British and North American industrialists.

Why is Africa poor? One scenario points to poor climate and soil for agriculture, disease, drought, and environmental limitations coupled with a traditional village-based society that does not lend itself to national development. The second view points to the recent orgy of industrial imperialism that divided the continent and only began to relinquish its hold in the last few decades.

A more complete picture of global socioeconomic change comes from recognizing that these three elements are often intertwined and work in concert.

Capitalism provides the search for profit, growth, and efficiency. Industrialization provides the means of expanded production. Imperialism provides the raw materials and markets.

The rise of commerce and the rise of science in the fifteenth century in small European countries and city-states began a series of world-changing repercussions. The first result was the science of war, shifting from war horse to gun boat. The second result was the expansion of industry, first in Britain circa 1740 with textile mills, and by 1840 in France, the German states, and the United States. Together these allowed expanded global penetration on an unprecedented scale. The rise of the West is predicated on several "weddings." The wedding of science and commerce gives birth to technology. The wedding of science and war gives birth to a new military science. Finally, the wedding of war and commerce gives birth to new economic imperialism.

Achievements in science and commerce have been made in many times and places, but only Europe and China had the scale of civilization to provide a "critical mass" of innovation, as well as the continuity to sustain a chain reaction of innovation once under way. The question is then posed, Why Europe and not China? The answer may lie in the nature of empire.

All large, powerful societies have had to cope with the issues of centralization versus decentralization, unity versus diversity. How can local-level solidarity, ingenuity, and productivity be maintained under an umbrella of centralized control? Each society must confront an interplay between its power structure and its opportunity structure (see North 1981). Each economy—regardless of its form from simple redistribution to markets, to capitalism and socialism in their various forms—confronts the risk that emerging power structures will monopolize privilege by closing the opportunity structure (see Weber 1979 [1922]; Parkin 1979). This problem has plagued, and ultimately destroyed, each of the world's great empires.

There are advantages of empire: large economies of scale, broad integration, lowered transaction costs through common currency, law, procedure, governance, and so forth. There are also great costs to empire. There is the stagnation of over-centralization: a reduced number of organization forms and channels, the loss of parallel forms of organization, an elongated hierarchy and the "iron law of oligarchy" Michels (1967 [1911]). There are only certain ways to advance and these become dominated by insiders. Those on the inside claim more and more of the benefits while those on the outside become further marginalized and an elite core and a social periphery emerges. Impetus for growth comes from the top but this is diffused through a limited number of channels which do not reach all points. As economy and technology change, insiders fight to maintain their privileged position (since now this position may be their only resource), even at the expense of the growth of the overall system.

Power structure constricts opportunity structure, and the socioeconomic system stagnates. This describes many great empires and massive states. It is the China of the sixteenth century; it remains to be seen if it will describe China in the twenty-first century as well.

Three areas had the agriculture-friendly geography to maintain empires: East Asia, Southwest Asia, and Europe. Each had golden periods. But in Europe the early dominant empires were decentralized. The rise and fall of Rome and Constantinople gave Europe its common ideals: Greek learning and science and Roman language, law, and governance. But the power structures were the multiplexity of independent cities and duchies. These drew on common heritage, but followed independent local channels. Even as they consolidated they often did so as confederations or locally influenced unions: Swiss Confederation, German states, United Provinces, United Kingdom. Spain, France, and Britain each in turn attempted empire-building and foundered. The costs of these attempts may still be felt internationally, but each state, once stripped of its empire, has been reincorporated into the diverse amalgamation of Europe.

Europeans, clustered along a continent divided by a diversity of small mountain ranges, seas, and inlets, were never able to come together in a single empire (Diamond 1997). Many dreamed of recreating a Roman Empire that would stretch to the Baltic, but they never achieved it. That failure may have been their salvation. Instead of a single empire they had this multiplexity of broadly compatible cultures and economies under the banner of "Christendom," yet remained ever in competition with one another, always looking to gain the edge through practical innovation and through the possibilities of commerce on the ever nearby seas. China, built upon a vast plain with the great expanse of mountain plateau and desert to the west and the expanse of the Pacific to the east, was more isolated from the world beyond and more integrated within. The two great rivers founded two great civilizations, north and south (Chinese still distinguish between northerners and southerners in speech and manners), but once these were united into a single empire, the power structure became enormously centralized and remains that way to this day. The only empire that proved almost as enduring was the Russian, finally disintegrating in 1991—from stagnation, over-centralization, inefficiency, and stifled innovation. The events of 1991 were hailed as the demonstration of the failure of communism; they may have merely been a grand demonstration in the failure of empire.

States have prospered when forced to gain wealth through a combination of intensive production and expansive trade, and foundered when wealth could be extracted from tributaries. This implies that capitalism may not be first cousin to imperialism but at odds with it, at least in the long run. The great founding thinker of modern capitalism, Adam Smith, argued vigorously against the mercantilist school of thought that had guided the great empires. The global system that has replaced the arthritic old empires has far greater flexibility, yet continues the struggle between structures of opportunity and structures of power. It is based on three ancient foundations that have waxed and waned over time: curiosity, commerce, and desire for control. The global system is also based on three that continue to accelerate exponentially: population, technology, and the conquest of space.

Curiosity—the desire to know, experience, and understand far-flung elements of our world—and commerce—the desire to acquire the many possibilities of that world—are as ancient as the Old North Trail, the Camino Real, the Asian and African caravan routes, and as old as the Austrian Iceman. Yet they have fluctuated in intensity. Together they saw a great flourishing about 3000 B.C. in the "fertile crescent" of the Middle East, and soon in far flung river valleys of Asia. New mechanical devices, new materials, newly domesticated plants and animals built new societies that invented writing, built cities, and created that agglomeration of exchange networks we call civilization. These creative energies fossilized into empires that fought each other on depleted land until the deserts consumed them all. Another great burst of creative energy in about 600 B.C. saw a Greco-Mediterranean world of incredible ingenuity and of scientific and literary advance interacting across the trade routes of the Great Sea. They laid the foundation of the great empires of Alexander and the Caesars, which also in time fossilized and crumbled.

In the East the same period was the age of the great Indian and Chinese thinkers: Lao Tzu, Confucius, and Buddha among others. Yet ethical visionaries in both China and the Mediterranean saw the dangers in the imperial concentrations of power that threatened both the powerless and the life of the system itself. Hebrew prophets denounced the abuses of power while a mysterious Chinese sage offered an assessment that sounds very contemporary:

When the courts are decked in splendor
weeds choke the fields
and the granaries are bare
When the gentry wears embroidered robes
hiding sharpened swords
gorge themselves on fancy foods
own more than they can ever use
They are the worst of brigands
They have surely lost the way
                    —Lao Tzu, sixth century B.C.

New surges of curiosity and commerce came around A.D. 600 in the classical period of Mesoamerican civilization and the expansion of Arab civilization.

Accomplishments in everything from city building to mathematics laid the foundation of empires that both collapsed before the rise of Spanish power. The curiosity and hunger for commerce that kept an unsatisfied Columbus shuttling across the Atlantic bringing back new specimens to an always-unsatisfied Spanish monarchy was typical of the great burst of curiosity and commerce that was building from the 1200s on in the European Renaissance. In the realms of science and curiosity was there any question not asked by the likes of Leonardo da Vinci and Galileo? And was there any discovery not exploited to serve the wealth and power of competing patrons? The Renaissance Europeans regained their admiration for the similar burst of creative energy that enlightened Greece and both Rome and its Greco-Roman successor in Constantinople, but they never rebuilt the Roman world, nor even Byzantium. They remained in a fluid world of exchange and competition, of shifting alliance networks that spurred still more curiosity and commerce and attempts at control.

These three—curiosity, commerce, and control—have continued to wax and wane in modern times. Periods of global embrace are marked by periods of retreat and isolationism (Chase-Dunn, Kawano, and Brewer 2000). Could the current rush to globalism be followed by a great rush to isolationism and protectionism? Given the inexorable trend of the last five hundred years toward a common global system, this is unlikely. While political winds may always shift, three interrelated factors are each increasing at an ever-accelerating rate, leaving no way to turn back.

The first is technology. The rate of technological innovation has historically varied widely, with the possibility even that some innovations would be lost entirely. Yet since the beginnings of the industrial era, technological change has continued to accelerate. With the coming of the electronic era, the pace has only increased. Most of what has been learned (at least in quantity of data if not in ultimate importance) has been learned in our lifetime. With a daily stream of new information technologies generating new information flows and still more technological diversification, this is not going to be reversed.

The second is population. Population growth, like the growth of technical knowledge, has continued a broad, slow upward movement over the centuries, marked by significant reversals. Yet population since the industrial era has also followed a similar upward arc. Unlike technology, the rate of population increase is starting to slow but it will not end until we are all in much closer quarters than our ancestors.

Third, along with surging populations and technical knowledge, is the conquest, for better or worse, of environment and space. Globalization is rooted in the rapid movement of ideas, people, and products. This new level of social organization is built upon the computer, the airliner, and the container ship. The very terms we use for electronic integration, the Internet and the World Wide

Web, picture this new density of interaction: a great global net, a world web, connecting the collective knowledge (we can hope it is wisdom) of a billion motherboards and the brains of their billion owners. At the same time the jumbo jet can contain an entire village—a village of the air that can be transplanted within hours anywhere on the globe. Meanwhile, the container ship can carry the cargo of an entire city, ready to move inland by a waiting network of roads and rail without ever needing human handling.

These three form an ever-accelerating engine of change. Technological change constricts spaces and allows us to maintain ever larger populations. Growing populations fill spaces and demand yet more technological support and innovation. Shrinking distances constrain burgeoning populations and their aspirations, while bringing together the ideas and energy to foster new innovation. Jane Jacobs (1984) describes how the city has been a catalyst for change, bringing together all the vital ingredients with vital intensity. But now the entire world is such a city. The global village is a picturesque image but the global metropolis has become a daily reality.

The model of the global system offered here is based on the unfolding of three ancient vacillating forces—curiosity, commerce, and control—and three ancient but accelerating forces: technology, population, and the conquest of space. Along with these are two sets of structures continually in tension: that between the power structure and the opportunity structure, and that between local structures and global structures. Understanding the local-global dynamic is key to understanding the modern world, and the shifting tension between power and opportunity will determine this world's future.

To explore the global system that enfolds us, Chapter Two begins with curiosity and culture: cultural globalization. Chapters Three and Four look closer at the dimensions of commerce and work: economic globalization. Chapter Five looks at control and the world of politics at empire's end: political globalization. Chapter Six explores the growth of global technology and Chapter Seven looks at the world's growing and urbanizing population. Chapter Eight returns to the question of the global environment that made all this possible and now stands threatened. Throughout each chapter we will move between the local and the global, and between struggles for power and struggles for greater opportunity.

It should be no surprise that a complete and coherent theory of globalization does not exist. It is hard to explain a world that has not yet been fully born. Yet the ghosts of global humanity's past remind us of several key points. Humanity has always held a global vision and global curiosity, although these have been limited by distance, distrust, and discontinuities. Greater global interaction has always held a double edge. On one hand it brings bursts of innovation, creativity, and productivity. On the other, it can bring greater concentrations of power and greater global inequalities. We are seeing both of these effects, and both on ever greater scales. Global winners reap a world of profits; global losers have nowhere to flee. The delicate balance between opportunity and power is always open to be decided and the stakes in this decision are increasing.

2

WELCOME TO THE WORLD

Global Structures Enfold Local Cultures

[We] go down to the baggage carousel and watch our lives circling, circling, circling, waiting to be claimed.

—Pico Iyer

The answer to excessive globalism is not fiery nationalism but committed localism: the rediscovery of community.

YOU MAY BE THE SORT of person who finds accounts of distant times and places fascinating. Or you may be wondering what is the point of so much discussion of faraway places and times. More pressing problems are closer at hand. It's been a rough week. You're just getting over the flu (from Hong Kong), and all you want to do is slip into silk (from China) pajamas (India) and a heavy cotton robe (Native America), take your cold medication (made in Puerto Rico by a German conglomerate from derivatives of two Native American healing herbs), have a cup of tea (from India by way of a British-American multinational venture), and turn on C-SPAN for some satellite-relayed mindless diversion: shots of European royalty cavorting in the Caribbean while trying to avoid paparazzi (an Italian word for these Italian, French, and American photographers) outside their French-built, Japanese-financed, Afro-Caribbean-staffed hotel. For better or worse, the world is at your doorstep. History is repeating itself in your living room; for that matter, in your body. Like some physicist's model of a vortex in space-time, nothing is distant, and history and geography converge in your own experience. You may be simply unaware of how often. Remote now only refers to the buttons you hold in your hand; it no longer applies to any aspect of human experience.

The cultural fabric of the globe is changing daily. We have come to think of culture in national terms: Japanese or American culture. For most of human history, however, we have lived amidst tribal culture. The small country of Papua New Guinea has hundreds of cultural groups on one half of what is by modern measures a sparsely populated island. Every rise and valley brings a new culture: related but in some ways distinct. We have come to think of such places as "primitive." Yet Papua New Guinea is gradually coming together into a national culture while all across Europe states are splintering and minority groups are asserting their language and culture so that every rise and valley now seems to offer a new group with new aspirations. Both New Guinea and the new European states are immersed in global media, global exchange, and global structures. Will these forces bring us to a one-world culture? Or will they create new demands for local identities and distinctiveness? The answers to these questions will in many ways shape the character of the world to come.

New Strands in the Tapestry of Culture

Humanity has been compared to a great mosaic of cultures. Up close one finds infinite variation of hue and form in the tiles, stepping back reveals a great composite portrait of the fullness of humankind. This analogy also reminds us that any missing and lost tiles ultimately mar and detract from the whole. Since I have focused on how these cultures are interwoven, a better analogy yet might be a large, rich, and complex tapestry. Individual threads merge, entwine, and blend with others without losing their own distinctiveness. Out of these many interwoven threads, patterns emerge as one steps back. A few more steps back reveal that these patterns are part of a larger whole, a still grander design. If this is the tapestry of human culture, closer inspection will reveal more. Running the entire height of the tapestry are great warp strands that provide structure and bind the tapestry together. Close observation will also reveal that some of the smaller strands have become worn, faded, and frayed.

Tribal Culture

Prior to the neolithic ("new stone age") revolution of domestication, humanity roamed over open expanses as hunter-gatherers. Hunting provided concentrated protein as well as considerable excitement, while the gathering of plants provided the staples needed for daily survival. Hunter-gatherers lived in bands of relative equals with groups of men hunting and groups of women and their children gathering. Probably their roles often overlapped: hunters stopped to gather up a find of honey, women trapped and captured small animals to add to their gathering stores of roots, stalks, and nuts. Political decisions were limited to issues of where and when to move on. Where fishing resources were abundant, the first small villages could be formed and men and women probably worked closely together to exploit this resource.

When rising populations and declining environmental abundance forced people to begin to control the movements of animals and fend off predators, and to control the propagation of plants and root out competitor "weeds," the social as well as environmental place of humanity shifted. In dry country, animals that could turn grass into meat, milk, blood, and muscle power for humans were essential, and hunters became herders. The great pastoral societies were born. In wet locations where edible plant resources were abundant, it was the hoe and not the staff that was the essence of life, and gatherers became horticulturalists. People settled into clusters, villages, near crops and herds, and had to get along with their growing numbers of neighbors. Movement was still common: gardens exhausted the soil and had to be shifted, herds exhausted the grass and had to be moved, but now the group decisions were more complex. People turned to the guidance of elders and of people of proven wisdom or established prestige, and tribes were born. Since men often controlled and defended the herds, especially of larger animals, pastoral tribes were likely to be male dominated. Since women often worked the gardens and so controlled the essential economy, horticultural tribes often gave them greater influence, although it was still usually the domain of men to hunt, fight, trade, and talk peace.

In especially rich environments, men who could hunt, fight, trade, and talk with particular skill or ruthlessness rose in rank to have greater authority and became chieftains, ruling their chiefdoms with greater power than truly tribal leaders, but still often depending largely on their acquired prestige. These three forms of government: band, tribe, and chiefdom, comprised the entire social order of humanity for tens of thousands of years until the crowded cities of the agricultural river valleys faced problems that demanded greater order and facilitated greater coercion. The three types of political organization share much in common and grade into one another in levels of complexity, so that they can be, somewhat imprecisely but usefully, grouped together as tribal societies (Weatherford 1994).

For all their relative simplicity, tribal societies were not without power and potential. Hunter-gatherer bands crossed the ice-trimmed tundra of Siberia into North America. Hunting bands and their dogs sailed or drifted to Australia. Tribes found ways to harness thousands of plant and animal resources to occupy land from the Tibetan plateau to the Indonesian rain forest. Polynesian chiefdoms expanded over thousands of miles of open ocean to spread across the Pacific. In time, tribal peoples came to occupy every major portion of the earth's surface that was not under permanent ice. At the time the great European explorers set out, there was really nothing new to explore, only old relatives to encounter. The largest uninhabited place outside of Antarctica was no bigger than the island of Mauritius. The first global encounter had already been accomplished in moccasins, travois, canoes, and rafts.

The world of tribal culture was simpler technologically than the world we now encounter, but if anything, far more complex in its cultural diversity. We still have glimpses of this incredible diversity. On the island of New Guinea, a mountainous, heavily forested sanctuary of surviving tribal cultures, there are approximately one thousand spoken, living languages (Diamond 1993)—one thousand languages, one thousand identifiably different groups of people, one thousand distinct cultural expressions on a sparsely inhabited island. Compare this with Europe, which for all its diversity can boast only forty-five languages. Or China, with its billion-plus population and only a handful of distinct ethnicities and languages, a billion people speaking one of several dialects of a single language. The difficult terrain of New Guinea has been especially well suited to a multitude of languages and cultures, but rather than being an anomaly, it gives a glimpse of the diversity and complexity of the tribal world. When Europeans first came to the Americas they found a world with over one thousand languages. Even sparsely populated Australia had 250. But if those European travelers had had a better sense of history they would have recognized not an exotic and bizarre human situation but their own not-too-distant past.

At the time of the Roman empire, two forms of social organization dominated all of Europe and vied for its control: one was either a member (not necessarily a citizen) of the empire, or one was a member of a tribe (or perhaps more accurately, a chiefdom). To Romans the choice was simple: civilized or barbarian existence. To the myriad tribal groups to the north, the choice was equally simple: freedom or slavery to foreign imperialism. The Europeans who mocked, and sometimes envied, tribal peoples, were themselves the descendants of tribesmen only recently enamored with the idea of empire. When Julius Caesar marched on Gaul he faced a loose alliance of tribes, the constant movements of which troubled the organized bureaucracy of Rome. When he and his successors crossed the English Channel, they encountered tribes that were united only in their opposition to the newcomers.

The names which now evoke such national pride were grafted on to this complexity. Scotland was a complexity of clans loosely tied to more powerful chieftains. In time the name of a single group, in this case ironically one from the Irish island, the Scots, came to designate the entire region. England came to be named for tribal invaders from a single German chiefdom, the Angles. Germany itself was a complex fabric of family lineages variously organized as tribes and chiefdoms. The various names attached to that land reflect the lack of agreement on a dominant group: the English term "Germany" comes from one tribe, the Germani; the Roman world came to call them all after another tribe, the Alemanni; and the emerging nation came to adopt Deutchland from yet another tribal name. Even as rulers came to think in terms of nation and empire, the lived reality of the people was one of clan and tribe.

National Culture

The first challenge to tribal culture came as tribes were impressed into the great agrarian empires. Alexander's empire made Greek the language of the learned and powerful over a vast area. Rome spread the use of Latin and its later derivatives. Many of these, however, were merely imperial veneers over continued regional complexity. Both Alexander and Caesar were quite content to rule through the allegiance of local leaders tied to local cultures whenever possible. The greatest homogenization took place over the millennia of the world's greatest empire, that of China (Diamond 1996). Glimpses of an earlier time remain. The dark-complected people of the western Pacific with their myriad languages and traditions are linked to southeast Asia and probably reflect a bit of what this land looked like before "Sinoization." The distinct mountain cultures in the highlands of Vietnam, Laos, Thailand, and Burma are the remnants of an earlier complexity.

The European counterpart to Chinese nation-building came later, about A.D. 1200, and grew in intensity over succeeding centuries. France draws its name from the Franks, whose powerful chieftains began to extend control over a large region with Charlemagne finally crowned as emperor in 800. But Charlemagne, and the pope who crowned him, imagined an emperor along Roman lines, one who would rule over a diversity of subjugated peoples, not a single people. France remained a region of local affinities. Burgundy remained largely independent through adept political and military maneuvering—in at least one case, buying off their would-be conquerors with fine wine. Provençal in the far south remained distinct from its northern neighbors. Breton remained a bastion of the Celtic tribes that had swept Europe before the coming of the Germanic tribes (which included the Franks). In language and culture they were closer to other Celtic tribes in Scotland, Wales, and Ireland. A remarkable global embrace created Normandy. Norseman fleeing harsh Scandinavian lands came south as traders, raiders, and potential settlers. They fell in love with both the northern French countryside and its women. They not only took French wives, but adopted their language and many of the customs. They were no longer Norsemen but "Norman French." Combining their own considerable military prowess with new innovations of their land they became a military juggernaut. They became the "loose cannon" of medieval Europe and the Pope was never quite sure whose side they were on as they invaded and conquered everywhere from England to Sicily. When that short-tempered Norman, William the Conqueror, showed up on English shores, he was faced by an English King exhausted by trying to hold together diverse tribes while fending off new tribal invaders from across the seas. A veneer of Norman French control was established but the people's loyalties were often not to London, whether it be English or French speaking, but to local regions, the realm of recent tribes: Cornwall, Yorkshire, and so forth.

National identities were formed, and enforced, only as leaders decided that enduring power could not come from mere empire-building (the empires of Alexander and Charlemagne, for instance, did not outlive their founding conquerors) but from nation-building: forging a single people from many. In what was becoming France, the language and culture of Paris was to be emulated everywhere. Napoleon, that great pan-European empire builder, was, within the borders of France, a fervent nation builder. Common laws, common school systems, common language, must bind the French people together with a sense of solidarity.

In England, it was to be the King's English (the language of Westminster), common law, and common customs. Ferdinand of Aragon and Isabel of Castile began the process of building a united Spain—one speaking Castilian Spanish with common customs. Nation-building in Germany and Italy continued well into the nineteenth century, struggling to form a common identity out of incredible and entrenched diversity. The process continued right into the twentieth century. The last example of this style of nation-building was the creation of Yugoslavia in 1918. It was also the first European nation-state to collapse.

When Europeans launched their voyages of encounter and conquest, they took with them this emerging national idea. More so than ever before, language, law, and custom were exported to new lands. When these lands demanded independence, departing European powers tried to leave behind a patchwork of European-style nations. They had first encountered a few empires (the Aztec of Mexico, the Songhai empire in Africa, the Mogul rulers of India) and a myriad of tribes, but now they would leave nations. The first to win independence—with leaders of European heritage—formed themselves into nations. Simon Bolivar, the liberating general of Latin America, envisioned unity among the Spanish Americas, but saw leaders quickly divide the newly independent land into separate nations. The Arab world long envisioned a great pan-Arab land, but gradually came to accept a string of separate nations. Nowhere has this nation building been more difficult than in Africa, a place of great diversity and local identity that emerged from the colonial era carved into a series of nation-states whose logic was more apparent in Europe than anywhere in Africa.

For a time in this process, many political analysts argued that economic development would require "nation building." Development was after all "national development." Global organizations were assumed to work with this national model; they would be "international," linking nations, as the name "United Nations" suggests. Models of national development are still being vigorously pursued, most particularly in Asia, but by the late twentieth century, cracks in this national system were beginning to appear. Not only is Africa still struggling to create working nations, but in Europe itself the veneer of nationhood is splitting to reveal regional, linguistic, and ethnic loyalties. The growing headache that has plagued the U.N. is that not only are the nations not uniting into a common agenda, they are not united within themselves. Some have decried a return to tribalism, describing bloodshed in the former Yugoslavia, the former USSR, and such. This is probably a smear on tribes, who nurtured their people and local cultures more often than they went to war. Yet modern tribalism takes place in the more confining and combative enclosure of the world power structure.

The Coming of Cosmopolitan Culture

As surely as national cultures took hold at the expense of tribal, regional, and local cultures, so now national identities are buffeted by the transnational exchange of people, products, and ideas. The defenders of national culture have long realized that products can be cultural Trojan horses. Along with the offered item comes a great quantity of uninvited invaders: advertising to tell people that they need this product to live the good life and that they should be living a life in which the product is indispensable, attitudes about affluence and appropriate lifestyles, and sales and service personnel to model, promote, explain, and finance the product. An entire new way of life may be introduced. This happened first to tribal societies. Lauriston Sharp (1952) described how the "simple" introduction of steel axes changed the Australian aborigine authority structure, economic exchange, and view of the meaning of life itself. It then happened on a larger scale as poor nations came under the influence of the wealthy powers. Finally, the process has gone fully global as all nations are effected by transnational products, transnational media, transnational superstars, and transnational trends.

It should be no surprise that the country with the world's largest economy, the United States, should also have the greatest influence. Yet in the process of Americanizing much of the world, the United States itself is becoming globalized. World culture is not just American culture projected abroad, but a truly cosmopolitan blending of elements, giving priority to the most powerful players. In essence American culture was built in much the same way—a blending of indigenous and European elements with the greatest influences going to the most powerful parties.

One troubling aspect of this export of ideas is the tendency to export the worst of American and European cultures to new lands. As new health findings and lawsuits threaten to bring down American cigarette companies, they are making record profits exporting the very hazards Americans are increasingly rejecting. With tongue-in-cheek style, British development commentator Susan George proposes the SNOB (Social Naivete of Behavior) "theory" and its motto, "Nothing So Blind as a Colonized Mind."

George contends that the SNOB "strategy" exports the crasser and more questionable aspects of Western society that are being rejected by educated elites, while convincing the opinion makers and the upwardly mobile masses in developing countries that adopting these is the best way to be "Western, "modern" and "cosmopolitan." In the area of food, she notes that there is often an affinity of practices between Western elites and the simplest tribal societies, while the new urbanites of the Third World adopt the often-less-healthy practices of less educated, less well-off Westerners. Western elites, like tribal women, breastfeed, while poorer Westerners and newly urban "Third Worlders" believe they should bottle feed with expensive formula. Elite Westerners, like tribal people, tend to be slim, while newly rich Third Worlders are likely to put on pounds as a sign of prosperity, looking more like less well-off westerners who can't afford the health club. Western elites, like tribal peoples, eat diverse diets with whole grains and interesting vegetables, while newly prosperous Third Worlders tend to adopt the meat and fat heavy diets, and the junk food and fast food habits, of less well-off Westerners. Plastic is spurned by elite Westerners in favor of hand-crafted utensils, often of tribal or peasant design, while cheap plastic products from the West dominate in the homes of newly urban Third World consumers. To counter this trend to imitate, at great expense, the lifestyles that wealthy Westerners export even as they reject them, George suggests a new United Nations agency with offices open to Third World opinion makers.

It would be partially staffed with volunteers from the best families and would devote itself to the display of authentic upper-class Western lifestyles. Trendy New York hostesses could lecture on how they serve unpolished rice and perfect vegetable terrines (nothing quite so déclassé as a steak nowadays) at their most fashionable dinners. Their husbands would explain that "nobody" watches television or buys *anything* plastic when a natural substance is available. Elegant Britishers would put down polyester and nylon; Scandinavian industrialists' daughters would carry on pleasant conversations while breastfeeding their babies. French intellectuals would take participants to film festivals to watch esthetic movies about workers and peasants. The possibilities are endless . . .

Who knows? Western corporations could lose a few marginal markets, but Third World elites might begin to feel secure in their own traditions (George 1990, 92).

Eat Globally

Cosmopolitan culture can be seen in the foods we eat, and the ways and places for eating—long a domain of great intercultural variation. In today's world we find that variety has survived, but no region is far from the shadow of the golden arches. McDonald's and its many look-alike franchises first brought uniformity to the American countryside and then charted a global course. Only a few decades ago traveling across the United States meant sampling from a variety of hometown cafes, mom and pop restaurants, truck stops, and roadside diners. By 1920, hotel-based dining had given way to the advent of the automobile, and with it, roadside dining. Their advertising was simple, sometimes just a name: "Joann's"; sometimes just a command: "Eat"; or sometimes a questionable welcome to the world of food and fuel: "Eat here and get gas."

By the 1950s, this world was starting to give way to interstate highway interchanges and the orange roof of Howard Johnsons. The menu of "HoJo's" was long and diverse, but always predictable, unlike its predecessors where travelers would sample the unknown that ranged from "hidden gems" to "greasy spoons." This innovation in predictability soon gave way to the other elements of "fast food": speed, the seeming efficiency of streamlined operations, and the financial flexibility of franchising. These were hallmarks of the national culture, and they were carefully and consciously captured by Ray Kroc as he built a hamburger shop owned by the McDonald brothers into a huge national corporation.

As the American market became saturated, McDonald's went global. The beef could come from Australia, Argentina, or Costa Rica—what made the restaurant was the atmosphere and the advertising, and these could be endlessly exported. As soon as the former Soviet Union opened its economy, a first fruit of *glasnost* and *perestroika* was a Russian McDonald's. Somehow in a land of shortages, this huge restaurant (much larger than its American counterparts) could command the supplies needed. The greatest challenge was teaching the traditionally dour Russian counter attendants to smile and wish their customers a nice day in the best California style. The land of somber poetry and politics, of Tolstoy, Dostoevski, and Lenin, had just come face to face with the Happy Meal. The breakup of the Soviet Union and the subsequent further splintering of the Russian Federation only meant further opportunities for McDonald's opening in Belarus and the Baltic republics, adding to over one hundred other countries (Tahiti was the 101st). *New York Times* columnist Thomas Friedman suggested this expansion was good news, for no two countries with a McDonald's had ever gone to war (Chechnya, Bosnia, and Serbia have yet to be served). Is this peacefulness the result of the transnational cheer brought by the Happy Meal, the result of global prosperity, or the fact that in a McDonaldized world (Ritzer 2000) national boundaries matter less than the transnational billions served as federations give way to franchises? The World Burger is too new to be sure.

The greatest draw of these McDonald's seems to be not price, for the Russian hamburgers are very expensive relative to local foods. Nor is it even product, for McDonald's has now opened restaurants in India that serve no beef! Why would people pay a premium to eat soy on a sesame-seed bun? The answer seems to lie in the SNOB factor, and the desire to join a cosmopolitan cultural clique.

Of course McDonald's is not alone. In Cuernavaca, Mexico, McDonald's offers the only fast food on the central plaza, but further south along a well trafficked commercial strip it must compete with Burger King, Baskin Robbins, and even what would seem to be the ultimate insult, Taco Bell. Why these imports in a country famous for its cuisine? The answer is suggested by the patrons: mostly young, well dressed, well versed in American media, and eager to join the clique.

The United States is itself not immune from global gastro-economic influences. Restaurants have often offered opportunities for internationals and international experiences, and the choices keep increasing. The usual offerings of Chinese, French and Italian foods must now compete with Thai, Vietnamese, Middle Eastern, and many others. Further, a more cosmopolitan clientele has gained greater appreciation of regional differences: the ubiquitous Chinese restaurant may now specialize in the spices of Szechuan, the Italian restaurant is now Milano or Neapolitan. Influences travel in many directions, but they are also directed by the vectors of financial and advertising interests. Some places specialize in concocting cuisine, others in marketing it. A few years ago, Hispanic-American magazines triumphantly announced that Mexican-style salsa had surpassed that all-American favorite, ketchup, as the best-selling condiment in the United States. Mexican-American culture had gone mainstream. About the same time, however, U.S. business magazines noted that the best-selling salsa in Mexico was now made in Texas. No sooner had a cultural element been absorbed, than it was commercially transformed and reexported.

The Japanese have been doing this for decades, not in food but in industrial products and consumer goods. Many of the most popular four-wheel-drive pickup trucks are made by Toyota and Nissan. The rugged terrain and mountain scenery in the advertisements, like the desire to drive a truck through them, are purely American, but the engineering is done in Japan. It may be this sense of technological and market power that makes the Japanese so much more comfortable in welcoming American cultural influences—from music and media to the Disney complex near Tokyo. With sufficient industrial and financial might, many elements can be absorbed, commercially transformed, and eventually reexported.

World Beat

Music provides a classic example of cultural exchange in which artistic taste is heavily influenced by media power and finance. New sound and innovative combinations emerge from cultural exchange, but the dominant waves come from a few locations, especially the United States and the United Kingdom. English lyrics and pop melodies are thus the dominant medium in this exchange, sometimes incorporating, but often obliterating, local forms in the mix. The enormous power of the recording industry, now promoted by the worldwide reach of MTV music videos, assures this dominance. The late nights still bring Mariachi bands to the streets of Mexico City, but during the day the streets throb to the sounds of rap, some in English, some in Spanish. The combinations can be compelling, amusing, or disconcerting. Babydoll Alisha does Hindi versions of Madonna songs for an enthusiastic Indian audience. Yet one must wonder about the broader cultural ramifications as a culture still decorated by long cotton saris encounters Madonna's breathless world of brass brassieres.

Technology plays a central role in this encounter. MTV could only encircle a world filled with television sets and showered by satellite relays. Inexpensive cassettes and CDs (sometimes pirated, either locally or by a new generation of international pirates) make the music of a few global superstars often more available than the music of local artists. Within the United States, backup musicians find themselves replaced by prerecorded tracks. In Trinidad, an open lot filled with as many as one hundred drummers would provide the sound for local recordings. Now the same recording may be done hidden in a studio with multichannel recording mixes providing the backup (Barnet and Cavanaugh 1994). The song may be the same, but clearly the social and cultural impact of the process has changed.

Musical styles can encircle the globe so quickly now that the eyebrow-raising exchanges are endless. A leading *taiko* drummer in Japan is from a Chicano family in Los Angeles, while a leading Afro-Caribbean salsa group, Orquesta de la Luz, is from Japan (Lipsitz 1994). An Arab musician weds traditional Arabic lyrics and instruments to more familiar western intervals and creates cassettes that appeal to audiences from Cairo to Chicago. Bob Marley brought Jamaican reggae to the United States and is a cult hero in both Toledo and Tanzania. On the one hand, local traditions give way to global pop, on the other one of the hottest pop sounds openly acknowledges its roots in exchange, being dubbed "world beat." The ingredients of world beat are already polyglot: zydeco emerged when Cajun sounds came from France to Nova Scotia to Louisiana, where they blended with Afro-Caribbean rhythms. Enter new sounds from Africa, Brazil (mingling African, Spanish, and indigenous sounds), and the French, Spanish, and English Caribbean, add a technology of synthesizers, a new generation of multinational artists and world beat was born: local rhythms marketed by transnational corporations to a global audience. Is this preserving or undermining a musical tradition?

Popular music has become a powerful force for the global diffusion of ideas and lifestyles, especially among the young. Ten- and twelve-year-olds in Latin America who cannot come up with the name of the current leader of their country bear the names of global superstars and the dates of their latest world tour. The possibilities are doubled-edged. On a trendy Toronto street, an informal gathering of Asian, black, Francophone, Anglophone, and Latino Canadians spontaneously blend and experiment with dance styles, their efforts encouraged in Spanish by a young Latin-Caribbean band. Laughs and camaraderie come readily and young couples are joined by elders and children. It's a momentary vision of global harmony. At the same time, people around the globe wonder about the "pop" export of drugs, materialism, sexism and violence, and rebellion against cultural norms. Theirs is a vision of global greed and cynicism. In broader perspective, music alone is not likely to bring either the Age of Aquarius nor global apocalypse. Yet it reminds us of two distinct possibilities: the power of globalization to nourish creativity and culture, and its power to crush local traditions under corporate-sponsored conformity.

Cords That Bind—and Strangle

One way to view the multiplying strands of the web that binds our world is to look at the maps of major airlines and their international affiliates. In place of a few crucial links between international hubs, lines now crisscross the globe in growing profusion. They still cluster where wealth and power are clustered, yet few places are far from the crowded skies. Some of this density is due to developing technology—it is now possible to fly from Chicago to Shanghai direct, non-stop. It is also due to our long infatuation with other places, other ways of life, and what they might offer. Travel has long been sought as a means to personal enrichment, although once only available to the rich or the intrepid. The new ease of movement offers the possibility of new understanding between people, yet the ties of travel and tourism can strangle as well as bind.

Like the global flow of information, much of the flow of people is still unidirectional. Most of the world's tourists come from Western Europe, the United States, Canada, Australia, and Japan. They continue to visit one another in substantial numbers. The longtime American interest in Europe is now well reciprocated by Europeans seeking the natural and commercial wonders of the U.S. Pentax-packing Japanese tourists have become so commonplace that Japanese script on tourist brochures in the United States no longer looks unusual. Yet global inequalities make for a largely one-way street between the first and third worlds.

The third world offers the allure of bargains to the first, but the first is prohibitive to the third. Mexicans visiting their own beaches in the winter months expect to share them with many U.S. visitors (and in fact often visit during the bargain summer months), but Americans would be surprised to find Aspen, the Grand Canyon, or Yosemite crowded with Mexican visitors at any time. Since many wealthier countries are in climates with harsh winters, and many poor countries are rich in tropic sun, one of the dominant flows of international tourism has been toward the tropics in search of what has been termed the 4 S's:

sun, sand, surf, and sex. Canadians and Americans have fled to Florida, but now find better bargains just beyond in the ever-multiplying sites in the Caribbean and Mexico. Northern Europeans have long frequented the Mediterranean coasts of Spain, France, Italy, and Greece. They are now seeking fewer crowds and lower prices across the sea in Tunisia and Morocco, in the Indian Ocean in places such as the Seychelles, as well as India itself. A slightly longer flight offers current and former colonies in the Caribbean, the coast of southern Mexico, and the dangerous allure (despite high prices) of Miami Beach. The Japanese have rediscovered Southeast Asia, where they must share Bali and Bangkok with Australians and a few intrepid Germans. The annual migrations provide the host countries with eagerly sought foreign currency, but also a multitude of frustrations and dangers.

Travellers bring with them many things that cannot be confiscated at customs. They bring attitudes. In Barbados, residents are confronted with tourists who, to them, seem loud and brash, sexually brazen, and crudely materialistic and hedonistic (Gmelch 1993). With tourism comes crime, prostitution, and a drug problem. In Bali, the religious ritual that has bound together a multifaceted ancient culture is now a commodity for display. The land changes. Nature's preference for a tropical coast is often a mangrove swamp. Tourist development demands white sand, even if it has to be hauled in. The clamor for a room with a view can create a concrete and glass cliff of look-alike hotels bordering the beach. If a real cliff exists it will become filled with villas and condos. The laws change. Many Caribbean countries have added a fifth "S" to their package: slots. Gambling provides promised income but also a challenge to traditional values, whether in the Caribbean or the native reservations of the United States.

Mexico is one of the world's most heavily visited countries, and tourism brings in more foreign currency to Mexico than anything except oil. The vast majority of this is resort tourism and border tourism (Sernau 1994). In border tourism, U.S. day trippers cross over from San Diego, El Paso, and other border towns to shop and "see Mexico." Mexicans are adamant that what they see is not Mexico. It is instead a distorted market of loud hawkers offering stereotypical souvenirs to impatient buyers who will shuttle back across the border by day's end. Markets, both legal and illegal, flourish but at the expense of any authentic, enduring Mexican culture. Resort tourism also flourishes in a country blessed, or cursed, with two tropical coasts. The coasts that once exposed Mexico to military invasion now face an annual invasion of millions: Americans to the north and the Caribbean coast; French and other Europeans—and now some Japanese—largely to the south. The old fishing town of Mazatlan swells with American college students on spring break. Puerto Vallarta has grown explosively, blasting its niche out of the forested hills but offering cleaner beaches and more seclusion than Acapulco. Acapulco, like a scandal-embellished and aging starlet, holds on as a grittier but more interesting destination. More hotels per square mile fill Cancun than any other spot in the world. Here a once-remote spit of sand that is closer by air to Miami than to Mexico City was targeted by a tourism-bureau computer as the perfect mix of sun and sand. On the Pacific side, the computers and hopeful officials are targeting the five bays of Hautulco for the next Cancun, but with Japanese and European hotels. The benefits of all this expansion include new jobs, new roads, new airports, new schools, new municipal services, and new prospects. The price includes crime, noise, pollution, and the feeling of being, albeit seasonally, an occupied nation. Like people in tourist destinations everywhere, the recipients often find they resent the very intrusions on which they have come to depend.

The irony for visitors is that their presence can undermine the very cultural and natural ambience that they have come to seek. Just as the hotels built to accommodate large numbers may block the beach and spoil the skyline, so large numbers of people and their needs and wants, as well as the lifestyles and currency they bring, can all swamp local cultural ambience. The first intrepid hikers in the Himalayas of Nepal and Tibet were delighted at remote rural villages in which their very presence caused a sensation. Now they are more likely to be met in those same villages by children in sneakers and T-shirts hawking souvenirs. The trails are littered with refuse of previous expeditions, and the culture, while still interesting, is littered with the trinkets of mass tourism. Few visitors to Bali get beyond the dances staged for crowds of tourists to experience the island's unique culture. To see Polynesian culture many visitors to Hawaii flock to a dance center and museum near Honolulu run by the Mormon Church.

The first visitors to Puerto Vallarta and Zituatenejo in Mexico reveled in the quaint fishing village atmosphere, now immersed in the new development that engulfed the original towns. A cultural experience is now often limited to drinking margaritas at the hotel, bartering with underemployed hawkers of trinkets made elsewhere, or shopping in mini-malls that line the beach. Playing to the imagined paradises of tourists can be a trivial charade such as the ubiquitous hula girl greetings throughout the Polynesian Pacific. It can also have a much darker side, seen in a growing global sex trade from Manila to Bangkok and beyond, in which young girls are lured from rural settings with a promise of glamorous city employment. The employment may, in fact, be prostitution and a web of debt, drugs, and fear from which they can find no escape.

The travel industry maxim seems to be that tourists seeking the four S's must not be disappointed, even if those who hoped for an honest encounter with another culture often are. From the malls of Montezuma to the shores of Tripoli, intrepid travellers hoping to be one of the first ashore instead find, as they elbow through the armies of waiting hawkers, that they are trampling what they came seeking. If only we could be one of the very few to find the exotic!

This of course implies, however, that travel would be the domain of a very privileged few. Must the loving embrace of global tourism then mean the kiss of death for local cultures?

An alternative has been offered in the ideals of ecotourism and eco-cultural tourism. While the reality has not always met the promise of the vision in this approach (McLaren 1997), the goal is to shift from intruding tourist to respectful traveler. This approach has become the centerpiece of the Costa Rican travel industry. Costa Rica could offer the world two coastlines on which to sunbathe. It has offered the world beef raised on temporary rangeland cut from the rain forest. It is now finding new international prominence by offering the world glimpses of a remarkable interconnection of ecosystems that is fragile but still intact.

Madagascar, an island off the coast of Africa in the Indian Ocean, could offer the world a ring of sunny beaches, at least once all the forest was cut away. Much of the forest has already been cut by a growing and desperate population. But Madagascar also has wildlife unique in all the world. Zimbabwe has found that more income can be derived from tourists coming to see elephants on its well-managed reserves than by selling ivory, now banned on the world market. This is managed "wilderness," for Zimbabwe is still interested in selling the ivory of carefully culled populations. In prospering East African game parks, tourists may often exceed big game in numbers, but they have traded their guns for cameras. Their hosts are now guides rather than porters. The animals are frequently disturbed, but at least they are still essentially wild.

One key to ecotourism is to actively involve local people. In the Australian outback parks the rangers and guides are often drawn from the aboriginal people who have trekked this land for fifty thousand years (Breeden 1988). The new parks can also have their hazards: poaching remains a problem in Africa and India, and Mexico has national parks that exist on paper but seem to have few protections in practice. Yet in the newly emerging parks, in zoos that have moved from P.T. Barnum-style beast-in-a-cage to ecosystem displays, in museums that move from presenting native peoples as stuffed effigies to on-site interpreters and artisans, a new attitude is being cultivated.

The respectful inquiry of the true ecotourist naturally carries over into approaches to local culture. Various locales have found new interest in what has been termed, accurately if not very sonorously, "ecoarcheocultural tourism." The sun and fun that looked so compelling on the brochure can get old very quickly. Too much time in the sun is hazardous if not monotonous, and many find the same is true of too much time in the casino, which after all may look a lot like the casinos now floating in the Midwestern United States. The first attempt to combat this was adding adventures such as parasailing. New interest has been found in adding cultural and archeological attractions. Now those who tire of the beach at Cancun can add a visit to the fabulous Mayan ruins at Chichen Itza. These are still brief tours—visitors are back in Cancun for the opening of the discos—yet they do offer a glimpse of the country's heritage. Plans are underway to develop an extensive "Ruta Maya" through southern Mexico and on into the Mayan sites of Central America to draw travellers to adventures in the interior.

A lower profile movement has been fostered by the Smithsonian Institution. Its new National Museum of the American Indian has three traditional locations and a "fourth museum" that consists of community museums scattered throughout the hemisphere. These exist not to display cultures that have vanished, but to celebrate and nurture cultures that have endured. In community museums in Oaxaca, Mexican villagers manage the museum, and present a reawakened interest in folk art and indigenous culture. Tourism provides outside interest and income, but the main goal is local cultural renewal. The museum shops offer locally made crafts to visitors eager to escape the uniformity of coastal enclaves. Says a project planner, "In exploring their pasts, indigenous peoples are unlocking their futures" (Levine 1996).

Ecotourists are given the admonition to take only pictures and to leave only footprints. Well done, this tourism can bolster rather than bash the local culture and society. Travellers can bolster the local economy if their money goes to local artisans, shopkeepers, and hoteliers rather than to resort chains and cruise lines. Of course this tends to be quite small scale. Of the people who visit Mexico, only a small fraction explore the interior in any way. In fact, ecotourism must often be small scale. Too many footprints erode fragile environments, too many pictures disturb not only wildlife but the daily routines and rhythms of the local populace. Yet innovations in travel that respect and rejoice in local environments and cultures offer a glimpse of the possibility of a different type of tourism with a kinder, gentler embrace.

Tourism is by some measures the world's single largest industry (World Bank 1997). Ironically, tourism offers the possibility for either preserving the land or paving it. It offers the possibility for preserving cultures or commercializing them into Disneyesque reproductions of a forgotten original. Travellers discover again and again that places that are idealized and discovered can easily become trivialized and exploited. A key problem is that once again the exchange is not an exchange of equals. So long as tourism consists of the affluent few escaping their prosperous but tedious cities in search of a remote paradise populated by poor but happy—and presumably lovingly servile—people, it cannot help but lead to resentments and disappointments. Yet a world in which all localities prize and nurture both their local natural heritage and their local cultural heritage while at the same time maintaining a curiosity about the lives and accomplishments of others—a world in which prosperity and discretionary income and time is more equally distributed—such a planet offers other possibilities. One could envision Spaniards and Moroccans enjoying summer on the beautiful Norwegian coast, then hosting their Norwegian hosts on their sunny coasts when the winter sun leaves Norway in twilight. One can imagine a world in which Costa Rican and Mexican middle-class travellers walk through the redwoods of California, listen to country music in the Appalachians, and watch woodcarvers in the Ozarks, then invite their hosts to come enjoy their own music, crafts, and natural wonders. This is the real promise of ecotourism, but such a promise would obviously require a very different world social and economic structure. That route promises to be perilous and is yet to be adequately explored.

Tribal Resistance: Oil, Lies, and Videotape

The cords that tug at many of the world's cultures, especially the smaller tribal cultures, can be too much, causing the cultures to unravel and collapse. The Innu were proud hunters, trappers, and fishers of the vast barrens of Labrador. After a long period of outside intervention they were moved, entirely, to an island off Davis Inlet. They had been simply too remote for the authorities who wanted access by boat and seaplane. So a nation of hunters, not seafarers such as the Inuit "Eskimos," found themselves cramped on an island, squatters in plywood government housing, waiting for government deliveries of supplies with nothing, often absolutely nothing, else to do. By boat, by plane, and by satellite the Canadian government brought them the products and images of the outside world, but inadvertently (at least one would hope it was inadvertent) strangled one of the world's ancient cultures. On Davis Inlet, 95 percent of the adult population fell to alcoholism, succumbing on a colossal scale to this disease of displaced indigenous peoples from Alaska to Australia. The youth turned to sniffing glue, then to sniffing gasoline in mass suicide attempts. Said the Innu president, "The program made the people dependent on the government, for kids growing up there is no self-esteem, no pride in culture" (Scott 1993). Culturally and psychologically gutted, a people who had endured thousands of arctic winters might simply be extinguished in one last angry act of auto-suicide. With the magnitude of the desperation capturing outside attention, including that of the world press, a few have begun to press their demands. They want a new home, relocation to the mainland, a place with potential for jobs, a place where they can still move out onto the tundra. They may get it. Their once-remote tundra is, however, no longer a place of solitude and meditative silences. It is now frequently torn by the sonic booms of low-flying NATO jets—their once-home is now a test range—that terrify herds and children alike. They do, however, have their own allies as they fight the NATO alliance: a range of international environmental groups, international peace and human rights organizations, and—increasingly—transnational coalitions of native peoples (Chartrand 1991).

Their neighbors to the north, the Inuit, now have a newly recognized, self-governed homeland, the new Canadian province of Ninavuk, a vast land bigger than Alaska and California combined (Parfit 1997). Their neighbors to the west, the Cree, are caught in a struggle with the Quebec government, which wants to build a massive hydroelectric power project that would inundate much of their hunting ground. Quebec would sell much of the power to New York and the eastern United States. Their neighbors to the south, the Akwasasne Mohawk who straddle the New York-Ontario border, are battling a golf course and other intrusions. On the Alaskan northern slope, the Inupiat Eskimo have been able to use oil revenues to sponsor a program of cultural revitalization, Inupiat Ilitqusiat, "the spirit of the people," that translates traditional values, such as community acclaim for hunter success, into new values, such as community acclaim for educational success, and community revitalization (Olson 1992). The Inupiat manage large native-owned corporations, and keep their isolated schools connected to one another and the world through the Internet (Chance 1997).

The encroaching world that threatens native cultures also provides new resources for resistance, if only they can be harnessed. Deep in the Amazon basin, oil prospectors continue to press beyond agreed upon limits. With flaming wells that ignite the forest and toxic run-off that kills the rivers, they are quickly threatening the cultural if not literal extinction of many native peoples. In his book *Savages*, Joe Kane describes the struggles of a Huaorani leader, coming to the United States to contest these intrusions:

After we entered the industrial corridor north of Delaware, however, his face lost its glow. We passed a field of giant tanks used for storing chemicals; to Moi, they looked exactly like the tanks the Company uses to store oil.

For a long time he didn't say a word. Then he asked, "Chong, are there any Indians here?"

"No."

"Were there Indians here before the Company came?"

"Yes. There were Indians everywhere."

"Were they killed?"

"Yes."

"All of them?"

"Almost all." (Kane 1995, 245)

Moi and the Huaorani, like many other Amerindian tribes, pondered this and vowed to fight with "the spirit of the jaguar."

And fight they have. In response to illegal incursions onto their Brazilian lands, a Kayapo warrior, brandishing spikes from his painted face and head, slips silently through the underbrush carrying his weapons. He carefully notes the movements of the intruders, then draws his favorite weapon from its case. Methodically sighting the cross hairs on the illegal intruders, he precisely fingers the trigger, then relishes the satisfying whir as he unleashes his video camcorder. The tape will be evidence in Brasilia, at the OAS, at the U.N. The Kayapo have learned the importance of the world forum for calling attention to their plight. Led by a media-savvy chief in full paint and traditional regalia, they show up at major conferences, and hold their own press conferences often accompanied by taped footage and international celebrities such as the politically oriented rock star, Sting. They have already defeated a major hydroelectric project that promised to flood their land, and proven that native peoples can adeptly navigate the tangled jungles of international law and multinational agreements.

A stark drama of the struggle between centralized power and the myriad threads of localized culture has been played out in Central America between centralized, often militarized, and often authoritarian governments and the heirs to the Mayan realms that once emerged from this land. Guatemala became a strategic pawn in Cold War struggles, and the predominantly Mayan inhabitants of the Mexican state of Chiapas see themselves as pawns in the grasp of world capitalism. Their spokesperson is the mysterious ski-masked but university-trained Sub-Commandante Marcos, who types his communiqués on an old typewriter in the field, but then faxes and e-mails them to sympathetic academics and journals around the world. In the name of the indigenous commanders (he himself is mestizo), he denounces colonial exploitation in its various forms:

Chiapas loses blood through many veins: through oil and gas ducts, electric lines, train cars, bank accounts, trucks and vans, boats and planes, through clandestine paths, gaps and forest trails. This land continues paying tribute to the imperialists: petroleum, electric energy, cattle, money, coffee, banana, honey, corn, cacao, tobacco, sugar, soy, melon, sorghum, mamey, mango, tamarind, avocado, and Chiapan blood flows as a result of the thousand-some teeth sunk into the throat of southeastern Mexico (Marcos 1994, 9).

Chiapas remains poised between reconciliation and open rebellion. An uneasy peace has been reached in Guatemala after four decades of incredibly brutal conflict, while the future of the other nations of the region remain uncertain and precarious. Guatemalan indigenous leader Rigoberta Menchu has received the Nobel Peace Prize for her efforts on behalf of her people, and world markets have taken notice of the beautifully distinctive colors and patterns of Mayan fabric, yet the future of the people and their culture also remains uncertain and their lives precarious. Their situation exemplifies the struggles faced by small-scale, traditional, and indigenous people around the world.

Colors Dancing
Scott Sernau

Colors dancing,
Dancing upon the loom.
Reds upon oranges
Latching under yellow,
Gathering azure to magenta.
Images emerging,
Faces of fancy,
Of fear and of flight.
Hope of life
Cast in dye.

Colors dancing,
Dancing in the market.
Men, women weaving together.
Scarlet calzone
Past red rebozo,
Fringed sombrero
Tipping by ivory gardenia,
Set upon tied strands of jet.

Colors dancing,
Telling the history
Of three millennia.
An unbroken tapiz,
Art made of the passing
Of common threads
Time-twisted to endure

But the olive drab
Is marching, marching
From barracks to barrios
From sierra to selva.
Baggy cotton
And oiled leather,
An image of order,
Snapping and clicking,
Seeking enemies.

The olive drab
Is marching, marching,
From scuffed corridors
To diesel-stained streets,
From distant commanders
To charred village husk.
For marchers progress,
Dancers do not.
A world to be won,
Or crushed,
Like petals
From a time when the world
Was young with dreams,
Young enough to dance.

Cultural Resistance: Make the World Go Away

Benjamin Barber sees two opposing forces at work in the modern world: tribalism, which he terms "Jihad" from the Muslim term for holy war, and globalism, which he terms "McWorld" in view of global corporate dominance and uniformity.

Just beyond the horizon of current events lie two possible political figures—both bleak, neither democratic. The first is a retribalization of large swaths of humankind by war and bloodshed: a threatened Lebanonization of national states in which culture is pitted against culture, people against people, tribe against tribe—a Jihad in the name of a hundred narrowly conceived faiths against every kind of interdependence, every kind of artificial social cooperation and civic mutuality. The second is being borne in on us by the onrush of economic and ecological forces that demand integration and uniformity and that mesmerize the world with fast music, fast computers, and fast food—with MTV, Macintosh, and McDonald's, pressing nations into one commercially homogenous global network: one McWorld tied together by technology, ecology, communications, and commerce. The planet is falling precipitantly apart *and* coming reluctantly together at the very same moment (Barber 1992, 53).

As Max Weber (1979 [1922]) foresaw, the forces of economic rationality and market integration continue to undermine national barriers. At the same time, a resurgent nationalism calls on commonalities of history, culture, language, and religion to define separateness. The problem continually confronting nationalists, however, and the reason that nationalism can be so explosive, is that these forces rarely follow national boundaries. The Soviet Union divided into constituent republics, but what of a place such as Chechnya with provincial status within the Russian Federation? Yugoslavia also divided into constituent republics but now faces continued turmoil over provinces within the Republic of Serbia that have historic Serb ties but Muslim Albanian majorities.

Language is no less contentious. The referendum for a separate and independent Quebec was heavily favored by French-speaking Québécois, who wanted a linguistically defined nation. Yet the vote was narrowly defeated in the province, in part due to the votes of the significant immigrant population from Asia, Eastern Europe, and the Caribbean, and the Native Canadian population such as the Cree. None of these groups wanted to be part of a nation based on French language and heritage, a nation that might be less sympathetic to their own distinct linguistic and cultural diversity.

If the multiplicity of languages are too diverse for coherent nationalism, religious nationalism may be too broad and encompassing. Religion has shown enormous power to pull people together and to define entire civilizations. Fragmented Europe found a common identity as Christendom, Islam brought together the diversity of cultures that spanned central Asia across to North Africa, and Hinduism has been a common chord in the diversity of India. It has also shown great power to divide as seen on the Indian subcontinent, in Northern Ireland, in Palestine, and elsewhere. Religion was a force for empire building from the padres who accompanied the Spanish conquistadors to the pressures to convert in Islamic empires. It has also become a powerful force for resistance and identity. Huntington (1996) sees the post–Cold War divides of the world as largely along religious lines: Islamic Civilization, Western Christian Civilization, Hindu Civilization, and Chinese Confucian Civilization. The limitation to this division by "civilizations" is not only that they themselves encompass great diversity, but also that the world's religious and cultural diversity now defies geographic boundaries. Where is the core of Chinese Confucian civilization when there are more practioners of Chinese folk religion in California and British Columbia than in Beijing? Where is Islamic Civilization when there are more Muslims in Chicago than in Mecca?

For over a century the key concept for the discipline of anthropology has been culture. This concept is certainly not abandoned, but the anthropological literature is now filled with more references to "identity" than to "culture." What has happened is that culture is becoming less the property of a particular locality and more the property of those who appropriate it as part of their personal identity. As cultures have become globalized they have also become localized, and even personalized. Cultural identity has become a complex—and at times contentious and political—matter. In resort locales the wholesale transplant of American culture is particularly obvious. But between the aging glitter of Acapulco and the brand new glitter of American, Japanese, and European hotels going up further south is a fascinating blend of cultures, with indigenous

Zapotec mingling with the remnant of a West African group brought over to work the sugar plantations. They have retained their cultural distinctiveness over the last four hundred years, so much so that neighboring Zapotecs shake their head and claim, "'Los Negros' have no culture and no religion." On the contrary, they have maintained both but with distinctly African forms. In small towns, the black Mexican population tends to hold to distinctive neighborhoods with distinct traditions. A funeral procession through one of these neighbor-hoods at first looks much like others in rural south Mexico: a truck carries the casket and grieving widow, while mourners follow behind, led by a small band. But this line of musicians is not the usual mournful trumpet-players, but four black men with sunglasses playing the blues on saxophones. This instrument's association with "black" music fits better with these black Mexicans' sense of self and identity than a "Mexican" trumpet. Yet looming above the funeral procession as they pass by is the countryside's only billboard, this one advertising Bancomer VISA credit cards. In the local cantina next to the river where people are washing their clothes, you can pay with plastic. The cantina owners note that many locals are already badly in debt (Sernau 1997).

Around the world the forces of "Jihad" continue to orchestrate demonstrations, rallies, festivals, ceremonies, and, at times, serious conflicts. Before we too readily dismiss ethnic and patriotic nationalism we must remember that it brings us both the colorful fireworks of the Chinese New Year and of American Independence Day. Before we too readily embrace such nationalism, we must also remember it has brought us the merciless shelling of Sarajevo and the bloody machetes of Rwanda. Yet once the demonstrations, celebrations, and conflicts are over, the inescapable bills still come from the equally inescapable forces of "McWorld." We can travel most of the world without a visa issued by any nation so long as the VISA issued by our banks has a credit line sufficient to pay the bills.

Global Education: Many Lenses, A Geocentric Focus

Globalization offers the possibility of a single cosmopolitan culture. Human needs and longings, however, seem to make this possibility unwelcome, and so unlikely. As much as we may like to sample the world's offerings, most of us also long for some sense of roots, some place of grounding. In an essay he titles "No-where Man," Pico Iyer, whose "school bus" by age nine was an airliner between an American home and a British boarding school, reflects on his situation.

The modern world seems increasingly made for people like me. I can plop myself down anywhere and find myself in the same relation of familiarity and strangeness: Lusaka is scarcely more strange to me than the England in which I was born, the America where I am registered as an "alien," and the almost unvisited India that people tell me is my home. All have Holiday Inns, direct-dial phones, CNN, and DHL. All have sushi, Thai restaurants, and Kentucky Fried Chicken (Iyer 1997, 78).

With ties to three continents, taking budget vacations in Bolivia, Tibet, and Morocco, he has fully embraced what he calls the transcontinental tribe of wanderers, "global souls" (Iyer 2000) forever heading to the departure gate. He and his worldwide network of friends find the intense passions of Jihad to be unfathomable, yet he also wonders about the passionless state of nonattachment to anything or anywhere. There is unprecedented freedom and mobility, but also a complete rootlessness. They are not desperate refugees nor angry exiles, just passersby and detached observers:

We see people weep, shout, kiss in airports; we see them at the furthest edges of excitement and exhaustion . . . But there are some of us, perhaps, sitting at the departure gate, boarding passes in hand, who feel neither the pain of separation nor the exultation of wonder; who alight with the same emotions with which we embarked; who go down to the baggage carousel and watch our lives circling, circling, circling, waiting to be claimed (Iyer 1997, 79).

As surely as humanity needs a home in which to settle, we also have a real need and longing for places that are not like ours. We crave contact but we also crave diversity, the simple delight of difference.

Can we fulfill this craving and maintain a diversity of local cultures amidst a global economy and what may soon be a global society? I suspect that some local distinctives will always remain, in part because they are so important to us. The new transnational multimillionaires can choose to use their wealth to patronize the arts as the wealthy have often done before, and much of this art is regional, idiosyncratic, and folk. The way to show that one is both cultured and cosmopolitan has become to collect and patronize a wide array of art forms: indigenous crafts and dance, ancient sculpture techniques, folk music and painting, and so forth. This is not without its dangers, but artists have often sought patrons in the wealthy and powerful. The new global middle class may tire of bland "bourgeois" sameness, glutted by the predictable menu of McWorld, and use its new resources of income and education to seek deeper roots—local, regional, and ethnic heritage—as we have seen in many parts of the world. Finally, the ever-growing global underclass may find itself shut out of the offerings of McWorld, with little diversion from the daily grind but the music, art, and life that can be cultivated from within the community. Diversity remains because we demand it.

The world may indeed become more like the United States, but the United

States is already a multicultural society. Says Federico Mayor Zaragoza, director-general of UNESCO, "America's main role in the new world order is not as a military superpower, but as a multicultural superpower." People interact in a common marketplace but also try to retain and renew ties to a distinctive cultural heritage. Interest in ethnicity is far from disappearing as seen in a host of organizations, dance troupes, religious festivals, and holiday observances. In *Ethnic Options*, Mary Waters (1990) speaks of the choices people make in claiming and reclaiming ethnic identities. Parents want to pass on ethnic traditions, the specialness of holidays, and a sense of both uniqueness and belonging to their children, and so engage in the trappings of "symbolic ethnicity." Teenagers may spurn the "blandness" associated with the white middle class and instead try on cultural forms from black and Latino classmates: "goin' gangsta and choosin' Cholita" (Bernstein 1995). Global youth culture is heavily American-influenced, but it is the voice of multicultural, multiracial, multiple-identity America.

In a poem by the same name, Aurora Levins Morales (1986), daughter of a Puerto Rican mother and a Jewish father, calls herself a "Child of the Americas," and "a child of many diaspora, born into this continent at a crossroads." She insists:

I am new. History made me. My first language was spanglish.
I was born at the crossroads
and I am whole.

Just as English is spanning the globe as a second language, North America is becoming a continent of bilingual nations: English and French in Canada, English and Spanish in the United States, and Spanish and English in Mexico. I can function well in English in Mexico City and Cuernavaca, and certainly in Puerto Vallarta or Tijuana, but I have needed Spanish in East Los Angeles, in rural New Mexico, and in suburban Miami. A bumper sticker now reads, "Monolingualism can be cured," and it may need to be if we are to fully understand and interact with the world in front of our door. We can resist mass-market cultural uniformity, but we cannot resist cultural change, and the accompanying personal changes. Complains Mexican American writer Richard Rodriguez:

In the U.S. I am accused by all sorts of people of having "lost my culture." My answer: Culture is not static . . . We are fluid; we are human; we are experience. And within that experience we are transformed by our contact with each other. I am Chinese because I live in San Francisco, a Chinese city. I became Irish in America. I became Portuguese in America" (Rodriguez 1991, 48).

WELCOME TO THE WORLD

The blending of cultures has not meant the loss of cultural identity; rather, that identity has become more individualized, fluid, and negotiated. Regions are also determined to retain identities, even if they are increasingly blended identities. Vermont is most certainly not New York (especially in the hearts and minds of Vermonters) after centuries of being economically intertwined. The economic booms of Texas, first in oil, then in electronics, only created executives in Brooks Brothers suits and oversized Stetson cowboy hats with Texas-sized state pride. California took millions of migrants and immigrants from north and south, east and Far East, and created a culture that is distinctively Californian.

Of course none of these are visions of perfect harmony. Multicultural America is a land fractured by racial mistrust and divided by growing class inequality. A multicultural world may be no more harmonious. One could imagine a world with the worst of both worlds: all the bigotries and animosities of a narrow, localized vision of "Jihad," and all the crass commercialism and gross inequalities of a globalized "McWorld." If diversity is to be exuberant and not merely divisive, we have to find ways to work as well as think globally and to celebrate as well as communicate locally. Ironically, the best answer to the global may be the local. The answer to excessive globalism is not fiery nationalism but committed localism: the rediscovery of community. An alternative to a uniform global society is a global community of interconnected communities.

Global education is learning about the world; it is also learning from it. We need the wisdom that comes from multiple perspectives. Surveyors need several points to take an accurate reading, just as stereoscopic cameras need more than one point of view to capture depth in a scene. So too we need several points of view from differing perspectives to capture the depth of our world. You cannot see an entire globe from one angle. Maps show us the world in one scene, but all world maps distort size or shape or have parts missing, or all three. A globe gives a more accurate representation in three dimensions but it must be turned and observed from various vantage points.

A good photographer needs multiple lenses and settings to handle diverse environments. A good global education provides multiple lenses: some wide angle for the big picture, some zoom for focusing on the small and overlooked details. We gain that flexibility as we grapple with other worldviews, other languages, other patterns for living. We need global citizens who are grounded in their own communities but who have the vision and empathy to welcome new ideas and to build new partnerships. Muller, a former assistant secretary-general of the U.N., made a plea for global education, stating:

We must give a global vision to all the world's children, teach them about the miracle and sanctity of life, the necessity for love for our planet, for our great human family, for the heavens and for the creator of all these marvels. We must teach them rules of good behavior toward our global home and all our human sisters and brothers, so as to ensure peace, justice and happiness for all (Kabagarama 1997, 3).

A food supply based on a single crop is poised for disaster should that crop fail, a diet based on a single food is always lacking in nutrition, and a world culture based on a single point of view is not likely to be any more resilient nor satisfying. If diversity is to remain it will be because we delight in it, we respect it, and we take the time to understand and nurture it. The world is indeed on our doorstep, the question is whether we can generate the cultural hospitality and generosity of spirit to honestly say, "Welcome."

3

WORLD MART

Poverty and Prosperity in the Global Economy

Seoul for sale,
Corporate nation, come buy a share.
Share in this feast of laissez-faire
Where the dollar can do what it pleases
And the poor die quietly of industrial diseases.

IN 1996, A FREIGHTER unsuccessfully maneuvering in narrow waters slammed into a dock in New Orleans, destroying a trendy waterfront marketplace, tying up the entire dock front, and narrowly avoiding causing massive casualty. The costly cleanup was second only to the disaster wrought by the *Exxon Valdez* in Alaska. As in the days when many intrepid sailors never returned from voyages on the seas, international trade still has its dangers. The most intriguing element is not the magnitude of the accident, but the question of where to assign the blame. Whose ship was this that wreaked so much havoc? This ship is a microcosm of our interconnected world: The freighter was designed by the Swiss, built by the Japanese, owned by a firm in Hong Kong, with a crew from mainland China sailing under a Liberian flag with U.S. grain bound for Korea. Who gets the bill for the repairs? Presumably it went to the British insurance company, which, in fact, is just a clearinghouse for financiers on three continents. The global economy is offering new opportunities everywhere in the world; it is also wreaking havoc with local communities and their populace. Yet, as with the wayward freighter, it is often hard to know just where to place the blame.

Meet Me at the Mall

Ever since farming produced enough of a sedentary life that people could specialize and accumulate, then trade their specialties, people have met at the marketplace. In much of the world, the open air market is still the place to gather. Yet where greater growth, prosperity, and trade provided the means, the open air market gave way to the shops of a main street. Britain traded the wares of its far-flung empire to become in Hitler's famous disparaging phrase, "a nation of shop-keepers." Americans quickly followed this pattern. Small towns developed what Disney now evokes as the ultimate in Americana, "Main Street, USA." Big cities had their grander versions: New York offered Fifth Avenue, Los Angeles had Wilshire Boulevard, and Chicago had "State Street, that great Street." As street-cars gave way to personal cars, the streets lengthened and moved out in "miracle miles," with clusters of "shopping centers." Add a roof, since people still had to walk in and out of stores, and the great American mall was born. "Main Street, USA" is now visited by Disney-goers as a nostalgic relic, as many real small town Main Streets have lost clients to the Walmart on the edge of town and the new mall in the nearest small city. The United States has become a nation of shopping malls. Malls are now the American meeting place: here is where teenagers and pre-teens meet, flirt, hang out, and hope for excitement, seniors walk for fitness in this always-warm linear park, families satisfy their varied culinary demands at indoor food courts, 4-H youngsters display their animals, modern artisans display their wares in craft shows, the seasons are announced (albeit prematurely) in changing displays and decorations, Santa and the Easter Bunny hold court, the Red Cross checks blood pressure, and on it goes. Malls have become the new Main Street, USA, the circus maximus of American commercial culture, predict-able in their city-to-city sameness, yet also providing a window on the world. Not to be left out, let's take a trip to the mall (any one will do, most look alike) but instead of examining price tags, let's have a look at the "made in" tags, and I'll fill you in on a few of the stories behind those tags.

Turn into Kaybee toys and examine the array of action figures, stuffed ani-mals, and this year's "must have" items. Note the preschool aisle (the three- and four-year-olds know it by the bright primary colors), edge past the young girls in the hot pink aisle (they know Barbie lives there), don't get run over by exuber-ant boys in the khaki aisle (it's hard to play quietly with GI Joe, who is stationed here). If you did this fifty years ago you would have found items made in Ohio, Pennsylvania, and the industrial heartland. A decade later, a great deal would have said "Made in Japan." Yet another decade and the stamps would have read "Made in Taiwan, ROC" and "Made in Hong Kong." Now overwhelm-ingly the labels you find on everything in this store read "Made in China."

Toys tend to be light and easy to ship but are also often labor-intensive and so they especially tend to move where inexpensive, dependable labor can be found. At the turn of the millennium, this is China. A full 40 percent of all toys sold in the United States are made in China, and this grows every year. A trans-Pacific entrepreneur described his frustration with rising wages and rising costs in Taiwan, and his eagerness to move operations to the welcoming, dependable production facilities of Guangzhou (colonialists called it Canton) and on to the special economic zones of Fujian. His product? Tiny clothes and plastic guns and boots for GI Joe. The country that only three decades ago trained its children to fight against a feared invasion by real GI Joes (then fighting in Vietnam) now outfits the doll. A country that Westerners associate with the all-purpose, all-blue Mao suit now sports row after row of inexpensively but brightly dressed young women stitching, molding, trimming, not only GI Joe's gear but also Barbie's entourage of sequins, satins, and shiny silver and bright pink accessories. The officially atheist state also has managed to dominate the Christmas ornament market. In fact, they have come to dominate so many markets that Chinese production of toys and consumer goods amounts to a forty-billion-dollar invasion of the U.S. consumer market. Some have suggested that the American concern about working conditions in China is really a concern about an exploding trade deficit that exceeds the deficit with Japan (which also now runs a trade deficit with China).

But not all the toys are made in China. The vinyl soccer balls are, but the more expensive balls by Nike and major competitors note they are "hand-stitched." Closer inspection notes this is done in Pakistan. In fact, balls for American children have been stitched in South Asia by children as young as five years old, for as little as six cents an hour (Schanberg 1996). These children, crouched over their work, consider it a privilege to stand up, let alone play.

This talk of Nike suggests a visit next door to the Foot Locker. The profits here are found in the growing market for an incredible diversity of athletic shoes. One can pause to wonder why a nation that is so berated for its sedentary lifestyle needs such a quantity and so many varieties of athletic shoes—maybe it is to walk through these unending mega-malls—but don't get distracted. Read the labels. The market is dominated by Nike and Reebok, two recent American-based firms, as well as a few competitors such as the German-owned Adidas. Yet none of the athletic shoes are made in the United States or in Europe (a few off-brands once tried plants in Yugoslavia). They are overwhelmingly made in Asia. Philip Knight, the founder and CEO of Nike, once wrote a paper for his University of Oregon business school class on marketing athletic shoes made in East Asia. He has done just that and, with some help from famous names like Michael Jordan, he has become one of the country's richest men. Knight has accumulated over six billion dollars, while Jordan earned a mere twenty million for his publicity. Knight's earnings, in fact, have been greater than the salaries of all the workers who made the shoes combined! Reading the "Made In" tags is a wonderful refresher in the geography of Southeast Asia. China is also featured, but Malaysia and Indonesia are currently most favored. Young women, mostly urban and predominantly Muslim, provide crucial income to often large and often impoverished and otherwise underemployed families by stitching together the bits of suede, synthetic rubber, and nylon mesh that are on sale here for $120 as Air Jordans and the myriad lesser varieties. Continuing down the mall, the Victoria's Secret store catches everyone's attention with exotic underwear and erotic nightware. Most quickly look away with a bit of self-conscious embarrassment, but be bold enough to walk over and turn over the tag under the lace on that exotic underwear: "Made in Israel." Israel? Certainly not in an ultra-orthodox settlement, one would suppose. In fact, they are made by a Jordanian firm who employs veiled Palestinian women to make the delicate stitches, then adds a "Made in Israel" sticker to take advantage of the favorable trade status that Israel has with the United States.

Gawk too long at Victoria's very prominent "secrets" as you walk by and you will fall over the flower stand set up in the midst of the mall. Evoking a bit of the feel of an open-air stall, at least here must be a local product. Don't count on it; turn over the tag on the plastic wrap: "Introducing exclusive bouquets from Colors From the World, specially grown and hand selected in the Andes Mountains of Ecuador." Yes, Ecuador. These bouquets are "specially packed and shipped overnight from Ecuador by Airborne Express" to arrive in this mall only forty-eight hours after their cutting by Quechua-speaking highland *campesinos*.

Down the aisle is B. Dalton Bookseller. Dalton came to dominate a market once filled with small competitors in part by strategic placement in large malls. The real competition now comes from the super-stores, Borders as well as Barnes and Noble, who have become meeting places in themselves, offering Starbucks coffee, children's programs, civic activities, chess matches, and in effect trying to host, and so capture, many of the functions and maybe some of the ambience of a European sidewalk café and an American town hall. Dalton's has the select grinds coffee shop across the aisle and the community and children's activities out in the mall, and so can focus on packing as many books as possible in a small space. As you look around, American authors clearly dominate, as do New York publishers, many with familiar names. But our task is to look under the cover, and the copyright page can be very confusing. Several of those familiar imprints belong to the British-based publishing empire of Rupert Murdoch, several others to the influential German conglomerate, Bertelsmann. Reference to rights always includes international reprints. Editorial offices listed may include New York, London, Toronto, Sydney, Auckland, and Tokyo. One publisher lists seventeen offices, including the above as well as Paris, Bonn, Singapore, Melbourne, Madrid, and more. As you examine the fine print more closely you will notice that many of these books, regardless of the location of the editorial offices, were printed in East Asia, especially Hong Kong and Singapore. This is particularly true of children's books and photographic books in which printing is a major expense.

As you tire of books, the flashing LED lights beckon you into the high-tech world of Radio Shack. Here you won't be surprised at the Japanese names—Sony, Panasonic, Toshiba—and so forth, for the Japanese movement into what was once a largely American monopoly has become legendary. In fact, only one large American television manufacturer remains, Zenith. But now look on the back of that Zenith television: "Assembled in Mexico." The component parts are made in the United States with transistors from east Asia. They are then shipped across the border to Reynosa, Mexico, where they are assembled. Shipped back to the United States (duty free) they are labeled and sent to national distributors. The computers offer a range of brand names, but they all have Intel circuitry made up of microchips manufactured by young women in white coats with microscopes in Malaysia and Indonesia. Component parts and assembly are also done by young white-clad workers, overwhelmingly female, in the Philippines and Mexico. Specialized assembly may be done in the "Silicon Valley" region near San Jose, California, often by Mexican-American and Asian-American immigrant workers who look and work no differently than their sisters at the twin plants back home.

Enough of electronics—try The Gap next door. Resist the sale tags on the items on the table to examine the "Made In" tags. You have your choice of Indonesia, China, and Hong Kong. If not here, certainly in a place with the down-home Americana name of County Seat you would hope to find U.S. labels. In fact, tag reading will be a good refresher course in Asian geography: India, Bangladesh, Nepal, Cambodia, Myanmar (that's Burma, if you're not current), and Hong Kong. Stitching jeans in Hong Kong sweatshops is several decades old, but why would a manufacturer choose to locate in remote Nepal, war-torn Cambodia, or the isolated military dictatorship of Myanmar? Clothes production is readily relocated, needing only willing women, thread, and some export capacity. Shops have been known to close overnight and reopen within days in new facilities and new countries. Trends to rapidly changing styles and quickly filling specific orders place a priority on smaller operations with very low labor costs, and some of the lowest production costs in the world are today found in South Asia. You can search the mall in vain for a single store dominated by American-made clothing, and you will have to shift to upscale boutiques to find European-made (rather than just designed) clothing. Even Eddie Bauer, filled with rugged looking American-style outdoor wear, repeats the story. Check out the sweaters on the table as you pass by: "Northern Marianas Islands." They are in the Western Pacific near Guam, if you wondered.

Walking through the large "anchor" department store to get out of the mall, randomly pick up items as you pass. From clothing to housewares, the items are made in diverse and distant locations. The J.C. Penney display near the exit features relaxed outdoor styles to compete with Eddie Bauer, and the images and the brand name, St. John's Bay, are pure North American back country nostalgia. The labels, however, remind us how hard it is to come home again. It is back to Asia for Sri Lanka, and then one American nation stable and poor enough to compete in this clothing market, Honduras. On the way to the car, the mall-based travel agency is touting posters for cruises, "ample opportunity for sightseeing and shopping in exotic locales." One wonders why anyone would bother.

Global Embrace: Reaching for the World

The Land Never Ends

Not everyone loves meeting at the mall, or they are too busy paying for previous purchases to have time to travel to shop. The result has been a boom in mail order catalogs: "direct merchandising." This idea is as old as the once-treasured Sears catalog that brought mass marketing to rural America. The big Sears catalog is gone, replaced by hundreds of specialty publications trying to target the interests and tastes of continually updated, specialized mail lists. If you have taken to shopping for clothes at home, your name has probably found its way onto the mailing list for Lands' End, one of the fastest growing direct merchandisers of clothing. Their name reflects their original specialty in sailing apparel, but they now cover a wide range of outdoor apparel and casual classics. Their styles may be classic Americana that have changed little over several decades, but the catalogs are filled with tidbits about South American cotton, Indian Madras, Nepali cashmere, and Shetland wool. All that is needed to access a world of fabrics is to call their 1-800 number. This number does not ring in a high-rise office tower in New York or Chicago, but rather in Dodgeville, Wisconsin. Land's End did, in fact, begin in Chicago but moved to the rural ambience, open space, and presumably lower wages of southwestern Wisconsin. The cheerful person who answers your call in the evening (they're open 24 hours) may well be a farmer's wife, or at least a farmer's daughter, who works second shift and whose wages are now vital to the family income. She knows a lot about the durability of South American and Egyptian cotton and about the type of weave and the number of stitches, but she and her co-workers do not stitch anything themselves—unless they quilt when they go home.

The stitching is largely done in China. Much of it is based in Guangdong Province, but sewing is not as tied to expensive facilities as is electronics and much of it can be subcontracted to outlying areas, many of them well into rural China. Workers, many of them farmer's wives and daughters, can gather in a tiny shop with six to twelve sewing machines owned by a village entrepreneur (who in some cases is the former village communist cadre, see Nee 1990). Their work is then sent to a central source in Guangdong, then trucked into Hong Kong, and then shipped to warehouse districts in the United States from which distributors can quickly send out the right size and color.

This is the global economy at work. Notice that it doesn't simply link a handful of "world cities" such as Hong Kong and Chicago and their cosmopolitan workforces; it spins its international strand from the threads of rural contacts as well: a small cotton farmer in rural Egypt, a seamstress in rural China, a switchboard operator in rural Wisconsin, and a consumer anywhere in North America. The new international division of labor has so spanned our planet that this company's name is an anachronism (like the term "switchboard"). For global distributors the land never ends; it has been woven together by purchase orders, fiber optic cable, and shipping lanes into an interwoven mesh as dense as Egyptian cotton.

The International Division of Labor

When British imperialists set out to claim the world, they had a simple idea of the international division of labor that would propel Britain's industrial progress. Overseas colonies would provide raw materials that would be worked into finished products at home. The dockyards on the Thames would be filled with Virginia and Carolina cotton, Scottish wool, Irish linen, and Egyptian flax in great unfinished bundles. The spinning, weaving, and sewing would happen at home. What could be mechanized would be done in great factories—first water-powered and later coal-fired. Hand-work would be subcontracted to local cottage industries (often literally housed in worker's cottages). The idea was challenged by Irish weavers and New England woolen mills, yet into the middle of this century, India provided cotton, but England made the cloth. Gandhi's great symbol of defiance was a spinning wheel to spin his own cloth within India. This principle extended to all forms of production that needed foreign materials: the Malay peninsula provided the rubber but home-based Rolls Royce commissioned the tires and built the cars. The arrangement was altered not so much by demands from the raw-material exporters as from the demands of local labor forces for higher wages. As domestic workers gained bargaining power and political power, two solutions to rising wages presented themselves: import cheaper workers or export the production process itself. Both solutions were tried and continue to this day. Britain, with a vast empire, led in this area as well. Lenin claimed that the British could maintain a "laboring aristocracy" only because they had exported the lowest paid work to India.

With few colonies and vast internal spaces, the United States tried the other approach. Just as a southern aristocracy provided the nation with its cotton not through importing raw materials but through importing slave labor, the industrializing north imported labor. From the mid-1800s until 1920, cheap labor poured into the country from Europe and, in the earlier years and often on a temporary basis, from China. This was followed by cheap labor from the South in the form of African-Americans escaping the poverty and repression of "Jim Crow" segregation laws. Finally, during the years of industrial expansion in the 1940s and 1950s, cheap, temporary labor was recruited from Mexico through the Bracero (manual laborer) Program. The Mexican *braceros* worked in the agricultural fields to feed new legions of urban workers, but increasingly they were used as low-wage industrial workers themselves. Like the Chinese of a century earlier, these were intended to be labor migrants and not immigrants: they were supposed to go home when the work was done. Finally in 1964, a nation declaring war on poverty decided it didn't need to import any more of it.

The Bracero Program ended but was replaced with the logical alternative strategy, what was called the Border Industrialization Program (BIP). Rather than importing workers to work in American factories, American companies would send their light assembly work, first in textiles and then soon in electronics, across the border. The "imported" components would be assembled by low-wage Mexican labor, and then "re-exported" back to the United States to be marketed. The BIP made this entire process "duty-free," that is a free-trade zone with no import-export taxes or duties. A string of twin cities along the U.S.-Mexican border made this idea extraordinarily simple: Tijuana-San Diego, Juarez-El Paso, Reynosa-McAllen, Laredo-Nuevo Laredo. U.S. executives could live on the U.S. side and yet make day visits to plants in which Mexican wage rates, labor laws, and regulations were operative. The idea boomed, and the new plants, dubbed *maquiladora* from the word for machine, mushroomed to by far the fastest growing component of Mexican industry (Fernandez-Kelly 1983, Sernau 1994).

The idea has proven so successful that export processing zones, free-trade enclaves that operate like the Mexican border program, are now found across the world. This is the new international division of labor, the global assembly line. Instead of poor nations only marketing raw materials, now the greatest raw material of many poor nations is their vast pools of cheap labor. This arrangement has changed the face, along with the faces, of work around the world, with ripple effects felt in both rich and poor nations, in both city and countryside.

Global Visions: Rethinking Paradigms Lost

Smith: The Wealth of Nations

Who benefits from this global network? An old line of economic thought that is very much in currency now suggests everyone will. This view is neoclassical economics or neoliberalism, harking back to its roots in British utilitarian philosophy in general and the economics of British economist Adam Smith in particular. Ever since the 1500s inaugurated a period of European dominance based on extracting great wealth from the Americas and controlling trade with Asia, the thinking of European powers had been dominated by a line of thinking known as mercantilism. In this view nations were great competing merchants, and for several centuries European countries looked just like this—each trying to grow wealthier than the others by accumulating, and hoarding, gold. Gold was power, gold was glory, gold was wealth—every good monarch since King Tut had known this. Now the vast expanses of the Americas with their huge mines worked by slave labor could provide Europe with previously unimagined amounts of gold and silver. Spain garnered the lion's share, Portugal got some, and Britain and the Netherlands soon began to steal what they could.

This was not just a European obsession: the one thing the Europeans had that interested the Chinese emperor was gold and silver, and so they could buy riches from the East. The Spanish monarchy embarked on a huge effort to steal gold from the Americas faster than Francis Drake and the British pirates could steal it from them. But an odd thing happened. Spain's "golden century" of the 1500s gave way not to ever greater prosperity but to decline. Inflation made the more abundant gold, and especially the now very abundant silver, worth less. Gold meant goods and services could be bought abroad, but the more that was bought the less was produced at home, and the idea was to hoard and not to spend the gold. The great hordes were impressive but they produced nothing and Spain fell into decline. Portugal eventually followed. China accepted nothing but gold and silver coins for its products but it didn't grow rich—it fell behind the aggressive traders of northern Europe.

At the beginning of the 1700s, Adam Smith saw this and wrote his famous treatise on The Wealth of Nations. Amassing gold, by whatever means, did not bring wealth and prosperity. Trade, commerce, and ever-expanding production brought prosperity, and the gold-grubbing monarchs only hindered this process. Since production and trade brought prosperity, Smith believed it should be unfettered. The important actors were not kings but merchant capitalists and their armies of investment bankers. As they competed freely the nation would grow rich. Smith knew this was only an ideal, for he noted that the great East India Company was growing rich as a result of a government-sanctioned monopoly, yet his endorsement was for vigorous competition. The concepts that developed around this line of thinking defined the emerging field of economics and so became the "classical" line of thought, espoused by the "liberals" who rejected the old monarchial order. Later thinkers added more sophisticated formulations on the effects of supply and demand, consumer confidence and preference, and the value of trade that is free from regulation except to control coercive force and fraud, and this became the doctrine of neoclassical economics, or neoliberalism.

Long established—although not always followed—in Britain and the United States, neoliberalism became the driving force behind Thatcherism in Britain and Reaganomics in the United States. The terminology can be confusing: while Ronald Reagan was clearly not a "liberal" in the current American political usage, he was the arch-"Liberal" in the older European economic sense of the term. This economic neoliberalism continues to dominate the practices of both countries, so that the once-champion of Kennedy-style American liberalism, Bill Clinton, became a champion of Adam Smith-style neoliberalism: fighting to gain passage of NAFTA, fighting to bring down trade barriers, fighting to get "fast-track" authority to conclude new free trade treaties around the world. Likewise in Britain, the Labour Party regained power after almost two decades by distancing itself from the language of the welfare state and democratic socialism, with Prime Minister Tony Blair embracing the language of Adam Smith and free trade and applying it to a new world situation.

This is also the language and ideology of powerful international organizations such as the International Monetary Fund (IMF) and the World Bank, launched in Bretton Woods, England after the Second World War to create a stable world economy in which free trade could flourish and prosper. To be fair, neither Clinton Democrats, nor Blair Labour partisans, nor the World Bank believe in complete laissez-faire ("hands-off, let-it-happen") capitalism. Neither did Adam Smith. The government must prevent unfair monopolistic practices, unfair labor practices, and shady deals (such as employing force and fraud). In the new thinking of Clinton and Blair, it must also invest (and therefore tax) in infrastructure to foster productivity and in education and worker skills—what economists call "human capital"—to foster worker productivity. Yet the engine of growth, the bearer of prosperity, is an ever freer market.

Marx: The Turmoil of Nations

This view has not gone unchallenged. In the middle of the 1800s, while Britain eagerly pursued a nationalistic version of Smith's philosophy (the empire grew in grand Spanish style and Queen Victoria got the glory with such titles as "Empress of India," but the bankers kept, and reinvested, most of the money), a bedraggled German exile sat in the British Museum and wrote a different story. Smith was correct, he contended, that free market capitalism (Smith, in fact, did not use the term which later became popular) unleashed incredible productive forces that would spur economic growth everywhere, but there was a great contradiction. Rather than Smith's "invisible hand" that would spread prosperity everywhere as people sought their own economic gains, free-market capitalism was an iron fist that crushed workers, both at home and abroad, beating them down into ever greater misery.

The poverty and misery that Charles Dickens described in London was exceeded only by the poverty and misery in Calcutta and Bombay. The overworked Bob Cratchets and the displaced Oliver Twists struggled in lands controlled by equally desperate capitalist Scrooges, who struggled to maintain profit margins amidst cutthroat competition in which at any time they and their businesses might perish. This was the contradictory logic, the inevitable outcome of industrial capitalism according to its most famous critic, Karl Marx. Marx credited Smith and his like for overturning the old bankrupt feudal systems, and he believed that the beast of capitalism must be unleashed to set in motion this great surge of productivity. But then it must be destroyed by the world's workers, who everywhere shared in its misery but not its benefits. In a speech of January 1848 (see McLellan 1977), Marx endorsed free trade in large measure because it would speed the revolution!

In a post–Cold War world with communism in decline, it is easy to dismiss Marx. Yet in 1848 Europe did erupt in revolution. Workers did demand changes, but the compromises favored the liberal reformers, the nineteenth-century Blairs and Clintons who wanted to amend the system, and not the communists who wanted to bring it down. Marx and his co-author Engels called on their communist followers to work with the liberal reformers where they could, and a whole host of their recommendations were indeed followed: minimum wage laws, workplace safety laws, bans on child labor, limits on work hours, and so forth. Yet the system itself remained intact. Workers accepted their gains, and a growing middle class identified with the bourgeois capitalists, and found too great a stake in the system to see it overthrown.

That free markets would ever provide prosperity was much less obvious in the former European colonies, and their allegiance to free market principles has been much slower in coming. When Latin America won its independence from Spain and Portugal, a long and bitter fight ensued in many countries between "conservatives" and "liberals." Conservatives were a landed and church-supported elite that favored a Roman Catholic plantation-based aristocracy inherited from the old world as the system to guide independence. With the exception of their strongly Roman Catholic religious background, in many ways their views and interests were similar to the plantation owners in the pre-Civil War U.S. South. Marx would have called them feudalists. They were opposed by Liberals, who were capital "L" Liberals in the sense of favoring free markets and unfettered commerce, and a government that while democratic would act on behalf of business. Marx would have called them bourgeoisie.

Just as the United States was torn by a civil war between these contending factions, so were many Latin American nations. It is not surprising that one of the most famous of the Latin American Liberals, Benito Juarez, "Mexico's Abraham Lincoln," found such consistent support from the real Abraham Lincoln. While Lincoln fought southern landowners, Juarez fought a conservative-imposed and French-backed Austrian Duke, Maximilian, who had been installed as Mexico's emperor. No sooner was the American Civil War over than Lincoln started moving troops to the border to ensure an end to the Mexican struggle. Lincoln won, Juarez won, and across the Americas Liberal republicanism was firmly established.

The Latin American Liberals were true to their promises to business, if not always true to their promises to democracy. One of Juarez's Liberal generals, Porfirio Diaz, ruled for thirty years before being toppled in the decade of confusion known as the Mexican Revolution. In the 1920s, a Nicaraguan Liberal, Antonio Samoza, came to power in a dynasty that lasted until the Sandinistas toppled the regime in the 1970s. Diaz and Samoza promoted exports and trade, and the new railroads and highways to make this possible. They angered peasants and workers who stayed poor, and eventually angered even their business backers through excessive graft and cronyism (seemingly forgetting that warning about force and fraud).

Many of those who opposed these aging Liberals found their inspiration not in neoclassical ideas but in neo-Marxism, attempts to update the thinking of Marx's political economy. The Nicaraguan nationalist hero Sandino may have hesitated to claim Marx as he fought foreign (largely British and American) influence, but the Sandinistas who claimed his name did not. The Mexican revolutionary Zapata was also reluctant to claim Marxist "bolshevism" as he led his peasant armies at the same time as Lenin led his, but the Zapatistas who claim his name in the Mexican state of Chiapas are not reluctant to draw on Marxist analysis of the "capitalist beast" they believe is bleeding their state (Marcos 1996). Throughout the middle of this century socialist and neo-Marxist thinking emerged across Latin America, even if briefly. Socialist fervor brought Presidents Arévalo and Arbenz to power in Guatemala before the latter was deposed by the CIA and a junta of neoliberal generals. The socialist Allende won a confused election in Chile before being deposed by General Pinochet with the substantial backing of American corporations. Pinochet is a neoliberal who favored business, opposed unions, and sought an export-oriented trade policy. Pinochet is still credited in some circles with bringing a surge of economic growth to Chile, although like the Guatemalan generals, he seemed to favor the invisible hands of the secret police and the death squads to Adam Smith's invisible hand of the market.

Frank and Cardoso: The Dependency of Nations

As the economies of the third world, essentially the former colonial world, continued to struggle, thinkers in the United States and Britain proposed the line of thinking that became known as modernization theory. According to this view, the entire world was moving from traditional to modern ways of thinking and living and conducting business (see Inkeles and Smith 1974). Yet such a transition was slow and the developing world was hindered by a lack of modern ideas, modern institutions, and modern technology. The modernizing efforts of old Liberals had built modern capitals but had failed to fully modernize a backward countryside. The answer to this problem often involved foreign trade, foreign experts, and foreign aid which would bring these modernizing influences (for example, see Weiner 1966). If multinational corporations could bring modern ways of doing business, modern organizational structures, and the latest technology, then ultimately the benefits of the modern world of industrial capitalism would reach everywhere.

Opposing this line of thought was a group of Latin American scholars who developed the alternate explanations that became known as dependency theory. In Mexico, Gonzales de Casanova (1965) took his inspiration from Marx and Lenin's descriptions of the immiserization of workers under international capitalism. In Brazil, Cardoso (1977, 1979) argued that Latin American development took place in the context of dependency on the first world and was always distorted by this relationship. A European transplant to Latin America, Andre Gunder Frank (1967) argued that colonial relationships had underdeveloped Latin America, and that neocolonial relationships kept Latin America underdeveloped and poor. World trade did not bring prosperity because the terms of trade were stacked against the developing countries, who paid high prices for imports while getting little for their resources and their labor. Latin America was poor, the dependency thinkers contended, not because it was traditional, but because its economy was exploited, its politics dominated and its society distorted by relations of international dependency. The multinational corporations and international institutions like the World Bank were merely agents of that exploitive relationship.

By the 1970s, modernization theory was dying a slow death in universities, slain by dependency critiques and its own Eurocentric worldview. Dependency thinking began to shape government programs, yet many programs brought few immediate results and heavy debt. By the 1980s, a resurgent neoliberalism came to dominate in politics. In Mexico, the party of the revolution (PRI) that has been in power since the 1920s had shifted ground. Their television ads still showed Zapata leading the charge, but their leader was Harvard-trained economist Salinas, who promised to cut debt, control inflation, support business, and privatize government industries. Salinas was the neoliberal who first proposed the idea of a North American Free Trade Agreement (NAFTA). In Chile, the populace finally rid itself of General Pinochet and his politics of repression, but installed an elected government no less committed to free markets and free trade. The Chilean "economic miracle" continues to provide dramatic growth, although at the cost of dramatic poverty and dislocation. The government has championed MERCOSUR, a South American free trade bloc, and is now promoting itself as the next NAFTA partner. Why the southernmost nation in the hemisphere would be part of the North American Free Trade Agreement defies geographic sense, although the agreement is built on the triumph of business over geography. In Brazil, the president is none other than the "radical" sociologist and dependency theorist Fernando Henrique Cardoso, elected on the popularity he built as Finance Minister when his free market reforms curbed inflation and fostered economic growth. Cardoso (1997) winces at being called a neoliberal; he prefers "neo-social" in that he remains committed to alleviating the misery of Brazil's vast poor population. Yet his economic policies, if not his politics, echo that of the Brazilian generals who led the Brazilian "miracle" of growth in the 1960s.

No countries have embraced the idea of free trade as vigorously and wholeheartedly as Britain, the United States, and their Latin American trading partners, but this view is clearly dominant around the world. The growing economies of East Asia are built around vigorous export economies. They have often not been ashamed of direct government involvement on behalf of their nationally based industries in what some economists call national corporatism and what American politicians have sometimes denounced as unfair trade. In the land of Lenin, reformers continue to struggle to privatize industries and promote exports, guided by Harvard- trained neoclassical economists. China is officially still communist yet has exploded on the international market with a vigor unmatched in the world. Europe struggles between protecting vulnerable sectors and a welfare-state social contract, while still merging into a truly common market with a common currency and unfettered trade.

Africa continues to struggle with economic and social upheaval, but is also hoping to find answers in the new global economy. Ghana, once the home of Nkrouma's pan-African socialism, has now followed Kenya in seeking international investors. Tanzania under former president Nyerere promoted village self-sufficiency and an authentically African socialism, and now looks to privatization and export promotion. Across the continent, generals and presidents-for-life, socialists and Islamic nationalists, eye the tiny country of Mauritius in the Indian Ocean off the African coast. Mauritius's many nationalities (none of them indigenous, this was the one uninhabited place at the time of European discovery) don't fight each other; they all work together in foreign-owned factories, looking more like Singapore than their African neighbors. Around the world, at least for the moment, neoliberalism and the free trade of World Mart have triumphed. Yet many continue to have their doubts, including American populists as diverse as ultraconservative columnist Patrick Buchanan, House Democratic leader Richard Gephardt, and billionaire industrialist Ross Perot, all of whom would blanch at being called Marxist. Some look at the miseries of the global assembly line and wonder if, even if he was badly mistaken about the glories of communism, maybe Marx was dead right about the evils of capitalism (Cassidy 1997).

Ricardo: Comparative Advantage

The driving idea behind the benefits of worldwide trade is what the classical economist Ricardo called comparative advantage. The idea of comparative advantage is quite simple: if everyone, and in this case every country, specializes in what they do best, and then trade their products for what others do best, everyone will be the better off. Rather than the British trying to grow tea and coffee on their cold, damp island, they should do what they do best—let's say raise sheep with especially warm wool—and then trade their wool for tea from India and coffee from Africa or Latin America. When thinking in terms of products based on natural resources this makes eminently good sense.

The picture gets thornier when the focus shifts to finished goods, and even more so in the case of services. George III thought that the American colonies should provide raw materials—cotton, tobacco, lumber, sugar—and should import, from British merchants, almost all of their finished goods. New England emphatically disagreed that there was any natural comparative advantage in this. It may be quite obvious that Iceland should not specialize in growing bananas and that Bolivia should not specialize in marketing cod fish. It is harder to see that Japan, with few iron resources, has a natural advantage in making steel, or that Hollywood has a natural comparative advantage in making films and television programs (except, perhaps, for Baywatch and surfer movies), or that the Swiss landscape is naturally ideally suited to the growth of banks. These are socially created comparative advantages, not natural endowments, and they are the result of historical forces, including perhaps forces of domination and exploitation. The Latin American poet Eduardo Galeano (1973) wrote, "The division of labor among nations is that some specialize in winning and others in losing."

Comparative advantage takes on a darker side when applied to the new international division of labor. Is it just good economics to say that a location has a comparative advantage in cheap, docile labor, or in an environment available for polluting? Is the ability to use child labor or the ability to suppress dissent a legitimate comparative advantage? Here the social and political construction of advantage becomes even more sharp edged, and we have moved from economics to ethics.

With the shift from a comparative advantage in natural resources to an advantage in labor resources, the land under the global assembly line has shifted as well. Natural resources can be depleted but they provided some stability: Bolivia produced tin, Zaire copper, Indonesia rubber, Colombia coffee. Producer nations were at risk that substitutes would be found for their products—synthetics replacing natural materials such as rubber, plastics replacing metals, and so forth—or that market forces would cut the price for the product. Yet nature itself was constant. Dole could shift its pineapple production from Hawaii to the Philippines, then on to Kenya, but they needed certain rich volcanic soils and tropic climates; they could not decide to plant next year in Bangladesh. Large facilities often represented a major investment as well. But people are a resource in great supply throughout most of the developing world, jobless people in particular. Light assembly plants are quite portable, and governments eager to attract jobs may even pay the cost of moving and setting up a new operation.

Freed from the constraints of nature and geography plants can move, and move they do. U.S. workers have seen this occurring domestically as states struggle to outbid one another to capture production facilities on the move. Nations can also enter into bidding wars to attract plants, offering tax breaks, and promising cheap and reliable labor. The result has been more frequent movement, and an interesting pattern of movement. Vietnam-era Cold War strategists warned of a "domino effect" across Southeast Asia in which one country after another would fall to the communists. What we have seen instead is a game of Asian dominoes, or maybe *mahjong* tiles, in which one country after another falls to the capitalists.

Japan revived its war-torn industries in the 1950s and 1960s by particularly targeting electronics, toys, and small consumer goods for an export market. The "Made in Japan" tags were everywhere, but Japanese wage rates started to climb with growing prosperity. American, European, and now Japanese executives looked beyond to the ready-to-work, low-wage yet diligent workforces of South Korea, Taiwan, Hong Kong, and Singapore. Intensely anti-communist and often authoritarian governments assured a pro-business climate. Production boomed, air and water were polluted, labor unrest was quashed, but incomes also rose. Success brings its price, however, as well as higher wage rates. Thus now American, European, Japanese, and now Taiwanese and Hong Kong and Singapore-based Chinese executives started looking further afield. Sometimes the foreign-owned plants just moved, sometimes they retained an office in Hong Kong or Taipei, Taiwan, but the work was subcontracted further afield. Malaysia, Indonesia, and Thailand were eager to join in the prosperity of the original "four dragons" and had waiting labor forces. As the cost of business climbs in these countries, many, including a few Thai, Indonesian, and Malaysian executives, are looking further on—to Mauritius, to Bangladesh, and beyond. Would it work in Kenya or in Khazakstan? We may very well soon find out.

In the meantime, how should we view these trends? Is this the triumph of free market economics, the spread of modernity, or the torch of prosperity being passed from one nation to the next? Proponents can point to dramatic growth rates and to rising wages in select Asian countries. As one country learns the system, it in turn passes on the benefits to yet another, and so forth until all are modern, prosperous producers and cosmopolitan consumers. We will all meet at the mall, too prosperous to remember old animosities. Others are not so sure.

At the moment many of the Asian dominoes seem to be crashing in disarray, taking their proud, new stock markets with them. Thailand, a later comer to this game, built huge facilities in Bangkok, found very effective ways to turn village girls into urban laborers, and despoiled its beautiful coasts preparing for a new export industry and wealthy Asian tourists. Development demands its price. Now with the social and environmental costs already in place, the boom is not materializing, and facilities stand vacant. China has entered this great *mahjong* game with such dominance that it may trump all its smaller rivals, and what does this mean for the smaller Asian hopefuls? What does this mean for Latin American and African hopefuls as well? To prosper Japan had only to do more work for less than American unionized labor, Taiwan had only to do more work for less than Japanese labor. Now to become the next Taiwan, Mexico or Brazil or Ghana will have to do more work for less than China, with its very low wage rates and government supported, and often controlled, labor. There seem to be ever fewer booths at World Mart, they cost more, and they return less. Some look at the despoiled environments, the huge social costs, the harsh working conditions on the global assembly line, the destruction of local economies and cultures, and wonder if maybe Marx was right: this passing torch will scorch the earth in the name of prosperity. It is more like a great transnational plague passed from land to land.

The debate is not merely academic but intensely political, as politicians negotiate new agreements and their constituencies angrily debate the outcomes. American business leaders promote the expansion of NAFTA and the World Trade Organization (WTO) as well as "fast track" authority for the president to conclude still new agreements to lower the barriers to trade. American labor is trying to unite to oppose all of these. European countries move toward open markets within the European Union, while local interests demand continued national protections. The IMF insists that countries seeking new loans go through "structural adjustment," a series of changes that include reducing government spending, especially deficit spending, devaluing currencies to increase exports, and deregulating private enterprise and trade. Many poor countries acquiesce. To some this is reform and good government (Brown 2000), but angry labor and peasant groups complain that the books are being balanced on the backs of the poor.

We must remember that NAFTA, hardly a north-to-south giveaway, was controversial on both sides of the Mexican-American border. For those with secure positions and incomes it offered new opportunities and less expensive products. Yet U.S. labor leaders feared that it would continue to erode the position of the U.S. working class, while Mexican small farmers and small businesspeople worried about an avalanche of cheap products that would put them out of business. Both fears have proven well founded.

Global Redistributors

From Reciprocity to Big Men

Exchange has been the lifeblood of human communities since their beginnings. For the simplest societies that are our common heritage, personal success in the day's hunt or the day's gathering could never be assured. Assurance came in the knowledge that the abundance of the most fortunate would always be shared, for the next day might reverse people's fortunes and today's benefactors would be tomorrow's beggars. In economic anthropology this is reciprocity, an economy based on sharing among relative equals. It was the way humanity lived its first millennia (Harris 1989).

As human populations grew and their goods became more complex, simple reciprocity became cumbersome. Rather than an ever-growing matrix of exchange relationships it was simpler to have a central redistributor who gathered surpluses and returned them in times and places of need. As human societies moved from hunting and gathering bands to growing horticultural villages they became more dependent on redistributors. The first headsman (they were generally men) could often do little more than trade the hard work of themselves and their families for prestige and the loyalty of a few followers. They gave gifts that could not be returned in kind, and so reciprocity became redistribution. As these redistributors grew in power they became chieftains who attained considerable authority and power.

Once chieftains operated in a system large enough that they were no longer personally accountable to each follower it is not surprising that they began to claim greater benefits from their privileged pivotal position in the web of social exchange, and their wealth grew. This is a very simple but compelling explanation for social inequality. Inequality did not begin with unequal talents, for talented hunters were always obliged to share their bounty, as well as work with and "mentor" the less talented. Inequality starts rather with ambitious redistributors who can claim the right to a portion of the surplus in return for their services.

Around the world, the great rulers were largely big redistributors. The great Inca Empire in South America had markets, but the economy was based on the redistribution of the great Inca, from whom the Spanish drew the name for the entire system. Ancient Egyptian pharaohs came to claim they owned all Egypt, so they demanded all its spoils from their now peasant subjects, and then redistributed the booty as they saw fit. The Old Testament has Joseph counseling the Pharaoh to gather grain for seven years so as to have vast stores for seven years of famine, a grand redistribution scheme that extended the Pharaoh's power beyond Egypt's borders to hinterlands desperate for food. In feudal systems, used both in Europe and in Asia, minor lords acted as intermediate redistributors for the kings and emperors of still larger systems. There were money and markets but many peasants never held any money and never visited a market. They lived on what they produced, their lord claimed a portion of the surplus as his right, and they looked to the lord to provide them with protection and any items they couldn't produce as part of the lord's "benevolence."

Surely it would seem that as this feudalism gives way to full-blown capitalism, we would also see the final triumph of markets over redistribution (Nee 1989). In fact, what we tend to see is redistribution on a grander scale. People are not free to travel the world and trade face to face, so global merchants act as the new redistributors. They deal continually in money and markets, but they can also control and manipulate those markets, standing like the big men redistributors of an earlier time at the nexus of a network of exchange. They too can claim a share for their services but now this is called profit. Both Smith and Marx saw market capitalism as something quite new but in this description it is starting to sound like the second verse of a very old song. The new capitalist bankers are clearly redistributors, standing between investors and debtors. A "free market" may be free from the interference of government redistributors but it is not free from the control of market redistributors.

With the exception of the simplest open air markets, or their "farmer's market" imitators, trade is rarely a face-to-face transaction between producer and consumer. It is usually mediated by a party with particular access to information and resources in the social network. The wealthiest tycoons have been the most privileged and aggressive of these go-betweens. Likewise, the wealthiest nations have often not been those with vast resources but those with a privileged or powerful position in large networks of trade. This was true in the rise to wealth and power of Portugal, the Netherlands, and Great Britain. Redistributors vary in their positions of power and influence, however, from mere middlemen to true moguls.

Middleman Minorities

In many times and places merchants were men without a country (female vendors have been common as well, but were more likely to be tied to a local market). Sometimes drawn from outcast or suspect groups, their ties were to the world of commerce rather than to nationality or locality. This pattern continues in middleman minorities, who operate small shops in the neighborhoods of other ethnicities. The "overseas Chinese" in Southeast Asia, Asian Indians in East Africa, Korean green grocers in Latino and black neighborhoods of New York and Los Angeles, Lebanese shopkeepers in the Middle East and urban areas in the United States, Jewish American and Chinese American small business owners on both coasts of the United States. The risks in small business are always high, in middleman business in changing neighborhoods the risks are even higher, but the opportunities for the person with an unusual but strategic place in an exchange network can be many. They are most appealing to those who are not able by their background, language, or other situation to obtain more secure professional positions. These positions also appeal to those willing to make high stakes wagers on their luck and ability. Sometimes the payoffs are considerable.

Immigrants who come with many skills and high aspirations but few local credentials often find their best opportunity in the middleman minority role. Small businesses in lower income neighborhoods, usually dominated by other minorities, provide the risky but profitable environment to make a beginning. This strategy has been successfully used in the United States by Jews, Lebanese, and Chinese, and now more recently by other Middle Easterners, Koreans, and Caribbeans. Once in place, a network dense with personal ties and contacts to other entrepreneurs creates an environment rich with information on business opportunities and possibilities. In a study of immigrant entrepreneurship in Los Angeles (Nee, Sanders, and Sernau 1994), we found fascinating examples of the possibilities. One Korean woman got her first encouragement, and her first loan, to start a liquor store from new friends at the Buddhist temple. However liquor-store entrepreneurship may accord with Buddhist teachings, it clearly accorded well with the immigrant subculture they were creating. The risks of this type of business are exceptional, but at times so are the rewards.

While many of these businesses start as family enterprises, they often expand to reflect the diversity, and the hierarchies, of American metropolises. An example of this is an employment agency in Chinatown specializing in restaurant workers. Now a majority and still increasing number of the many applicants at this agency are not Chinese but Mexican and Latin American. Fewer Chinese immigrants want to wash dishes as their options have improved and Latin American immigrants have taken their place. In many restaurants the owner, manager, hostess, and most of the wait-staff are bilingual Taiwanese, while the cooks and much of the kitchen help are from the PRC and often have weak English skills. The dishwashers may also be Chinese, but are just as likely to be Latin American. As businesses grow their ethnic diversity often increases. In particular, as customers become more diverse, the advantages of hiring a more diverse work force increase. Noted one Taiwanese man:

Hiring was word of mouth, and we had very, very few Chinese applicants . . . I have to admit this is a French Continental Restaurant. In the first place there are very few Chinese applicants, but also the fact this is a French Continental restaurant, we have to maintain to a certain extent the so-called environment, the mood . . . that's why it's basically white Americans and Mexicans.

This entrepreneur sees no incongruity in a Chinese-owned French Continental restaurant with Latino kitchen help and Anglo waiters. Likewise a Korean entrepreneur was in no way perplexed by the irony of Middle Eastern importers selling winter jumpers to a Korean shopkeeper to meet the demands of his black clientele. In the competitive urban marketplace of Los Angeles, business appears to acknowledge few impermeable boundaries.

Variations on this pattern are not limited to Los Angeles. Miami's Calle Ocho is still lined with Cuban restaurants and other businesses. A brief inquiry into the origins of many of the cooks, dishwashers, clerks, and other workers, however, reveals many Dominicans and Central Americans. Just as upwardly mobile Chinese Americans are not eager to wash dishes and bus tables, so too Miami's upwardly mobile Cuban community seems to provide entrepreneurs with a diminishing supply of low-wage workers. This supply problem was first ameliorated by the Mariel immigrants in the late 1970s, and now by a steady supply from the Caribbean and Central America. In this case the businesses can continue to operate in Spanish, but different nationalities serve to maintain the divide between owners and workers. Whether these interconnected ethnic labor markets reflect chains of opportunity (see Wilson and Portes 1980), or chains of exploitation (see Sanders and Nee 1987) is akin to the arguments on export processing. Yet it is obvious that the international division of labor is very close to home.

The potential profits are as dramatic as the experience of a Jewish pushcart salesman named Woolworth. The history of the dangers of this business and its resentments are just as dramatic. The Los Angeles riots of 1992 were just one of many uprisings in which middleman minorities found themselves to be vulnerable targets of deep-seated anger. Just as the middleman role has been a strategy for success of small and otherwise powerless minority groups, it has also been a strategy for small but strategic nations. Middleman trade between Northern Europe and the Byzantine city Constantinople, and later the Ottoman Empire, made the swampy salt-flats of northeast Italy into the glories of Venice. Many of the current middleman nations are the homes of the middleman entrepreneurs we have noted. They have included Lebanon before trade was crushed by civil strife, Israel despite Arab-led boycotts, and most notably now the Chinese-dominated cities of Hong Kong, Singapore, and Taipei.

Despite the much touted success of middleman nations and individuals, they tend to remain somewhere in the middle, far better off than those at the bottom, but still the small shopkeepers of World Mart. The real payoffs are reserved for those at the top.

Middleman Moguls and the New Big Men

The potential for well-placed redistributors to claim a share of the rewards of exchange increase as the system size increases. In the global exchanges of

World Mart, the magnitude is truly staggering. This is true for government redistributors with an eye to personal gain: Ferdinand and Imelda Marcos were able to garner enough of the returns from the participation of the Philippines in the new international division of labor to become fabulously wealthy. In income-poor but resource-rich Zaire (Congo), former president-for-life Mobutu Sese Seko also used his cultivated position at the center of import-export trade to become one of the world's wealthiest men. Private enterprise is every bit as profitable however. The United States alone now has 170 billionaires, almost all of them garnering their money from the profits of large corporations, most of which are international. The returns to these global marketers far exceed that of the most famous superstars: even though Michael Jordan receives a few million over several years for playing basketball, and millions more for his Nike endorsements, he still cannot touch the income of Nike CEO Philip Knight. As Disney films, parks, and products were encircling the globe, CEO Michael Eisner's annual income was as high as 300 million. The rise of Microsoft operating systems to the world standard (not the best, many users attest, just the standard) has earned Bill Gates a staggering fifty to sixty billion dollars. Internet middleman moguls have made the most recent spectacular gains. Amazon.com founding employee Nicholas Lovejoy left at age twenty-eight, a multi-millionaire after only three years, to travel the world. "We had this one trip on a sailboat for three weeks where we were totally out of contact with civilization," he said describing a South Pacific voyage, "And when we got done, the stock had tripled" (New York Times, Feb. 11, 2000). Lovejoy admits that such a world is "bizarre" and now devotes his time to social and environmental philanthropy projects such as starting community gardens in Seattle.

In some cases the returns even dwarf the revenues of governments, whose ability to tax and redistribute is severely constrained under free market philosophies. The net worth of the world's top billionaires is greater than that of many nations. Bill Gates net worth is greater than the gross national product of all Central America combined. This is no longer just the case with small nations. In a gesture of international philanthropy, Ted Turner of Turner Broadcasting pledged to give the United Nations one billion dollars. This is more than the entire debt to the U.N. owed by the United States, a debt the United States claimed it could not afford. No big deal, says Ted, this only represents the unexpected appreciation of his global assets over nine months! Turner's pledge is just the largest of a new series of huge gifts, in which private philanthropists can undertake huge social programs that governments now insist they cannot afford. This is a dramatic indication of the decline of government power in a global free-for-all market but also the dramatic rise of a handful of corporate redistributors.

Robert Frank and Philip Cook (1995) call this the rise of "winner-take-all" markets. Globalization plays an important role in creating these markets. Once the world listens to the same music, a few global superstars can dominate the airwaves of the planet, while others, maybe almost as good, languish in obscurity. More significantly, their record distributors can dominate the world market, individually or in great international interlocks such as have been recently concluded between U.S. labels and Japanese electronics firms. In international business, the search for a common standard, such as computers with Intel circuitry and Microsoft operating systems, means enormous returns for those who control these systems, while the multitude of alternatives, perhaps almost as good or ultimately better, are crowded out. For the winners there is a world of profits to gain, for the losers only the chance to try again, or hope for a job with the worldwide winners.

Misery at the Mart

The world is becoming a vast social network of trade relations. This network is not a smooth, even mesh but a web with key central positions, nodes of power, privilege, and prestige. Geographically there are still centers of power, although these now span at least three continents, and within the market there are key positions of power. As the system grows in magnitude and complexity so do the possible returns to well-placed redistributors. Also magnified are the constraints on self-sufficiency and the price of being cut off from the system.

Economists speak of the idea of economies of scale. It is more efficient to produce ten thousand automobiles of the same design than ten, better yet to produce ten million. This is part of the logic of export industrialization. During the ascendancy of dependency thinking in Latin America, many Latin American countries attempted what they called import substitution industrialization. The idea is that if countries are dependent on trading low-price raw materials for the finished industrial goods of the advanced industrial nations, then the way to break this dependency is to develop their own industries that will make products to replace the need for imports. The problem with this idea is that not only is it hard to get the necessary capital and expertise to produce a first-rate product, the internal market for the product may be very small. As a result, rapid industrialization has always been export industrialization (Sernau 1994).

Great Britain led the way into the industrial world by dominating world markets and exporting finished products far beyond its own limited domestic market. For almost two decades following World War II, the United States dominated world industrial markets. Americans began to think of ever bigger production, ever better wages, ever stronger job security as the natural order of things. Yet this prosperity was possible to a large extent because the rest of the world was either too poor or too war-shattered to compete with U.S. global dominance. As Europe and Japan recovered, and as new players entered the game, U.S. dominance diminished, and so did the assurance of rising wages and broad-based prosperity. What suddenly struck American workers as the ugly new world was in many ways the world of their grandfathers in a time when the United States competed with many rivals for world markets and world ascendancy: insecure employment, stagnant wages, and uncertain fortunes tied to the roller coaster of world economic fortunes. This is the world of 2000; it was also the world of 1930, 1910, and 1890.

The new global upstarts, meanwhile, made their market not with import-substitution industrialization but with export-oriented industrialization. The internal markets of South Korea or Taiwan could never support an ambitious foray into automobiles and electronics, even Japan could not have done this with internal markets, especially since these countries were all relatively poor with little consumer purchasing power. The key was the expansive global markets.

A problem is embedded in this, however. Mass production is most efficient at colossal economies of scale that far exceed local capacity to consume. Therefore the success of large industry is always tied to dominating vast, preferably global, markets. But if a few super-producers satisfy global demands for consumption, what happens to the rest? The answer seems to be that they find their work in service activities that cannot be centralized, they join the cadre of subcontractors making or assembling parts for the super-producers, or they do very little at all, locked out from the global factory, and left to scavenge in the dumpsters behind World Mart.

Exploitation and Exclusion

The global assembly and distribution of World Mart has filled the planet with products. More opportunities for more varied consumption are available to more people than ever before. A new global middle class has also been created, eager to begin flexing its purchasing power. By some measures India now has a larger middle class than the United States. It also has many more poor, of course, but the nation is so large that in the midst of great wealth and great poverty, there are now as many as 200 million middle-class Indians.

For those with a steady middle-class income, the prices at World Mart are lower than ever before. But for those excluded from the new world economy, the vulnerable working class and growing underclass, the price of this economy itself is very high. The informal economy, bolstered by workers who have no access to formal employment, continues to be the fastest growing sector in many developing countries. Meanwhile, unemployment in France and throughout much of Eastern Europe is a source of continued political and social turmoil. In the United States many workers find themselves trapped in cycles of short-term, no-benefit, low-commitment precarious employment. Underclass, marginalized, disenfranchised, underemployed—all of these terms seek to grapple with the social exclusion of the new world economy (Bhalla and Lapeyre 1999), increasingly an "economy of exclusion."

Alienation and Dislocation

World Mart has also produced huge human dislocations. Tijuana boasts some of the highest wages in Mexico, yet few Mexicans are eager to make it their permanent home. For many jobless transplants it is a place of rootlessness and impermanence, of crime and crass commercialism that deplete the soul. In Jamaica "barrel children" wait for barrels shipped from the United States by absent parents who hope that a new pair of sneakers will substitute in small measure for their prolonged absence in the lives of children they may rarely ever see (Larmer 1996). In the United States the enduring relationships of work and family have been replaced by frequently transient relationships in both (Rubin 1996). We have created a world without assurances, what Henry Louis Gates, Jr., calls a "free agent society."

The great abundance, great promises, and yet closed doors of World Mart have created a whole new criminal opportunity structure. The fear and control of the Russian KGB has given way to the fear and control of the "Russian Mafia." Gangsters now prowl the rich Crimean vacation spots once reserved for senior bureaucrats and their agents. In Hong Kong "entrepreneurs" who do little to hide their crime syndicate connections have survived the change in governments, and continue as a second, secret government (Dannen 1997). Worldwide trade generates opportunities for worldwide networks of violence, drugs, and extortion: "steal locally, syndicate globally."

A global advertising campaign of "get yours, you deserve it" reaching a world that has gotten mostly broken promises has spawned a surge in urban street crime. In Mexico City, the mayor had to cancel his big anticrime speech when his notes were stolen from his car. The U.S. State Department has issued crime advisories for travelers to Mexico City—while German travellers are warned about violence and theft in Miami. We have come to fear the street crime that is extolled in "gangsta' rap" now heard around the world, yet often lose far more to "suite" crime that manipulates the profits of world trade (Reiman 1998). The "get-rich-quick-or-stay-poor-forever" world of the new economy has fostered what Cornell West (1993) calls a "pervasive gangster mentality" that reaches from the streets to the suites.

WORLD MART

Seoul For Sale
Scott Sernau

Seoul for sale,
Corporate nation, come buy a share.
Share in this feast of laissez-faire
Where the dollar can do what it pleases
And the poor die quietly of industrial diseases.

But Bangkok boasts more bang for your buck,
Golden calves beckon in bordellos without borders.
Why reckon with the poachers of human skins,
Can't MasterCard pay the price of our father's sins?
Don't you know, dignity died of the new world disorder.

Surely there is no shame in Shanghai
Where daughters of the revolution learn to sew
Dainty drabs for GI Joe.
Peasant armies marching to purchase orders
Get with the program,
Put it on a chip,
Patent the people,
Pass the slip.

Common interest can be forgotten,
Look what compound interest has begotten:
A world of bonds and bondage,
Where world trade towers tall—
Built with minor foreign assistance.
Marvel at the grandeur of it all—
Built on the graves of the resistance.

Words of the profits scroll
On the monitors that monitor us all
Congregating in convention halls.
Pay no attention to the toll,
Pray the stocks rise even if the people fall.
Come, let us gather at the mall.

Remake the Market: Seeking Equity and Opportunity

In 1995 the United Nations held a major international conference in Copenhagen on the topic of social development. The U.N., particularly through UNESCO, the United Nations Economic and Social Council, has attempted to continue the dialog on social development through its Human Development Reports. In these reports the U.N. offers an index of human development—economic factors such as income and employment coupled with social factors such as health and education. The index shows a world that has made some progress, but with continued disparities in power and performance.

Economic growth alone will not carry us all ever upward. In the global currents, rising tides do not raise all boats, they swamp some and drown others who are stranded on the beach. The Copenhagen conference called for broad-based inclusive efforts at attacking poverty, building solidarity, and creating meaningful employment. Ferdinand Mayrhofer-Grunbuhel of Austria contended: "Social development should no longer be a byproduct of economic development, but should be pursued as an independent goal. In the future, security will mean not only the absence of military threat but also the freedom from distress and social exclusion" (UN 1998, 4).

At the heart of this is growing inequality, according to Jean Francois Giovanni of Switzerland:

This new, often invisible form of poverty is the result of emerging forms of exclusion and marginalization, particularly long-term unemployment. The breakup of society into the privileged and the underprivileged, which is found in all countries and between countries, is a major failure of the social plans developed at the end of the Second World War. Not only does it fly in the face of the moral imperatives of human solidarity, it contains the seed of growing social conflicts and may even result in social disintegration (UN 1998, 6).

This was echoed by Anas of Indonesia: "People should be put at the center of development . . . First, policies should be established for broad-based economic growth, to provide income-earning opportunities for the poor. Second, access to education, health and other social services should be improved, to allow the poor to raise their living standards" (UN 1998, 8).

We must find new links between people and between development approaches. Scholars of economic development have long searched for the key to a more balanced, inclusive, equitable economy: investment in basic needs (Streeten 1977; Samater 1984), promotion of entrepreneurship and enterprise generation (Schumpeter 1949; Hoselitz 1957), and investment in skills and education, sometimes termed "human capital" (Denison 1965). Each model

Table 3.1 Income and Well-Being in Thirty Nations (1995)

Country	Real Purchase Power	Life Expectancy at Birth	School Enrollment Ratio	Human Development Index (HDI)
HIGH HUMAN DEVELOPMENT				
Canada	$21,916	79.1	100	.960
France	21,176	78.7	89	.946
Norway	22,427	77.6	92	.943
United States	26,977	76.4	96	.943
Netherlands	19,876	77.5	91	.941
Japan	21,930	79.9	78	.940
Sweden	19,297	78.4	82	.936
United Kingdom	19,302	76.8	86	.932
Australia	19,632	78.2	79	.932
Germany	20,370	76.4	81	.925
South Korea	11,594	71.7	83	.894
Costa Rica	5,969	76.6	69	.889
Mexico	6,769	72.1	67	.855
Poland	5,442	71.1	79	.851
Brazil	5,928	66.6	72	.809
MEDIUM				
Saudi Arabia	8,516	70.7	57	.778
Russia	4,531	65.0	78	.769
Iran	5,480	68.5	67	.758
South Africa	4,334	64.1	81	.717
Indonesia	3,971	64.0	71	.679
China	2,935	69.2	64	.650
LOW				
Kenya	1,438	53.8	52	.463
Pakistan	2,209	62.8	41	.453
India	1,422	61.6	52	.451
Cambodia	1,110	52.9	62	.422
Nigeria	1,270	51.4	49	.391
Bangladesh	1,382	56.9	37	.371
Haiti	917	54.6	29	.340
Mozambique	959	46.3	25	.281
Ethiopia	455	48.7	20	.252
COUNTRY AVERAGES				
All Developing	3,068	62.2	57	.586
Least Developed	1,008	51.2	36	.344
Industrial	16,337	74.2	83	.911
World	5,990	63.6	62	.772

Source: United Nations *Human Development Report 1998*.
Note: "Real purchase power" is gross national product per capita adjusted for differences in the cost of living. School enrollment is the ratio of children in primary and secondary schools to the total school-age population. Quality of life index is composed of measures of health, education, and income.

addresses an important need but by itself still offers limited horizons. Basic needs provision cannot be sufficient or sustainable if low-income groups are only recipients and never participating providers. Entrepreneurship, on the other hand, already abounds in urban centers, but it is often a trade in trivial, or destructive, products that contribute little to fundamental needs. Human capital investment is critical but it must be linked to its means of application or it will only result in creating overeducated underemployed, and will be dismissed by the poor as a poor investment. The Brazilian educator Paulo Freire called for a new style of education, a "pedagogy of the oppressed," that would help people to understand their condition and be empowered to change it. We need to extend his ideas to the new ranks of the excluded, and develop an adequate "pedagogy of the dispossessed" (Sernau 1994).

Most needed are human capital investments linked to the needs of expanding enterprises that directly target the meeting of basic needs. One example of this is in housing: when local residents receive the training, materials, and property rights to address their most critical housing needs, they also build transferable skills and an altered community image, in dramatic contrast to the stigma and dependency that often goes with "public housing." It is ironic that places of the greatest unemployment and underemployment are often the places where there is the most work waiting to be done in addressing human needs. The role of social policy must be to restore those broken linkages between ongoing needs and stable employment.

Calls for better education and employment in the United States are often couched in the language of competitiveness. In campaigns for everything from president to school board, global competitiveness is the new buzz word. But we must move beyond the language of competitiveness, which is still neo-mercantilism—assuming nations are all in a head-to-head race to get the gold. Competition is no longer purely along national lines. What does record sales of Chrysler-Daimler cars with Mitsubishi engines mean for the economic competition between the United States, Germany, and Japan? We need a new worldview that extends beyond global competition to a recognition that we live in a world of transnational winners reaping global profits and transnational losers who must come together in new transnational solidarity. World Mart brings new opportunities but also huge concentrations of power; together we must insist that opportunity and empowerment are extended to all. The exclusive mall of World Mart must embrace the excluded and become something more inclusive and democratic, perhaps more akin to an open-air market.

4

BROTHERS AND SISTERS AFTER ALL

Gender, Work, and Home

> What I regret the most is not the pain of working at something so degrading, so meaningless. It is instead the pain of knowing that we, the laborers, are capable of so much more.
> —Juana, Mexican assembly worker (quoted in Peña 1997, 6)

I TEACH SOCIOLOGY at a mid-sized Midwestern American university. I like to begin a course with introductions, and ask students to share, as much as they are comfortable, something about themselves that relates to the course theme. In a course on the family this is one's current family or household setting, in a course on work it is one's current job, and so forth. My classes may be typical of many around the United States these days; they are certainly not typical of those in a small Midwestern community only a few years ago. Let me introduce you to a few people in a typical class.

Margaret is married with two older children. Her husband works three jobs, one seasonal and two part-time. She worked for Whitehall labs making pharmaceuticals. The Caribbean Development Initiative passed Congress during the Bush administration and was intended to promote new enterprise and thus stability in the Caribbean basin, but instead it merely gave tax advantages to U.S. companies to move their existing production off-shore. Pharmaceutical production is hard to move just anywhere since it is supervised by the U.S. Food and Drug Administration. But Whitehall could shift much of its production to Puerto Rico to take advantage of lower wages while still remaining in a U.S. territory and this they did. The company was then bought out by a German firm, Bayer, who still locally hires chemists and accountants but few production workers. Margaret was laid off and is using her severance to help pay for her return to college. She wants to be a nurse and her husband is mostly supportive, but she has a long way to go and will not begin earning a second (or in this case, a fourth) income for the family until after the children are due to begin college themselves.

After a stint in the military, John went to work for American Motors General, making Humvee military vehicles. A temporary lull in orders for the "Hummers" led to his layoff and his decision to return to school, where he is also in the nursing program, one of a growing number of men. He works part-time as a paramedic and has a steady girlfriend but feels he can't afford to get married.

Angie returned to school after both she and her husband were laid off from Johnson Controls, which shifted their particular production line to a twin plant in Reynosa, Mexico. Her husband grew frustrated with working odd jobs but was not supportive of her return to school to pursue an interest in social work, a degree that will take her at least another four years. They divorced and her three-year-old son spends school days in the on-campus daycare.

Ellen began school in Florida while living with her father, then moved north to live with her mother and continue her education. She is engaged to a carpenter and is seeking a teaching degree. Edward has transferred between three different schools, running out of money each time. He works nights at an Italian restaurant while pursuing a computer science degree. Flora's family ties are limited, since she lost her parents and all but two siblings in the genocide in Rwanda. In her entire extended family, of Tutsi background, these are the only survivors, one in Belgium, one in New York, and Flora who studies psychology here.

Karen often misses classes for court hearings as she is locked into a custody battle with her Jordanian former husband who would like to have their two children return with him to Jordan. Tanisha sympathizes, saying her situation is probably better; she hasn't heard from the father of her two children in six months—at least he doesn't interfere.

Tonya wears a backwards cap and a leather jacket that advertises every major rap group currently popular. She's struggling to finish her papers on time but not because she is always at concerts as I might first suppose. The jacket and cap are her teenage son's (she hardly looks old enough to have a teenage son) which she grabbed in a hurry on the way out the door—nothing else was both warm and clean. A single mother of six, she works for the local office of our congressman, and it's been a busy month. She's an honor student but that status is now precarious since the triple burden of home, work, and school are taking their toll.

Clearly my classroom would look different if I taught at the selective private university across town, or in a different location, yet this class is not atypical of many around the country. Still, my students are not likely to begin their courses with much awareness of the historical and geographic context of their situations. This classroom has the faces and stories it does in part because this community led the way into rust-belt deindustrialization with the closing of Studebaker in 1963. Civic boosters reject the rust belt label and proudly point to a robust economy with low unemployment. This is not the same economy as that of 1963, however, as is evidenced by the long row of abandoned brick factories and warehouses with broken windows that scowl from the shadows behind a new line of chrome and glass offices that now adorn the riverfront. In complex but compelling ways, the seemingly very private affairs of changing households are linked to changes taking place around the world. Margaret, John, Angie, Ellen, Flora, Karen, Tanisha, and Tonya have more in common than they at first realize. In particular, both their households and their aspirations are bound up in a rapidly changing world of work.

Working the Global Assembly Line

Many a U.S. worker has complained, "My job went to Mexico." Yet the job opening in Mexico, Asia, or the Caribbean may not be the same job that left; a transformation occurred as it crossed the border. The industrial jobs that remain within the United States and that shift between states are also being changed by the forces of global technology and the global economy. Henry Ford did not invent but refined and expanded the emerging idea of the assembly line. The idea had been around since the dawn of modern capitalism, maybe as old as the Venice Arsenal of 1438 (Peña 1997)—the way a highly commercial state could use its production skills to match the military might of larger neighbors. Ford, however, adapted the assembly line idea to fit the American economy and society at the beginning of the twentieth century. It was large, systematized, supposedly rational and efficient (industrial workers often wonder about this), and machine-driven.

The doctrine that became known as "Fordism" was not just about technology and production but also about economics and distribution. Who would buy all these Fords that rolled off the assembly line in record numbers? Ford's answer was that the new production process would allow prices to be low enough, and his highly productive workers' wages high enough, that they themselves should be able to afford a basic Ford automobile. Encapsulated in Ford's idea of the industrial revolution is a kernel of the American dream. No more crowds of workers walking from the dingy factory back to their dingy tenements nearby. No, work hard all day and you too can *drive* home in your Model T. Ford recognized that the depersonalized, routinized, machine-driven factory floor held what he termed "the terror of the machine" for workers, but it also held the entry ticket to the American dream.

Yet as assembly lines become global, many find the dream elusive while the terrors are very real. New times and places create new visions of the efficient work place. And an export orientation means there is no need that the workers are ever able to buy the products they manufacture. Devon Peña claims that "if Henry Ford had gone to Mexico he probably would have built a *maquiladora*"

(1997, 3). The assembly lines that stretch out of the twentieth century are quite different from the ones that led into it. Have a look at the new world of work.

Electronics

Juárez, Mexico — Juana Ortega works at an RCA plant on the U.S.-Mexican border, one of the first of a series of electronics *maquiladoras* that now dominate the economic life of the city. She gets up at 5:00 in the morning to make breakfast for her three children as well as her sister and her uncle. Then she crowds into a van for the ride to work. The plant, like many here, is new and expansive with a U.S.-style corporate campus, yet she feels her life is as cramped and stifling as the hot, crowded ride in the van. Says Juana:

This job is a terror. The noise. The monotony. The constant danger of the machine . . . In the factory the line is the worst, it crushes your fingers and in the end your mind as well. They stuff us into vans. They stuff us into factories. They stuff it to you at work. It's stuff! Stuff! Stuff! . . . You work till your bones hurt. You work till your eyes hurt. The engineers make you work till you think you will drop . . . always watching and hovering, stopwatch and clipboard in hand (Peña 1997, 6).

She goes on to describe acts of collective sabotage against the line, breaking parts and the belts themselves, that workers use to slow its relentless speed-up. Workers play stupid and play sick, and sometimes revolt in wildcat strikes against what they see as the inhumanity of their workplace. The plant manager sees the situation differently:

This [repetitive labor] also reinforces discipline and self-worth. We are helping Mexico become more modern. The technology we use here is high-tech. We are upgrading Mexico's technological infrastructure, and this is a big part of the progress we are bringing to our good neighbors south of the border. And so this opens up new possibilities for the girls who work for me. I mean, these girls don't have a lot of other options: stay at home, sell trinkets or candies on the street, work at a sewing factory, or, worst of all, prostitution. People accuse us of exploitation, but we are bringing a superior technology, good jobs at decent wages, and a better business climate to Mexico" (Peña 1997, 14).

Juana describes a familiar triad of dependency: exploitation, domination, and distortion. Her phrases echo Marx's century-old description of alienation in industrial capitalism. Her manager's counterpoint is that the plants bring what Mexico needs, the familiar modernization triad: modern technology, modern institutions, and modern personalities.

Penang, Malaysia — Julie was proud to begin a new job at a modern American-owned plant with its smart green uniforms and ample technology. That pride has faded into fatigue as she spends her nights crowded into a small room she shares with three other women, and spends her days in the demanding drudgery of "scope work." "Her job involves peering all day through a microscope, bonding hair-thin gold wires to a silicon chip destined to end up inside a pocket calculator, and at 21, she is afraid she can no longer see very clearly" (Ehrenreich and Fuentes 1981, 53).

Commenting on this problem, one industry executive admits that it is now hard to find women to do "scope work" in Hong Kong, but not in Malaysia and the Philippines. "They like scope work. And it's true that if they don't follow procedures they can diminish their eyesight a little. But these girls are 16, 17. They can take a lot of abuse. They abuse their bodies a lot" (Gray 1987).

Malaysia as a nation is hoping to escape the Asian economic woes and continues its dramatic 8 percent annual economic growth rates. The National Day parade features not military uniforms but the workers of Celcom, Malaysia's first private telecommunications company, parading in perfect formation in glistening futuristic silver costumes complete with silver bicycle helmets. The nightly government television assures viewers of their place in the new economy in a jingle, "Malaysia, you can be a star!" (Reid 1997). "See what the future can bring," the new armies of workers are told; Julie will do well simply to be able to see.

San Jose, California — Not all scope work can be exported, especially specialty work or that involving quick turnaround times. At an electronics assembly facility, the vast majority of the workforce, however, is nonetheless of Asian background. Recent mainland Chinese immigrants and second generation low-income Filipino-Americans sit next to Vietnamese and Cambodian refugee women. A new group added to the mix are young Hmong women. Trained from very young to do the precise needlepoint embroidery for which they have become famous, the Hmong are not much good at fast machine sewing, but they have the careful coordination ideal for scope work. One generation ago their parents farmed the mountains of Laos with buffalo and spoke an unwritten language; now these, their daughters, assemble the latest in micro-circuitry. As the women work in their clean uniforms, a guest quickly surveying the lines of microscopes would be hard pressed to tell this plant from its counterparts on the other side of the Pacific.

Apparel

Juarez, Mexico — Maria Patricia applied for a position at a local garment *maquiladora*. She is taken onto a floor filled with old sewing machines and metal folding chairs for a "test." The test consists of sewing on as many pockets as she can to blue jeans. There are no parameters to this test, and her production is added to the total output. Her task is to grab pocket material with one hand, garment pieces with the other, place the pocket exactly by sight, quickly stitch it with contrast thread and then, with one movement, shift it to another pile and grab a replacement. Her pile of unsewed material is continually replenished and grows as she becomes overwhelmed trying to match the pace of experienced workers at this "unskilled" task. Her assignment: sew a pocket every nine to ten seconds, 360 to 396 pockets every hour, between 2,880 and 3,168 pockets every shift. Her questions about the nature of the test and job are met with a curt response from the supervisor: "I told you already we do piecework here; if you do your job you get a wage, otherwise you don't. That's clear isn't it? What else do you want? You should be grateful! This plant is giving you a chance to work! What else do you want? Come back tomorrow and be punctual" (Fernandez-Kelly 1983, 114).

Waiting in line for another job application, she talks with Xochitl, whose family demands had kept her doing piecework at home despite holding a certificate from a private technical school in fabric cutting. The certificate shows a shiny eyed young girl quite different from this worried and prematurely aged woman, now thirty-two with four children and a husband who cannot support them peddling home-made refreshments. So she sews at home, making beach dresses for which she receives about eighty cents each. She sews from 6:00 a.m. to 3:00 p.m., then turns to her many homemaking tasks.

Xochitl is engaged in a domestic extension of the assembly line that dates to the beginnings of the industrial revolution. In New York at the turn of the century, it was not uncommon for immigrant families to sit huddled together in small tenement flats with everyone over about age five stitching together bits of leather, and putting soles onto shoes that would then be returned to the factory for a piece-rate price.

As with electronics and other manufactures, the contrasts between the assembly lines of Asia and Latin America and those within the United States are not as great as might be imagined. Sewing was long a staple employer of non-unionized women in the Southern United States. J.P. Stevens fought decades of anti-union battles in an effort to maintain low-cost production within the United States. Those factories are now idle, but domestic U.S. production remains in sweatshops in both New York and Los Angeles employing largely immigrant labor. According to one large employer: "Most of my workers are immigrants; if native, they're minorities. The shop is predominantly Haitian, then Jamaican, Spanish, some native black, with two Italian ladies and two Jews. If there were no immigrants, the needle trades would be out of New York" (Waldinger 1986, 115).

The "needle trades" also remain in specialty production scattered across the country. I encountered one such operation in the unlikely locale of Boulder, Colorado, in the back room of an upscale leisure clothier. Hidden from the customer's view, and perhaps from the immigration service, is a room of eight sewing machines worked by eight Spanish-speaking women. They quickly fill special orders and stitch garments to meet changing customer tastes. The room is also used for storage but the manager is uneasy until I return to the showroom with its huge posters of Anglo-Americans enjoying their leisure in both the wilderness and the theater, wearing the latest fashion.

Food

Arkansas — Imagine an assembly line. The workers have all punched in, they are all in their places wearing their smocks, tools at the ready. The line starts up and down the conveyor come—chickens. Live chickens. They come squawking, pecking and attempting to get away. One can hardly blame them, I suppose. The workers are comprised almost exclusively of black women, many of them single mothers or otherwise the sole support of their families. The workers are poised in waders, calf-deep in blood, knives poised. Their task is to grab the chicken off the line and lop its head off without getting pecked or scratched or slipping in the blood. With deft strokes successive workers butcher the still-jerking chickens and send them down the line—quickly, without pausing. Knife strokes must be precise to deliver appealing looking filets, a difficult task since the chickens are odd-looking even before their heads come off. Many are covered in tumors. The chickens are fed a feed mixture that includes a variety of residual products, including the unused chicken parts. The company denies that any unapproved hormones or chemicals are used, but these chicken cannibals seem to develop in unusual—and unappetizing—ways. It doesn't matter, most will not go as whole fryers anyway but as filets to be frozen. They will be boxed and shipped to fast food outlets, to supermarkets, to schools, and overseas.

This is Tyson chicken, which has been battling union organizers. The women complain not just of the cuts, scratches, and falls, the long hours and low pay, but also that their own hands develop unhealthy looking growths. The company suggests greater attention to protective gloves. The women claim they can't work fast enough to meet line quotas with too much on their hands. The union claims gross exploitation of the most vulnerable workers. The company claims they are providing work opportunity in a place with very few opportunities.

They also claim they are caught in an ever more competitive market. Even though they dominate the domestic market, the lucrative Asian market is being challenged by Thai chickens. Thailand is making a major push to develop its agricultural as well as its industrial exports. Chickens can be "subcontracted," that is raised on small farms, then mass processed for export to Japan, Taiwan, and South Korea. Processed food now makes up 30 percent of Thailand's manufactured exports, meeting the demands of fast growing Asian cities, and helping Thailand establish itself not just as an NIC (newly industrialized country) but also an NAC (new agricultural country)—Asia's new supermarket (McMichael

2000). Low wages and a vertically integrated system that includes the Thai government and the Bangkok Bank assures their competitiveness.

Tyson executives are acutely aware of their competition with the NACs to feed the hungry workers of the other NICs. The women on the floor are too busy trying to feed their families and stay out of the blood to investigate the NIC-NAC problem. They have no knowledge of the women in Thailand raising and butchering chickens, or whether they should be struggling against them or struggling with them. Their hope is that union activity will improve their work without costing them their jobs. The chicken industry does have other options. In Southern Indiana, a chicken factory employs Mexican-American migrant women, as well as recent immigrants, some of them perhaps undocumented, and none of them likely to organize there. Meanwhile, the options for these workers in Arkansas are few. The international competition may be intense, but in this corner of Arkansas, the competition for their skills is nonexistent.

Mississippi — There is at least one factory seeking similar skills, and similar workers, just down the Mississippi. This one specializes in catfish. These fish don't come from the river itself but are raised, like the chickens, on high-production farms. The catfish are trucked from the fish farms to the factory where they await the assembly line. The workers—also women, also black, also poor— are ready for them in their waders, looking like a female angler's society. But these women mean business. The fish come down the line, slippery and flopping. The sawyer grabs the fish and lops off their heads with a band saw, tossing the bodies back onto the line while the heads drop into a bucket. Down the line, women with razor-sharp filet knives make several deft cuts to eviscerate the fish and turn them into filets to be frozen.

Many of the longer-term workers have lost fingers, especially to the saws. The company says they fail to follow directions and get careless. The women say they are overworked. They say they get tired. They say they slip in the fish guts that fill the floor. But through it all, the assembly line, like Paul Robeson's Ol' Man River, "just keeps rolling along." The line that threads between these rows of black women is operated by a tall white man who supervises from a raised control booth, adjusting the speed of the line, and noting the workers' efforts. One watches and wonders: is this the face of the new south or the old south? And what of what Marx called the "social relations of production"; is this the assembly line of the future or the plantation of the past under a metal roof?

These facilities are the culmination of the process of industrialization of food production and preparation that began in the twentieth century. Already in the 1890s, mechanical conveyors were used in Chicago in the "disassembly" of livestock carcasses. Most of our food products now are consumed in some form of packaged, processed form. This is not just to meet the demands of convenience, but also to facilitate shipping and storage, key elements in a global food regime. Even the fast food restaurant has taken on the look of an assembly line, with compartmentalized work controlled by a line of machinery. Food is not prepared, but arrives pre-prepared for onsite assembly. Mass production, distribution, and consumption are the foundation of the operation. The McDonald's sign used to record how many millions had been served, then how many billions, until finally they just borrowed a phrase from Carl Sagan, "Billions and billions."

The way a society feeds itself is its "food regime." U.S.-style agribusiness feeds a growing nation and competes very effectively, some would say ruthlessly, in the world market. In the process, however, it consumes enormous amounts of water, chemicals, soil, energy, and it consumes many workers' hopes and dreams. We are long overdue for a new recipe.

The Web of Kinship

A cartoon in the *New Yorker* by Frascino shows a Neanderthal-like man with his wife, explaining to another, "I hunt, she gathers, otherwise we couldn't make ends meet." Family, work, and gender have been inextricably linked for a long time. Economic changes bring family changes, and the structure of the family and that of the economy mutually reshape one other. When men hunted and women gathered, they tended to have fairly egalitarian, generally monogamous, and at least somewhat enduring marriage and family relations. Where a growing dependence on horticulture gave women—who controlled the gardens—greater control in the economy, they also often had considerable say in the life and politics of the community. Agrarian societies, in contrast, have both men and women contributing to the tasks of survival but with privileged men owning the land and controlling the society.

Industrialization brought some women, often the poor and displaced, into the paid work force, originally in industrial extensions of domestic work such as textile mills. By the beginning of the twentieth century, one-fifth of all women in the United States were in the paid work force, many of these from immigrant families. Other women worked alongside husbands in family farms and businesses. The "emancipation" of the Progressive Era early in the twentieth century brought women both the right to vote and expanded roles in the workforce. The dismal male employment prospects of the Great Depression made income-earning women essential for an even greater number of families. The height of World War II saw unprecedented numbers of women in the industrial labor force in both the United States and Europe as "Rosie the Riveters" assembled mechanized weapons as quickly as their absent husbands could wreck them on the battlefield.

Only with the postwar prosperity that brought the return of the "American

Dream" to the United States were American women told that their patriotic duty was now to return to the home to raise large families and make room in the factory for returning veterans. Some never left, but many were eager to relinquish the assembly line, others had no choice. Just as this atypical period of world dominance became the American ideal of work opportunity, this very atypical decade became the American ideal of the family (Skolnick and Skolnick 1999). Women in the paid labor force had been increasing over the century, now female labor force participation plummeted. Marriage and fertility rates had been declining, now young marriage was fashionable, as were large families. Divorce rates had been steadily increasing over the century, peaking in 1946 at a level that would not again be matched until 1973, but now divorce rates dropped, and divorce was often again highly stigmatized.

A pattern of work and family was idealized and projected into American homes by the growing influence of television: true American families had a hard-working, prosperous male provider. Smiling in his shadow was a nurturing woman who tended the suburban home and its ample supply of children and pets in a nuclear family household with little reliance on kin or anyone else. Those who couldn't afford this lifestyle, as well as those who would not be welcomed into these suburbs even if they could, were simply not portrayed, and so a historically and demographically atypical family ideal became fixed in popular imagination as the "traditional American family" (Coontz 1992).

In Europe, where harder times didn't permit such prosperous dreams, earlier trends continued, and many European countries still have lower birth rates, lower marriage rates, and more employed women than in the United States. Family in much of the rest of the world still resembled the earlier models inherited from pastoral and horticultural roots (in Africa in particular) or from a still-dominant agrarian heritage (especially in Latin America and the Asian rim).

Family patterns everywhere are changing, however. To modernization theorists, traditional patterns have been giving way to modern ones. From this perspective, the pattern seems clear: with the arrival of electricity, the dowry gives way to the disco. In fact, the world is experiencing a radical realignment of the structure of the economy and the family in ways that are just beginning to be apparent. Latin America and mainland Asia are industrializing, and industrial pressures were realigning the family there as they had in Europe and North America:

Under the impact of industrialization the family in newly developing societies becomes more egalitarian, emotionally freer, and less sexually stratified . . . The sceptre of patriarchal authority does not exactly fall from nerveless male hands; sometimes the wife, emboldened by her new freedom of power, snatches it brusquely form her husband's grasp. More often, however, a process of negotiation takes place during which men agree, though not without some reservation, to share power with their wives . . . Thus marital relations in an industrial society become more openly friendly or more hostile, and sometimes both (Rosen 1982, 3).

Advanced industrial societies, meanwhile, are shifting from production to service economies. The economic changes that come with this rudely interrupted the American Dream and the European Concord, and accelerated shifts in gender roles and family structure. New concerns about global competitiveness brought stagnant wages to laborers. New demands for flexibility brought increasingly precarious employment with a rise in non-union, temporary, and seasonal work. This undermined the role of the working-class male provider. It opened new demands as well as new opportunities for women. Women were already well-represented in the routinized service economy of clerical work and personal services, and these greatly expanded. Industrial demands shifted from strong backs to dexterous fingers. A century earlier, the Bob Cratchets of the industrial world gave over many of the clerical tasks to female stenographers and switchboard operators. Now, as the production process itself came to be dominated by keyboards and circuit boards, the female work role was expanded.

Beth Rubin (1996) describes fundamental shifts in the social contract that underpins society, from long-term stable social relations to short-term flexible relationships. This shift is occurring in both the workplace and the family. Marriage has taken on new meanings, and around the world divorce and separation have become more common. In the United States, marriage remains popular but faces many new uncertainties. U.S. divorce rates are some of the highest in the industrialized world, in part because the United States still has high marriage rates. In Europe, delaying and foregoing marriage has become more common, suppressing the divorce rates since some parting couples never married in the first place. Japan is almost alone in the industrialized world in having both high marriage rates and low divorce rates. In many respects this reflects marriage forms that echo an earlier time when expectations of love and romance and even personal compatibility were less and marriage was a contract of kinship, property, honor, and duty, as it had been in the agrarian West (Kristof 1996). As these attitudes are being questioned by younger Japanese, family patterns are sure to change at an accelerating rate.

In the developing world, the changes were uneven and unpredictable. Parts of Latin America started to become post-industrial without ever fully industrializing. In Mexico, the percentage of the labor force in industry now is no higher than it was in 1920. What has changed is the nature of that work and the composition of the labor force. Male-dominated heavy import substitution industry is in decline and smoke stacks stand idle in Mexico as they do in the United States. In its place, female-dominated light export-oriented industry has spawned new industrial parks as in the United States. As a result, in Mexico, Brazil, Venezuela, and elsewhere, men and women are still rethinking old agrarian roles and the impact of urban industrialization even as their countries are rushing ahead to suburban new industrial and service economies.

Likewise in Asia, families only beginning to accustom themselves to women being co-wage earners may find that women are their sole or primary wage-earners. Strains are greatest for the poor but the middle classes must also adapt to the changes. In South Asia and the Middle East the changes can be striking to outside observers: female physicians in New Delhi clipping their beepers onto their saris, and veiled female engineers in Pakistan and Iran pulling cellular phones from their cars.

Newly independent African nations faced the prospect of leaping from horticultural and herding societal structures directly into the high-tech global economy, bypassing agrarian and industrial production all together, or of being left completely behind. Some African countries tried to avoid the leap and stagnated, some leaped and crashed, some remain tottering on the precipice with one eye on the horizon and one on the abyss. In each case, however, the world of family and work has been altered forever.

Despite differing histories and backgrounds, common participation in the global economy is creating some common experiences in family and gender. If we see these changes merely as personal choices, say a problem of growing selfishness, or as a problem of a particular culture or sub-culture such as "the troubled black family," we miss the reality of the underlying structural causes of change, as well as their roots in economic relations.

One striking pattern emerges when comparing American racial groupings: many characteristics are shared by African-American, Native-American, and Puerto Rican families. These three groups have the highest rates of single parenthood, low marriage, and high divorce rates, and high rates of impoverished female heads of household. Yet what three groups could be more diverse in their cultural heritage? Certainly something more than traditional culture is at work. What these three groups do share is common labor market experiences. All three have rural roots and made large-scale rural-to-urban migrations, largely in search of work, earlier in this century. All three moved into urban areas that were hard hit by deindustrialization, and being newcomers with little seniority and limited higher education, now face very high rates of unemployment, especially male unemployment. All three have their dramatic success stories, but now also show similar signs of widespread family distress. From economic structure comes family structure. One might carry this a step further and suggest this then becomes cyclical: the children from impoverished single-parent households in declining cities will have far fewer economic opportunities as well. Family structure reinforces economic disadvantage.

Versions of these hard-times blues are now being sung around the world. Migrants flee depressed countryside for the call of the city, sometimes across international borders, often within their own country. They trade the support of rural kin for a patchwork of limited and overtaxed urban services. They trade the prospect of endless rural poverty for the unknown prospects of the city. Often what they find is a mélange of informal and unprotected low-wage employment for young women; informal marketing and homework for older women; dangerous, seasonal, unpredictable and possibly illegal activities for younger men; and nothing at all for older men. As this persists, the young men leave or die, the older men drink, the young women age quickly, and the older women care for the children and cry for the lost.

Some version of these blues are played out among poor families regardless of race and geography—this is South Los Angeles, South Chicago, and the South Bronx; it is replayed in Mexico City, Sao Paulo, Lagos, and Manila. It is not so much the "culture of poverty" as Oscar Lewis (1968) described it, as the modern structure of poverty. We know it best as urban poverty, but as city and country economies merge, we can find a country version of the same song. It is sung in rural Kenya, rural Mexico, and rural South Carolina; sung in many languages by workers whose experiences are more intertwined than they likely realize.

Overburdened Women and Displaced Men

The interplay of work and family are evident in the experiences of Teresa in Juarez, Mexico:

There were about seventy women like us sewing in a very tiny space . . . When I was sixteen I used to cut thread at the shop. Afterwards one of the seamstresses taught me how to operate a small machine and I started doing serious work. Beatriz, my sister, used to sew the pockets on the pants. It's been three months since we left the shop. Right now we are living from the little that my father earns. We are two of nine brothers and sisters (there were twelve of us in total but three died when they were young). My father does what he can but he doesn't have a steady job. Sometimes he does construction work; sometimes he's hired to help paint a house or sells toys at the stadium. You know, odd jobs. He doesn't earn enough to support us (Fernandez-Kelly 1983, 119).

Work and gender are bound up with global technology in the United States:

Pete used to be proud of the work he did as a machinist in an auto parts factory. Now he's just tired—and scared. Half the workers in his plant have been laid off because carmakers have been buying parts from Japan. On top of that, his company is automating in order to compete. "[That] means they only need a quarter of the workers they used to." Pete says, "and if they move the plant or write new job descriptions that get around the union and seniority, they can hire women. With the computer running the operation they don't need my muscle. And they don't need my skill with the lathe and the drill presses anymore" (Astrachan 1989, 221).

Tony lost his job in a chemical plant to layoffs that were never recalled in spite of promises to do so. A long wait for a recall, followed by a long job search, landed him nothing but a dishwashing position that not only was low paying but that he found humiliating. The changes nearly cost him his self-esteem and his family as well:

I was just so mad about what happened; it was like the world came crashing down on me. I did a little too much drinking, and then I'd just crawl into a hole, wouldn't even know whether Marianne or the kids were there or not. She kept saying it was like I wasn't there. I guess she was right, because I sure didn't want to be there, not if I couldn't support them (Rubin 1994, 219).

Constanta's day begins with a trek across one of Africa's fastest growing cities. She begins her day in cramped quarters on the edge of Nairobi. She travels by bus to semirural markets where she buys a range of vegetables. Then she continues her journey to a small booth in an open air market near the city center. She at least has a fixed spot, although she hopes to be able to afford an indoor space in a large market building down the street—an informal version of the American mall, and a more secure and more protected place to sell. To do this, she will need to secure a small loan from a micro-lending agency that specializes in women entrepreneurs. She supplements her income by travelling around to each of the luxury hotels that soar in the city center and cater to foreign tastes. Negotiating at the back door with an assortment of cooks and chefs, she tries to provide the key fresh ingredients they will need for the day's offering. Her work takes her between dozens of locations, and between the labels we might use to define her situation. Is she rural or urban? Part of the formal or the informal economy? A poor underemployed worker or a rising entrepreneur? Her family status is just as ambiguous. She has a husband, but rarely sees him as he drives a truck on long cross-country routes, shuttling pineapple, coffee, and tea from the Kenyan highlands to the coast. Sometimes truckers bring home good wages, sometimes they bring home little or nothing, sometimes they bring home AIDS from tiny settlements along the way that have no viable trade other than prostitution.

Marketing, both formal and informal, is a survival strategy used by women around the world. Africa has a strong tradition of market women that has spawned new entrepreneurship. In a village with many heavy beer men, the women have formed a cooperative to make and sell the beer, thus at least retaining the profits from their husbands' excesses. Elsewhere the markets are larger and merge into international streams of goods. The African market tradition was brought to Jamaica and has been kept alive by multitudes of women vendors, "higglers." Female higglers handle as much as 80 percent of Jamaican food products (Bolles 1992). Some have moved into the international economy, selling imported goods from North, South, and Central America in the markets, while higgling Jamaican products to the resorts and tourist hotels. Some have built a trade circuit that encompasses several islands by small boat.

Female street vendors, often with children at their side or perched on a crate behind them, fill markets in the Philippines and throughout the sprawling cities of Latin America. Capital investment is low, experience is gained on the job, and they can work with siblings and children (Mitchell 1989). Street life is lonelier for rickshaw drivers in New Delhi, often young men displaced from the countryside. One such man runs his cart through the heat of the day and on into the late night, never being spoken to except to be hailed, directed, and dismissed. He sleeps a few hours under his rickshaw, then returns to his runs in an effort to earn the coins to survive. No one asks his name but it echoes with great irony a very different vision of his life that his parents must have imagined when they gave their first son a name that means, "The Lord King."

Domestic work, a longtime mainstay of female employment, continues in much of the world, now driven by growing middle classes with demanding careers that leave them little time to devote to home. In Mombai (Bombay), India, the families of entire shantytowns may be supported largely by women who, together with their children, clean the homes of the established wealthy and the new apartments of the middle class. The work relations are often degrading, the pay is poor, and yet this is their one venue into the urban economy (Mitter 1991). Where there is not this huge supply of available local labor, it can be imported, as with the large number of Filipina maids in Hong Kong. Newly prosperous Hong Kong couples are promoted by agencies as the "all time favorite employers" for the Filipinas: small urban apartments to clean, no aging parents to take care of, and maybe even fashionable hand-me-down clothes to inherit (Constable 1997). Importing maids when domestic supply dwindles has become common around the world. The U.S. market was once dominated by African-American women, but now looks to Polish and Caribbean immigrant women on the east coast and Latinas on the west coast. The number of Washingtonian families employing informal, and at times illegal, immigrant women to care for their homes and their children has several times provoked national scandal.

Locked In and Shut Out

When local systems collapse under more powerful international forces, it is often the men's roles that are the most completely erased. This is exactly because the men tend to hold positions of power, influence, and independence that are usurped by new forces and new masters. Ancient raids sometimes killed the men and captured the women. Modern colonial and corporate raids often do the same, albeit figuratively. The men's roles of authority and autonomy are replaced by more distant authorities. The women's roles of caretaking and daily provision are still needed, and so are harnessed to the new system. Poor women become locked in to the global economy, poor men are shut out. Because the women are closer at hand than distant and abstract forces, they may become the objects of the men's anger, frustration, and violence. While this violence is abhorrent and its consequences devastating, it must be recognized as a secondary reaction of the powerless to subtler but more powerful violence.

Examined side by side, common themes emerge from the repeated refrains. Women frequently bear the brunt of poverty. They continue to have primary responsibility for the care of children, as well as of sick and elderly family members. They continue to face discrimination and handicaps in the labor market, and attempts to gain greater education, independence, and upward mobility are frequently met with suspicion and outright hostility on the part of employers, fathers, husbands, and others. "When people who've had a little bit of education suddenly start acting uppity, they get slapped down," Jesus Sanchez told his daughter in the Mexico of a generation ago. "Take a look in the mirror and tell me what class you belong to, what your place is in society" (Lewis 1961). Versions of these harsh words are still heard in many places and many families, especially in regard to ambitious daughters.

A global perspective also shows that women, poor and middle-class alike, are frequently overburdened. Around the world, women work longer hours than men, and mothers longer hours than anyone (Scarr 1989). Women have become primary and important wage earners in many families, yet this is often only accepted, and then grudgingly, so long as they carry out all of their traditional homemaking and caregiving responsibilities. In some cases, the women themselves may feel that home is still their responsibility, and feel guilty about neglecting home, husband, and children. Almost regardless of the setting, upon entering a messy home it is the woman who quickly apologizes for the mess. Thus not only do single mothers bear a double burden of breadwinner and caregiver, but increasing numbers of married women also feel the double burden of home and work. This is true across many income levels and across geography. Studying middle-class American homes, Arlie Hochschild dubbed this pattern "the second shift" (Hochschild and Machung 1989). In Mexico, it is the *doble jornada*, "double day's journey."

In increasing numbers of homes, the men are just not there at all. Whether divorced, deserted, or just abandoned for long periods, the women carry on without male support. North Americans denounce "deadbeat dads" and "absentee fathers," Latin Americans murmur about the "machos" who prefer the streets to home, Africans wonder why their traditionally strong families are now so often supported by networks of female kin with few men to be found. These are sometimes called "matriarchal" families, a term that is misleading, for it implies that the women are powerful, when in fact they often feel overworked, overburdened, and victimized. A more accurate term is "matrifocal," focused or centered around the mother and female kin, and they are increasing in number on every continent.

So where are these men: the deadbeats, the dead broke, the machos, the bums, the deserters? The world has never lacked for individuals who have a difficult time enduring great responsibility, and certainly cultural patterns around the world contribute to this, but again we do well to look beyond personal and cultural peculiarities for structural causes. In their defense we must realize that many men have been displaced by forces they cannot control and may only partly understand. Traditional male roles, especially those which involved strength, independence, bravery, and self-reliant providing, have been severely undermined. Despite cultural variations, male roles in many societies have emphasized just these traits (Gilmore 1990). The man comes home from the hunt, the battlefield, the voyage, or the marketplace, tired and bruised, but loudly tosses down the goods and enjoys the acclaim of a waiting family and community. No more.

Surveying the last century and a half, one of sociology's first prominent female scholars, Jessie Bernard (1981), noted the "rise and fall of the good provider role." Family sociologist Frank Furstenberg, Jr., (1988) has noted that this "fall" created broader, more humane roles for some, but no successful and socially approved roles at all for other men.

The unemployed steel worker in Gary, Indiana, and the laid-off auto worker in Flint, Michigan, who once won approval for their ability to withstand the heat and grime and physical demands of their professions, now find themselves competing with teenagers for minimum wage jobs that the teenagers do better. They subsist on severance, on savings, and on women's employment. They drink beer, watch sports, and realize they have become a liability rather than an asset to their families. The same story is repeated in East Africa, where proud herders who once withstood the heat and grime and physical demands of their profession now are idled on government supported settlements, where they drink homemade beer and come to the same conclusion.

Women often find themselves locked in: locked in to a home full of never-ending demands, locked in (sometimes literally) to the demanding drudgery of an electronics or textile plant. Men often find themselves locked out: locked out of the labor market and eventually out of their families. Fatherhood around the world is shifting. While some men have the skills and background to become the nurturing, involved "Cosby-style" dad, many others find they are no longer needed or respected, no longer capable, at either the demands of the new marketplace nor the new home front (Furstenberg 1988). They become bitter, they become despondent, or drunk, or violent, or they just disappear. While the women may at least have the support of matrifocal families, these men may have very little at all. Some may follow any of a variety of organizations, usually with clear enemies lists and an angry agenda, but most have only the camaraderie of the street corner.

The new global middle classes clearly have access to more opportunities, but these also come with their own anxieties. New middle classes—whether they are African-American, Polish-American, Mexican, South Korean, or Indian—are often painfully aware of the precariousness of their position. A sudden economic downturn can result in an equally sudden plummet from privilege (Newman 1988). Raising children, ultimately an economic asset in agrarian societies, is an expensive and demanding proposition for the urban middle class. Often it requires two incomes from two separate professions. This creates demands that are very different from the side-by-side economic efforts of earlier families (Hochschild 1997).

Women working and economically contributing to their families is not new, women in professional careers is new. Wealthy women were educated to become cultured and poor women worked, but a new idea is the woman who combines education and work into a professional career. It has been suggested that the very idea of a career was created for a man who was largely exempted from family responsibilities (Slater 1970). This is not likely to be an option for career women. The woman faces criticism and guilt for neglecting her work if she invests too much at home, or for neglecting her family if she invests too much at work. The man feels that security in this precarious situation can only be won by heavy investments at work, yet knows that he is now also expected to be available at home. These present themselves as personal troubles but are in fact part of a global dilemma that must be faced cooperatively.

We Are the Children

The new world of work poses both opportunities and dangers. The benefits of new opportunities as always accrue to those with the greatest social power. It should be no surprise then that the greatest dangers have accrued to those with the least power: children.

Children at work is nothing new. In the simplest societies, the assumption of adult roles could be leisurely and natural. Children followed their natural fascinations: investigating the secrets of the landscape, gathering treasures, watching and chasing small animals and the like. When not off together, they could watch and help adults in their varied tasks. In time the skills learned, and the ability to work together, would become the very skills needed in more sophisticated form as adults. In many of the simplest societies discipline is quite lax, simply because more is not needed, the assumption of adult roles happens naturally. The natural world held its dangers but also opportunities to learn and explore.

This changed in agrarian societies that needed the labor of many hands to bring in yields. Children were valued as an important source of labor, especially as both they and their parents aged, until the time when the younger generation would provide for the older. Poor families without enough land to provide for and occupy all their children would often apprentice them out. Despite high birth rates, many poor peasant households were not that large because, as in times past, as many as nine or ten children could be out, largely on their own, as farmhands, as household hands, or as apprentices to craftsmen. These arrangements were supposed to benefit all, but often depended on the kindness or harshness of the new master, and the harshness of the times and conditions of survival. Colonial America continued this pattern with slave children in the fields, young indentured servants apprenticed to craft masters, and young girls working as domestic help.

Industrialization brought new possibilities for achievement and new demands for education. It also brought new possibilities for exploiting child labor. Industrialization in Great Britain saw children used in the mines and the mills—they ate less, fit better in cramped spaces, and had less leverage to leave or rebel. Industrial America soon followed suit, especially with immigrant children who sometimes labored alongside their parents or in their own labor brigades. Middle-class leisure was supported by working-class and poor children.

For every nineteenth-century middle-class family that protected its wife and child within the family circle, then, there was an Irish or a German girl scrubbing floors in that middle-class home, a Welsh boy mining coal to keep the home-baked goodies warm, a black girl doing the family laundry, a black mother and child picking cotton to be made into clothes for the family, and a Jewish or an Italian daughter in a sweatshop making "ladies" dresses or artificial flowers for the family to purchase (Coontz 1992, 11).

A jingle of the time chided the leisure class, "The factory is next to the (golf) links so the children can watch the men at play."

When Japan began catch-up industrialization at the end of the nineteenth century, they also found children to be a ready and pliable labor force and many worked to their deaths in the coal mines of "battleship island." Reformers in all three countries and elsewhere began to denounce the practices. The ideals of universal education and school as the appropriate place for all children were promoted. Yet the old practices persist and more children are now at work around the world than ever before. According to the International Labor Organization (ILO), there are 153 million children working in Asia, 80 million in Africa, and 17.5 million in Latin America.

The demands of changing economies and the perils of family poverty place many children at risk of cruel exploitation. Ten million children are in chronic labor bondage in India alone. More than a million children work squatting before dusty looms in Pakistani carpet factories. Pakistani children sew soccer balls for Nike, Adidas, and other foreign contractors for as little as six cents an hour. Working a ten-hour day to stitch one ball, they receive sixty cents for an item that wealthier parents will buy for thirty to fifty dollars. The balls enter the United States tariff free and proudly announce "hand made." No mention is made of whose hands. Schanberg reminds us to think of those hands:

Silgli is only three, barely able to hold a needle, but she has started to help her mother and four sisters in India, together they can earn 75 cents a day. Sonu spends his days cutting chicken feathers for shuttlecocks in a worker's slum riddled with tuberculosis. Amir left school after the third grade and now spends his days sitting on a concrete floor using his feet as a vise while sharpening scissors and tools for a Pakistani metal shop for 2 dollars a week (Schanberg 1996, 41).

These situations are not limited to South Asia. Children work in Honduran factories that make trendy garments, in Brazilian orange groves that supply American breakfast tables, in toy factories in China and Thailand and on assembly lines in Indonesia. Yet it is in south Asia where the extremes of poverty combine with a history of child workers to produce some of the greatest abuses.

In India the vista of child labor are much the same: eight-year-olds pushing wheelbarrows of heavy clay across brickyards; four-year-olds stitching soccer balls with needles longer than their fingers; fragile-looking girls carrying baskets of dung on their heads; little boys hacking up sputum as they squat before their looms, trying to do good enough work to avoid the master's blows. All this takes place against a backdrop of rising affluence enjoyed by the privileged classes—lavish villas with high walls topped by iron spikes and satellite dishes on the roofs, luxury cars driven by liveried chauffeurs (Schanberg 1996, 45).

Girls, in particular, face the added risk of sexual exploitation. In rural Thailand, village girls, often no more than eleven or twelve years old, are sold to labor contractors who promise to find them good jobs in Bangkok only to lock them into prostitution. In known prostitute villages in India, the prostitution is no secret and young girls are groomed for this by family members who believe they have no other options.

Some children are sold by poor families, some are stolen from powerless ones. Desperate families often face desperate choices. In rural Michigan a laid-off auto worker has turned to turkey farming to supplement his other meager income. The sheds he has to use are poorly constructed and a sudden freeze can send turkeys piling on top of each other seeking warmth and suffocating one another. Thus his young girls plunge into the dark sheds, tossing turkeys off of each other, breathing the minute barbed inner feathers that stick in the lungs, chasing after escapees with the desperation that comes from knowing that a few birds could make the difference between profit and disaster. The father seethes inside knowing what he is putting his daughters through, but sees no other way. The contractors who will buy the birds, of course, never need to know any of these conditions. It's not their sheds anymore than those soccer mills belong to Nike.

Often as cruel and just as crippling to young development as the exploitation of children is their abandonment and exclusion. In Guatemala City, close-knit groups ("gangs" seems a harsh term for ten-year-olds) of "Los Abandonados," the abandoned ones, sleep in abandoned buildings, beg for food, sniff glue to ease the hunger, and try to survive on the streets. Girl gangs are often encouraged to enter prostitution, boy gangs may find their only income from stealing car parts and fencing them to the many local informal repair and parts shops. In Rio de Janeiro, the street children are considered enough of a threat to local businesses afraid of petty theft and enough of an embarrassment to local authorities that they have become the target of death squads, which often include paid security guards and off-duty police. The actions are justified as a battle against gangs and street crime, but the gangsters who are victims of these squads are often nine- to twelve-year-olds who have fled abuse, abandonment, and abject poverty with nowhere else to go.

Neglected and excluded children are not limited to the large cities of Latin America, however. In *Savage Inequalities* Jonathan Kozol describes the dying dreams of youngsters who walk together through deadly neighborhoods to reach razor-wire encased, decrepit, collapsing schools.

The idea of rights of children is quite new but is being pressed around the world. Human rights must also include our most vulnerable. The United Nations Convention on the Rights of the Child asked to adopt a poem by Ina J. Hughs as its prayer and pledge. This poem concludes:

We pray [accept responsibility] for children who want to be carried and for those who must,

for those we never give up on and for those who don't get a second chance.
For those we smother . . . and those who will grab the hand of anybody kind enough to offer it.

Efforts are made, here and there, to address these problems once they come to light. *Savage Inequalities* sparked a nationwide debate and court battles for more equal funding of education in the United States. The role of child workers has gotten new worldwide attention. A campaign to rescue bonded child workers, championed by a twelve-year-old Canadian boy, Craig Kielburger, and led by an upper-caste Indian, Kailish Satyarthi, has freed many from the darkness. The South Asian Coalition on Child Servitude has freed over twenty-nine thousand children from the worst conditions. Kailish stresses education as the alternative: the children get basic schooling in literacy, social education to make sense of their experience and the powerlessness of the lowest castes that kept them subservient, and training in carpentry and tailoring to turn their skills toward a more profitable trade. Similarly, a girls school in Nairobi, Kenya specializes in street children. Girls who would be recruited into prostitution are instead given the basics of education and vocational training, and maybe a chance for a new perspective.

When they first enroll many of the girls resemble sad, elderly women," says the Irish-born director, "Now, to see those girls just laughing, joking, singing, dancing, and doing very well in school . . . I never realized human nature is so resilient and that we can recover from so many traumas" (Hackel 1996). In India, Dinesh, an eight-year-old boy rescued from a brutal loom owner, echoes her words, saying he feels like the fields after a restoring rain: "My body and soul are green again." Child labor is about economic justice and human rights but it is also quite simply about nourishing the dreams and joys that give childhood its beauty and delight.

Marietta Dreaming
Scott Sernau

> By the sidewalk,
> Legs tucked back
> and wares spread before,
> In a world of no-name knees
> Whisking by to go
> Where you haven't been
> And where you don't know,

It's easy to dream
A life of exuberance
To match the life of your soul.

Marietta, at age twelve
You could be learning
And trying and yearning to become.
But here where your black hair
Almost touches the blackened street
And a tattered blanket holds
A sampling of life's trivialities,
There's nothing to try and little to learn.
Just exchange your life for those coins,
What you need to feed the rest,
What you can do to help.

But when friends stop
You laugh and talk—
Mostly laugh—
And when they go you dream:
What could and might and should.
Where no one else will
These dreams accept your love,
Soak it in and bloom
With colors and storied detail—
And brightness.

People have left,
Promises are failed,
But a good dream comes back.
It settles in and holds your mind
Until the blanket is folded for the night.
Dream on, Marietta,
In a world of betrayals
Your dreams and your laugh
Are the only glimpses
Of what is real.

My Brother's Face, My Sister's Eyes

The 1995 United Nations Fourth World Conference on Women in Beijing, China, was a remarkable reminder of the growing global awareness of the common cause of women and the continuing risks and burdens facing girls and women around the world. Some at the conference would consider themselves feminists, some would have never heard the term. Yet this highly publicized gathering was a definitive demonstration of both the multiplicity of problems and the commonality of hopes and struggles. Hillary Rodham Clinton addressed these commonalities in her speech at the conference:

However different we may be, there is far more that unites us than divides us. We share a common future. And we are here to find common ground so that we may help bring new dignity and respect to women and girls all over the world—and in so doing, bring new strength and stability to families as well.

By gathering in Beijing, we are focusing world attention on issues that matter most in the lives of women and their families: access to education, health care, jobs and credit, the chance to enjoy basic legal and human rights and participate fully in the political life of their countries (Clinton 1995, 1).

Women's roles are changing rapidly around the world, yet the world remains a dangerous place to be female. Consider these reports from around the world (cited in Seiple 1998):

WHO (World Health Organization): More than twenty thousand women were raped during the Balkan war; more than fifteen thousand women were raped in one year in Rwanda.

Alan Guttmacher Institute: In the United States, some 74 percent of girls who had sex before age fourteen report that it was involuntary.

UNICEF: In India, more than five thousand women are killed each year because in-laws find their dowries inadequate.

National Center for Health Statistics: Homicide is the second leading cause of death in the United States for girls aged fifteen to nineteen.

London Times: Yearly more than sixteen million girls in India are killed by their mothers or village midwives.

South China Morning Post: Six million Chinese women are named *Lai Di*, meaning "a son follows quickly."

WHO: Some 585,000 women died from pregnancy-related causes in 1990; 99 percent in developing countries.

UNICEF: In Haiti, 74 percent of primary-school-age girls are not in school.

Population International: In Chad, adult women have, on average, less than one month of education.

United Nations: One million children become prostitutes every year.

These problems point to the particular vulnerability of women and children, yet also speak of the need for broader transnational awareness of human rights struggles. Hillary Rodham Clinton stressed this connection:

It is a violation of human rights when babies are denied food, or drowned, or suffocated, or their spines broken, simply because they are born girls. It is a violation of human rights when women and girls are sold into the slavery of prostitution. It is a violation of human rights when women are doused with gasoline, set on fire and burned to death because their marriage dowries are deemed too small. It is a violation of human rights when individual women are raped in their own communities and when thousands of women are subjected to rape as a tactic or prize of war. It is a violation of human rights when a leading cause of death worldwide among women ages 14 to 44 is the violence they are subjected to in their own homes . . . If there is one message that echoes forth from this conference, it is that human rights are women's rights—and women's rights are human rights" (Clinton 1995, 5–6).

When seeking to improve the lives of women and children it is natural to focus on the home and family. Yet around the world and across societies we have seen that economic power is often the key to social power. The single greatest burden on women and children is no different from that on men: economic uncertainty and the drain of ill-compensated, degrading and dangerous work. Improving home and family situations must be paralleled by changes in education and the workplace.

In a memorable reading at President Clinton's first presidential inauguration, poet Maya Angelou called on those gathered to have the grace to look across racial, ethnic, historic, and geographic divides "into your sister's face" and "into your brother's eyes" and to say with simple hope, "Good morning." That hope has proved elusive. In Europe and the United States it took decades of labor struggle for workers in different factories to see their common cause and several more decades for workers in differing industries to see their common cause. In the United States, it took still longer for native born and immigrant workers, and then for black and white workers, to see themselves as fellow strugglers rather than competitors. The current globalization of capital may require a similar globalization of labor organization.

We still live in a time in which workers in different countries are likely to see one another only as competitors, and maybe unfair ones, and in which men and women see themselves as competitors, each in a zero sum game in which someone's gain is someone else's loss. Yet in new ways men and women around the world are being pulled together to see their common stance as co-laborers, co-providers, and co-activists in reform. In a poetic speech 140 years before Angelou's, the Native-American Dowamish chief Sealth, known to whites as Seattle, reminded his white listeners of their common position: "Yet not even the white man can escape the common destiny. We may be brothers after all. We shall see." To which we can only add, "Yes, brothers and sisters."

5

THE NEW WORLD DISORDER

Culture, Conflict, and Power

The world is facing riots without borders.

We can't just "send them away"—in an intertwined world there is no longer a "them" nor is there an "away."

THE WORLD OLYMPIC games are intended to transcend national boundaries and bring the world together in sport. They do bring much of the world together in front of television sets, yet they hardly escape the world of politics. The U.S. boycott of the Moscow Olympics, the killing of Israeli athletes, and the many struggles over location and protocol are all unwelcome reminders of the continuing contentious world of politics. Nonetheless, it is a rapidly changing world: as contentious as ever but along shifting boundaries. Despite the ideal of the world coming together for sport, the Olympic organization is based on the idea of distinct nation-states. Like the U.N., the games are an international event, not a supranational global meeting. Athletes belong to national teams, wear national uniforms, march under national banners, and their victories are applauded by the playing of the national anthem. Host countries use the event to showcase their nation and national pride, competitors struggle for national medal totals and recognition. Perhaps it should be no surprise that the games can take on an almost martial fervor, for the original Olympics and many sporting events since have been touted as a less bloody alternative to war. Yet while politicians are still eager to capitalize on this national fervor to serve their ends, the national basis of competition is on ever shakier ground.

The 1992 Summer Olympics in Barcelona, Spain, were remarkable not just for the sporting prowess displayed, but also for the way the games highlighted just how confusing the post–Cold War world was becoming. The mayor of

Barcelona gave the opening welcome, and immediately drew shouts of acclaim and applause from the local audience. The "bravos" had little to do with what he said, but that he didn't say it in Spanish. The mayor addressed the home crowd in Catalan, the ancient and enduring language of Catalonia of which Barcelona is the main city. Catalan has been under siege ever since Ferdinand and Isabella of Castile united Spain. The king's Spanish became Castilian, and "Castilian," the language of Castile, is still used as the designation of the Spanish of Spain. Suppressed by kings and outlawed by nationalist dictator Francisco Franco, Catalan has not only endured, it has rebounded as an emblem of regional pride. Once the language of the isolated countryside, it is now the chic language of very cosmopolitan Barcelona. Visiting Barcelona you can put away your Berlitz Spanish phrase book; in Barcelona, the very cosmopolitan, very European, but also very proud merchants of Catalonia may well prefer to dicker prices in English, French, or German rather than the language of Madrid.

The national confusion in Barcelona continued. The perennial powerhouse had been the team from the USSR, but the USSR had disbanded the year before. Would the former-Soviet athletes compete for their newly independent republics or for the uncertain Commonwealth of Independent States (CIS)? Would they have one uniform or many, under which flag, with which national anthem playing? They ended up settling for marching under the Olympic flag as one common emblem—they came, after all, for the love of competitive sport more than the love of the vague and history-less CIS.

The composition of other teams was also in question. With more and more athletes holding joint citizenship or residing in a country other than that of their birth, which team should they claim? An American athlete of Spanish background found a place on the Spanish team. The United States does not often recognize joint citizenship of adults but Spain does, and he could make the Spanish team. The possibilities were intriguing: find the right claim to nationality and you could have a place in the Olympics, maybe cross-country skiing for Fiji. The U.S. team itself was bolstered, especially in gymnastics, by the children of immigrants and refugees.

If national identities were somewhat uncertain, other loyalties were clearly in the forefront—those to products and commercial sponsors. For the first time, a change in rules about amateur status allowed the United States to assemble a basketball team comprised of professionals, the so-called "Dream Team." The nightmare for the Olympic committee came when the basketball players were to play with uniforms bearing Adidas insignia. Adidas was a big Olympic sponsor. But some of the U.S. players had signed exclusive rights contracts to only promote Nike products. Michael Jordan flatly claimed to have "seven million reasons," the dollar amount of his current Nike contract, to only promote his sponsor. It seemed as if the flag on the uniforms of the competitors had become uncertain and unimportant, but the product insignia on their uniforms had become supremely important. Key questions shifted from which countries to include and which sports to include, to who would be the official credit card of the Olympics and whether Coca Cola or Pepsi would be the official soft drink. National interests were being superseded by multinational commercial interests. The Cold War over global spheres of interest had given way to cola wars over dominance in world markets. At the same time, national pride was superseded by regional pride, a pride both cosmopolitan and parochial. Welcome to the new world disorder.

The End of Empire?

No one seemed prepared for the events of 1989. A seemingly insignificant move by Hungary to open its border with Austria set in motion a chain reaction throughout Eastern Europe. East German "tourists" in Hungary could now slip through this one hole and show up in the living rooms of family members in West Germany. When it became clear that Gorbachev would not intervene with Soviet tanks, this one hole began the unraveling of the entire iron curtain. Like the storied hole in the Dutch dike, this one threatened to bring down the Cold War dikes and create a human flood of movement. Shortly other borders opened and the now-useless Berlin Wall served no purpose but as a pounding block for venting a generation of frustrations. When conspirators in the Soviet Union tried to turn back the clock with a political coup, their clumsy efforts resulted in the collapse of the Soviet Union. One republic after another declared independence, until Boris Yeltsin declared that Russia itself was now also an independent state. The Soviet Union that had withstood Hitler's *wehrmacht* was gone without a nuclear whimper.

Unlike the many highly touted summits that often accomplished little, the world-changing events caught U.S. President Bush fishing at Kennebunkport. Once back home and changed, he announced the New World Order. What the term meant was unclear, although it seemed U.S.-led democracies were to figure prominently. Yet it was anything but orderly. The newly independent states threatened each other and felt threatened by a newly nationalistic Russia. Entities that were not republics but part of the so-called Russian Federation, such as Chechnya, were not given independence, and a bloody fight for independence began.

Germany united politically, but had to decide how to unite socially and economically without massive upheaval. Euphoria was followed by renewed resentments between east and west, and a new suspicion of foreigners. No sooner had the two German states rejoined than Czechoslovakia divided into the Czech and Slovak republics. Guided by a playwright president, Vaclav Havel, this, like Czechoslovakia's "velvet revolution," was accomplished without violence. Less easy was the reforming of Bulgaria and Romania. And then came the bloody fracturing of Yugoslavia.

Yugoslavia was a fairly artificial post–World War I creation that had been held together largely by the personal authority of Tito. Cracks in the union had been building for some time. The Serbian republic contained provinces with Moslem Albanian majorities that were eager for greater autonomy if not outright independence. To the north, tiny Slovenia, which had always looked more to Vienna than to Belgrade, was eager to cast its lot with the more prosperous north than the foundering south. Its independence was opposed but not intensely. Slovenia is, unlike the other republics, largely of one nationality and identity, Slovene. When Croatia broke away next it was much messier. Not only was Croatia larger and more strategic, its borders encompassed many Serbs. Macedonia to the south also broke away, worrying the Serbs less than the Greeks, who have a province of Macedonia, which might someday want to break away and join its northern namesake of fellow Macedonians.

The republic that was the worst situated was Bosnia, with a population of intermingled Bosnians, Serbs, and Croats. A new term was coined to try to sanitize the bloodshed that followed: "ethnic cleansing." As the struggle brought unending civil war, genocide, and huge numbers of refugees, outside powers tried to intervene, first with U.N. peacekeepers, then with a Cold War alliance, the North Atlantic Treaty Organization (NATO). With NATO troops threatening and with little hope of a decisive military win, the opposing forces finally agreed to serious talks to be held in, of all places, Dayton, Ohio.

The history of the world has been dominated by empire building. The world order was the order imposed by the most powerful empires. The Yugoslavian states reflected the legacy of empires. The southern half of the country had been part of the Turkish Ottoman Empire. Bosnians are ethnically of the same origins as Serbs, but had converted to Islam under Turkish masters. Unlike Orthodox Serbia and Muslim Bosnians, Roman Catholic Croatia and Slovenia have looked north. They had been part of the Austrian-Hungarian empire. The architecture and much of the local culture reflects German influences more than the Greek and Turkish styles of the south. Dividing lines were recast by the council of Vienna, one of Europe's early attempts to define stable boundaries upon the collapse of Napoleon's empire. The imposed order had always been tenuous—it was the assassination of Austrian archduke Ferdinand in Sarajevo, Bosnia, that triggered World War I.

The "Great War," as it was known, was a struggle between the great European empires: Britain, France, and Russia on one side and Germany, Austria, and Turkey on the other. The war that created Yugoslavia also ended the empires of Austria and Ottoman Turkey. Germany's attempt to regain a great empire, along with similar desires in Italy and Japan—while France and Britain were eager to retain their empires—led to the Second World War. The bloodshed of the Napoleonic Wars had left Europe weary of empire building on the European continent and led to the council of Vienna. It was safer to limit empire-building to overseas possessions.

The bloodshed of the two world wars left most of Europe exhausted of the idea of empire building altogether. Still it took two more decades of struggle for the end of empire: Gandhi in India and Ho Chi Min in Indochina struggled against the remains of the British and French empires. The Algerian war of independence brought the struggle to Africa. By 1965 most of Africa was free of its German, Belgian, French, and British empires. In 1975, Angola and Mozambique were the last to be independent from what had been the first European overseas empire builder, Portugal. When South Africa finally gave up formerly German-controlled territory to become the country of Namibia, Africa was finally free of colonies, and the world largely freed of great empires.

In an odd way, the last empire to fall was the great Russian expanse. World War I had brought down the empires of Austria and Turkey, but had transformed the Russian empire into the Soviet Union. There was a new socialist agenda, but much of what followed—Russian emigres moving into outlying republics and taking the Russian language and institutions with them—looked like the old face of national empires. Stalin, in particular, adapted the old methods of empire. In seeking to restore some of the territory of the Czarist empire, he annexed the Baltic states and territory from Finland, and reclaimed half of Poland. Faced with Nazi invasion, he called his country from revolutionary communism to a "great patriotic war" against Hitler, and after a hard-fought victory "moved" the boundary of Poland to shrink defeated Germany while enlarging Russia, established a sphere of influence in the rest of Eastern Europe, and exiled enemies and strategically transplanted friends to extend control. This was the empire that fractured amidst a stagnant economy and resurgent nationalism in 1991.

What was to follow the end of empires, in the mind of the former empire-builders at least, was nation-states. These would consist of a nation, that is a group of like-minded and somehow related people, coming together to build a state, an independent political entity. This was Europe's vision for Africa and it became the guiding vision for the Commonwealth of Independent States. Trying to turn the ethnic mosaic of the Yugoslav Federation into distinct nation-states led to ethnic cleansing and seemingly intractable boundary disputes. The problem for Yugoslavia, as well as for Africa, is that people had been moving and mixing too long within the constraints of empire boundaries to form distinct nations. The states that were created reflected the accords and contrivances of the empire-builders far more than any logic of geography or ethnicity.

In 1990, in the midst of the unraveling of the USSR and Yugoslavia, and the reuniting of Germany, the world faced a new dilemma in the land of the ancient Babylonian empire. Saddam Hussein's Iraqi army invaded Kuwait. Hussein did not admit to empire building, but rather cited several grievances over oil and loans, and then offered an interesting justification for annexation. Iraq and Kuwait should be one country, he claimed. They had been under one administration, more or less, under the Ottoman Empire, and had been divided when the British empire divided up the old Ottoman Empire, creating the Emirate of Kuwait. Against charges from the U.N. that he was violating national sovereignty, Hussein claimed he was under no compulsion to recognize boundaries that were the arbitrary creation of imperial powers. The problem with his logic, not lost on the member states of the U.N., was that it could be applied with equal brutality almost anywhere in the world. Most national boundaries had been the creation of imperial powers, mostly European, at one point or another, and had no inalienable logic to them. Yet to completely reject these imperial creations would be to open the world to endless fighting over boundaries—and maybe to a new wave of empire building.

The nation-state idea at least provided hope of stability. Yet the nations themselves seemed increasingly unstable. As global forces came to the fore, nations seemed too small to handle the great global demands—global economy and labor, the global environment, and so forth—and too large to deal with increasingly local demands. As a result, the world was confronted with the dual spectacle of simultaneous national integration and disintegration. In fact, the two forces often complemented one another. One reason that a small country like Slovenia could hope to prosper under independence was the growth of the European Union with its common markets and open borders.

One common joke was that the Europe of the year 2000 would have only seven countries, one united Europe and the six fiercely independent and contentious former Yugoslav Republics. Yet it was the very process of European unification that often encouraged national disintegration into mini-states. The president of the European Union was from Luxembourg, and even smaller states such as Liechtenstein could thrive as part of larger transnational identities. Many of the Eastern European states were also eager to seek greater security in transnational security arrangements such as NATO. Independence was possible only by means of new alliances and allegiances.

The idea of the independent nation is certainly not dead. Some American conservatives have worried that the New World Order refers to a powerful world government, one that could in time become despotic. European conservatives seemed less worried about despotism than the heavy taxation and transfers that might accompany a Europe-wide welfare state with new, poor countries ever eager to join. Yet all these worries seem far from present realities. The U.N. is now more active in the world's trouble spots, but is still dependent on the voluntary involvement of member states to carry out its missions. Like national governments, it is also in the process of downsizing, cutting staff and bureaucracy. The independent national state remains the primary form of societal organization, and the key political actor on the world stage. Yet while not disappearing, its clout is clearly diminishing.

States command diminished loyalties. David Jacobson (1997) notes that while nationalism is alive and well, and while the state as a bureaucratic entity is alive and well, the nation-state as a common people with a common will is in serious trouble. States remain,

Yet the state is less the embodiment of the "general will" but rather the locus of "competing wills" (often of global character). National, ethnic, and social identities are increasingly independent of national borders, and are either transnational or "localized" in character. "Nation" and "state" are no longer wedded together (Jacobson 1997, 132).

States also command diminished resources. Even large states must often cooperate to achieve economic goals, and many are dwarfed by the international clout of private—or semi-private—corporations. National rivalries in space have given way to international cooperation, in part out of an attempt to share the great cost. Chinese rockets launch European communication satellites with Japanese electronic components at a discount in an attempt to compete with U.S. monopolies. One of the world's largest "economies" is Mitsubishi, bigger than Indonesia, bigger than almost all of Africa's states, bigger, in fact, than most of the African states combined. National empires are giving way to media empires and corporate empires.

The British empire utterly dominated the world for about one hundred years between the defeat of Napoleon and the First World War. This was the time when the sun never set on the British empire, the "British Century." At the beginning of a new century, the United States is still the world's dominant economic and military power. From its beginnings, however, the "American Century" marked the triumph of a global economic system over old-style empire-building. This does not mean, however, an era of equality of power and opportunity, only a more complex power structure.

Internal Colonialism: The Emperor's New Clothes

We have seen how national cultures have become increasingly global and how national economies are ever more global. The world is also witnessing the globalization of power relations. Patterns of colonial domination persist, yet with new twists. The era of great overseas empire building was the great age of colonialism—whether it was a golden age or a leaden age largely depends on whether or not the observer was in one of the great seats of power.

Colonialism in the old sense only exists in remnants. The new Russia has found itself fighting what looks like an old colonial-style war in Chechnya. China pretends that colonial domination of Tibet, with the familiar heavy military presence (one Chinese soldier for every ten Tibetans), the attempts to undermine indigenous language and religion and to transplant sympathetic parties, is an exercise in national sovereignty. China is continually embarrassed as most of the rest of the world finds the quiet words of the exiled Dalai Lama far more convincing. The United States offers new referenda to Puerto Rico, gained in a colonial struggle with Spain at the end of the nineteenth century, but finds no clear course between statehood, independence, and continued territorial status as a "commonwealth." The United States also retains its occupation of Guantánamo naval base on the tip of Cuba, also gained in the old colonial war, as a way to annoy and threaten Fidel Castro, pretending that a base only seventy miles from Florida is truly a strategic defense of the Caribbean in an age of supersonic strike aircraft. American and British naval bases still encircle the globe, old "coal" stops largely anachronistic to a nuclear navy and transcontinental air power. France insists on blowing up nuclear weapons under South Pacific possessions, seemingly gaining far more ill will than security. Still, these vestiges of colonialism look a bit like the horse maneuvers on the eve of World War I: obsolete vestiges of an old idea of power.

The dependency school of thought argued that as old-style colonialism retreated, it was replaced by neocolonialism. The old powers still economically dominate and exploit, politically manipulate, and militarily "protect" former colonies, while ostensibly acknowledging their independence. In this view, Africa still serves the corporate-dominated economies of its old European colonial masters, the United States continues to dominate Latin American affairs while warily eyeing other competitors, and Asia continues as a free-for-all for control between Europe, the United States, and Japan.

A related line of thinking focuses on the colonial relations that occur within national boundaries as "internal colonialism." The United States has never held many large formal colonies. It gained the Philippines, Puerto Rico, and Guam from Spain 1898, and immediately began fighting a colonial war against Filipino resistance. The United States held a sphere of influence in China about the same time, fostered an essentially colonial relationship with Hawaii, and often intervened militarily in Latin America. Colonial expansion was nonetheless minor and reluctant in a nation that itself was founded as a colony.

Robert Blauner (1972) has argued, however, that American race relations have a colonial cast. It may be that the United States needed fewer colonies to support its agrarian expansion and industrial development in that it could depend on internal colonial peoples. Rather than sending colonial regents to supervise

African plantations, the United States imported African labor to its own cotton and tobacco plantations. Britain, in contrast, withdrew from the slave trade earlier but maintained large expanses of colonial labor in Africa itself. The United States maintained colonial relations of political dominance with the American Indian nations, although finding them to be unreliable sources of labor. The United States never directly maintained the vast conscripted labor systems that Spain used in the Americas, but has often been willing to import laborers from Mexico and the Caribbean within its boundaries.

Likewise, the United States was slow to join in the partitioning and plundering of China that accompanied European (and later Japanese) spheres of influence, but for several decades imported Chinese laborers. These were not immigrants but labor migrants. Mostly men without families, they were to work hard, stay out of trouble, and then go home. When other groups, especially European immigrants and westward settlers, saw their jobs at stake, the Chinese were excluded in 1882. Eventually the wide open border with Mexico was also closed. The border patrol began in 1924, but Mexican laborers were recruited into the 1960s. The internal colonial argument is that each of these groups differ markedly in their experience from immigrants. They were incorporated into the American economic expansion with no or highly restricted options, their movements and governance were controlled, and their labor was extracted for minimum returns.

The United States is not the only country with an internal colonial heritage. Great Britain had vast formal colonies, but also maintained essentially colonial relationships with the people of its "Celtic fringe," Scotland, Wales, and Ireland, even as these places were part of the United Kingdom of Ireland and Great Britain, a single country (Hechter 1975). Scottish land, Welsh mining labor, and Irish grains were all essential to English economic expansion, yet they only participated peripherally in the benefits. The suppression of Irish resistance in particular was long and difficult. The transfer of loyal populations was attempted: Scottish farmers whose lands were needed to supply the woolen mills of England were shifted across the Irish Sea and given land in northern Ireland. Resources were extracted: at the height of the Irish potato famine, local populations starved while Irish grains still left from Dublin for London.

Internal colonial practices generate their own resistance and can prove as destabilizing as international colonialism. Yet the consequences of such actions endure. Some of the transplanted Scottish farmers tired of Irish hostility and came to America in search of more generous land as the Scotch Irish. Many joined the American Revolution against British transatlantic colonialism. Later the Irish fled the famines in large numbers, also coming to the United States, where they were again cast as colonial labor. The earliest examples of a dual labor market, one that would later repress the ambitions of black Americans, emerged as notices announced one hourly wage for native-born Americans, and a lesser wage for Irish. In Ireland itself, the strains between the Protestant transplants and the still-resisting Roman Catholic Irish continue to take lives and to plague London.

Internal colonial practices continued in the Americas after independence from Spain and Portugal. Local elites, largely of European heritage, continued to control the land and to gain income from neocolonial trade with Britain and the United States, while local laboring populations, indigenous and African, continued in poverty. Southern Africa, where the more temperate climate favored European settlement, faced internal colonial arrangements in Rhodesia, named for Cecil Rhodes, the prime minister of Africa and chief administrator of colonial activity and once caricatured as the colossus of Rhodes astride the entire continent. Independence only led to a protracted civil war, as the resident white leadership attempted to maintain control. They failed, and the country was recast as Zimbabwe, named for an ancient African empire. Despite an officially socialist black-majority government, white landowners continue to hold economic dominance, now challenged by land invasions and violence.

Global Apartheid

The classic African case of internal colonialism has been South Africa. First colonized by the Dutch, then seized by the British, it has a long colonial history. Seeking land, the Dutch trekked inland and came to think of themselves as sons of the soil, Afrikaaners, the white tribe. The British were more interested in strategic ports and refueling stops and often held to urban locations. After fighting a colonial war in 1902 to retain and unite the colony, Britain eventually gave the union its independence. Yet white South Africans, first with English and then Afrikaaners in control, maintained a complex internal colonial system. Black South Africans worked the profitable mines as well as serving as farm labor, but were excluded from political control and had their movements restricted by pass laws and the complex rules of "apartheid" or separateness.

The line between internal and external colonies blurred as independent states such as Lesotho and Swaziland were surrounded by and dominated by South Africa, Namibia was administered as a territory, neighboring southern African countries were politically manipulated and economically dependent, and nominally independent "homelands" were created for black African populations. The residents of the homelands, like the residents of the black townships, were still entirely economically dependent on white-controlled South Africa, and provided vast pools of colonial-style labor. Asians had been brought in as colonial administrators and survived in part as middleman minorities. Likewise caught in the middle were those of mixed racial background, labeled as colored. After years of internal resistance and years of global economic sanctions, this colonial complex finally collapsed. Yet colonial patterns are enduring and the task facing the former resistance leader and first black president, Nelson Mandela, was overwhelming. In particular, a colonial economic hierarchy has endured. In his inaugural speech, Mandela laid out the dimensions of the challenge:

We have, at last, achieved our political emancipation. We pledge ourselves to liberate all our people from the continuing bondage of poverty, deprivation, suffering, gender, and other discrimination. Never, never, and never again shall it be that this beautiful land will again experience the oppression of one by another . . . Let freedom reign. God bless Africa! (Mandela 1995, 621).

The South African government continues to struggle to dismantle the legacy of apartheid, yet in broad strokes the socioeconomic pattern of apartheid resembles the divisions of the planet. A predominantly white elite holds political power and much economic advantage. Asian middlemen stand between rich and poor, although a few of the highly successful have the economic, if not political and military, clout of the elites. The mestizo or mixed race peoples of Latin America stand a step below like the "colored" of South Africa. Near the bottom are the black populations of Africa and scattered locales like Haiti, with the least access to power or privilege. Not even represented in the South Africa statistics are the Khoisan peoples who Europeans derided as "bushmen." Though they have the longest roots of all in South Africa, insofar as they still exist within the country they are often the most destitute and most despised. Likewise, around the world, small indigenous populations often survive within larger nations as a "fourth world" with the least voice and power. This racial division of the world is not absolute, but it is also not accidental. Like the divisions of South Africa it is a colonial legacy.

The racial inequalities of the world are often mirrored within the inequalities of multiethnic states. Brazil is proud of its recent history of racial tolerance. In the last country to outlaw slavery, Brazilians of many hues now intermingle without significant racial tension. They do not, however, intermingle on equal terms. Brazil is one of the most unequal countries in the world, and this stratification sorts itself out along broadly racial lines that reflects Brazil's colonial, neocolonial, and internal colonial heritage. At the top are white Euro-Brazilians, sometimes with Portuguese first names and northern European last names; they are the heirs to immigrants who now control much of the land and much of the industry of this huge country. A step below are the darker complected mestizo and mulatto Brazilians of mixed racial background. Still poorer as a whole are the black Afro-Brazilians, and at the very bottom are Brazil's endangered indigenous peoples.

The inequalities in the United States follow a similar pattern. Poverty rates are lowest for whites, then Asian-Americans, then Latinos, then African-Americans, and the highest poverty rates of all are found on native reservations (U.S. Bureau of the Census 1995). These broad comparisons are generalizations comprised of differing histories and effects. Among Asian-Americans the best off are small select immigrant groups, such as Japanese and Indian-Americans, with high skill levels. Among Filipinos, recent arrivals reflect this more select immigrant pattern of higher skills, while earlier arrivals from the United States colonial period have higher poverty and unemployment rates; further, with Hispanic surnames and heritage, Filipinos show the complexity of categories. The greatest poverty among Asians is found among the Vietnamese, Cambodian, and Lao refugees from the long Indochinese Wars in which French, Japanese, Russian, Chinese, and American ambitions collided.

Likewise, among Latin American groups in the United States ("Hispanics" to the Census Bureau, "Latinos" on the West Coast), clear distinctions are seen between the best-off Cuban-Americans as select political exiles, Mexican-Americans with a blended colonial and immigrant background, and Puerto Ricans with continuing colonial status and also the highest rates of poverty. It has also been noted that many Cuban-Americans fit into American racial schemes as "white," while many Puerto Ricans would be considered "black." This raises the issue of the importance of racial bias and racism in the persisting disadvantage of Blauner's internal colonial minorities or "Third World peoples" in the United States.

In *The Declining Significance of Race*, sociologist William Julius Wilson (1978) presents a historical look at race and class in the American experience from plantation rule, to early industrial conflict, to advanced industrial economies. He argues that over this period race itself has become less important in determining one's life chances than class. Race and racism are still important in the political arena and sometimes in interpersonal relations in continued bigotry, but it is less likely to affect one's ability to get ahead than class position. Black Americans are now limited most by class, not directly by race. Historical racism, however, means that the black population was concentrated in inner-city, low-skill blue-collar employment that was hardest hit by deindustrialization, globalization, and technological change, and so are over-represented in the disadvantaged urban underclass. The black community itself is dividing into an established middle class and an impoverished underclass with few opportunities (Wilson 1987, 1996).

While accepting many of Wilson's economic arguments, philosopher and social critic Cornell West contends that we must always return to the fact that race is integral, not peripheral, to American society. The United States is, as a book dedicated to West contends, *The House That Race Built* (Lubiano 1997). West writes in the afterword:

The very construction of "race" is a European creation rooted in attempts to rationalize European superiority in oceanic transportation, military technology, and capitalist expansion resulting in imperial conquests and colonial subordination of many non-European peoples. The distinctive feature of the precious experiment in democracy called the United States of America was its profound and pervasive investment in white supremacy— in the expropriation of indigenous peoples' land and African peoples' labor. And one glaring aspect of our present-day society is the depth and breadth of racial polarization, balkanization, and de facto segregation (West 1997, 301).

The full extent of that segregation is documented by Massey and Denton (1993) in American Apartheid. They agree with Wilson's contention that global economic forces were at work in creating an urban underclass, but that it was racial segregation that turned this into a black (and Puerto Rican) underclass. Intense segregation concentrates problems, translates economic downturns into spirals of neighborhood decline, and increases social isolation. How severe is U.S. segregation? Massey estimates a segregation index, ranging from 0 (no segregation) to 100 (complete segregation). Average segregation in Brazilian cities is 40 to 50, accounted for largely by economic class segregation. In Canada, the index averages 35 to 45, accounted for largely by immigrant status, such as with black Caribbean Canadians. At the height of official apartheid South Africa managed an index of 95. The average for U.S. cities is 70 to 90. Living in separate worlds creates separate economic, political, and social realities.

West's argument that race stands as a central feature of U.S. society is certainly supported by Massey's figures on racial segregation, yet may also in its own way lend credence to Wilson's call to attack racial inequality with broad-based programs targeting joblessness and poverty regardless of race. Exactly because racism is interwoven into U.S. society, it is often difficult to attack directly. When blatant, old fashioned racism rears its ugly head it is easier to strike it down. More often, what we find, however, is that when poverty increases, when wages stagnate, when cities and countryside fall into decline, when environmental risks threaten, when crime threatens and police themselves react in threatening ways, then people of color bear an inordinate amount of the pain, in large measure because they fill the ranks of the poor and the powerless. When cutbacks come they get cut, when programs fail they are abandoned, when toxic dumping occurs they get dumped on. Racial issues must often be tackled in concert with others.

Poverty and suffering transcend racial boundaries but the color of the face in pain still seems to matter in how it affects us. The outpouring of response to Romanian orphans who were hungry, abused, and abandoned may have been due in part to the fact that we were not accustomed to seeing such pain and deprivation on little white faces with blue eyes and light hair. We have come to expect it from much of Africa. Yet the Romanian situation is also a reminder that whites are not immune to the suffering and pain of an unequal world system.

Just as colonialism and internal colonialism were often linked, the struggle for international equality and political rights often parallels the struggle for internal equality and rights. It is no accident that the struggle of African-Americans for civil rights in the 1950s and 1960s occurred simultaneously with the struggles for African independence. American civil rights leaders drew inspiration and impetus from the anti-colonial struggles in Africa. They read Fanon's (1961) angry denunciation in The Wretched of the Earth, drawn from his experiences in the struggle for Algerian independence. They read Nkruma's cries for a pan-African identity. They appropriated Nyerere's calls for ujaama solidarity based on African traditions of self- support. They followed Nelson Mandela's African National Congress through his resistance and imprisonment. While militants resonated with Fanon, Martin Luther King, Jr., borrowed non-violent ideals and practices from Mahatma Gandhi, practices Gandhi came to while reading Tolstoy in South Africa and later brought to the Indian struggle for independence. In turn, the success of African-Americans in coming together across divisions inspired African leaders to attempt the same in their own struggles. Today, even if African politics are often less than inspiring, the great cultural heritage of the continent continues to inspire an Afrocentric movement in the United States seeking to reestablish its Africanness as a source of strength and solidarity.

Strength and solidarity were also the rallying cries of the Chicano civil rights movement in the United States that borrowed the term La Raza. *La Raza Cosmica*, the cosmic race, is the grand sounding name of a book by the Mexican philosopher Jose Vasconsuelos. He argued that in Latin America the blending of the races produced a new identity that could lead the world in seeing how a racial intermingling would bring new strength and vision for the future. The new Latin American mixed race would be a source of pride not shame, and of power in place of poverty. The promise of La Raza remains elusive, yet a new pride in ancestry, including indigenous ancestry, took root in Mexico in the 1960s as well in politically conscious Mexican-Americans. The power of revolutionary resistance was also symbolized by Fidel Castro in his fatigues and Che Guevara, Argentine physician turned beret-donned revolutionary—both chomping Cuban cigars and demanding *"no mas"* to imperial control. Castro has given up the cigars and now struggles to hold on to power as a lone island of aging socialism, but the image of the slain Guevara, ever resolute in his beret, has revived currency as a symbol of the struggle for rights and equality.

The American Indian Movement (AIM) of the 1970s tried to forge a common agenda for the diverse indigenous peoples of the United States, and to look beyond to the rest of the Americas. Russell Means argued that the only group of humanity not represented at the table of nations was the Amerindians, who were isolated within countries that did not represent them. He voiced solidarity with the Miskito "warriors" on the Atlantic coast of Nicaragua, who had faced Spanish colonialism, British neocolonialism, and then internal colonial repression by both Samoza and his Sandinista opponents.

The more militant agenda of AIM has faded as casinos gain American Indians not only more economic but also more political clout than that achieved by takeovers and occupations. Yet the pride in heritage is stronger than ever. The native population of the United States is growing at a remarkable rate, far faster than could be accounted for by natural increase. What seems to be happening is that those who in the past chose to ignore or hide their native heritage now are seeking to explore, claim, and even vaunt it. Further, they are finding common ground with widely disparate groups. A conference in the Pacific brought together Native Hawaiians, Alaskan Aleuts, Polynesia Maori from New Zealand, Haida from British Columbia, Canada, and native groups from the western United States. Common issues of economic development, land rights and protection of the natural environment, and political voice carry across the disparate cultures.

The History of Hate

Given the widely varied groups that have come together under these sweeping pan-Indian, pan-African, and pan-Asian banners, one wonders that all these groups might not come together in unified opposition to global apartheid. Yet ethnicity remains a powerful force for mobilizing loyalties. It also, unfortunately, remains a powerful force for unleashing lethal vendettas.

Why does hate so often focus on racial and ethnic distinctions? Many observers of the modern world were certain that these divisions would diminish in face of class divisions in a global economy or national divisions in a global competition. Yet around the world ethnicity is alive and revived, sometimes bursting with pride, sometimes busting with hate (Smith 1981). Ethnicity is rooted in the idea of a common heritage, a family tie, even if that common ancestor is hard to locate (Horowitz 1975). It creates a boundary that distinguishes us from them, our group or our people from the others. Likewise, race lives on as the myth that won't go away. Race is a broad category based on presumed physical characteristics. The biological foundations are varied and shaky: is one dark enough to be classified as "black," are one's lips thick enough to be classified a "Tartar"? Physical anthropologists are dubious of any scheme to try to categorize the broad and intermingled diversity of humanity. Biological race may be an untenable concept, but social race, what a society construes to be a racial category, can be very powerful.

The attributes given to races have always reflected more about the prejudices of the beholder than any anthropological reality. The imperial British saw themselves as bearers of civilization, bearing the "white man's burden" to carry enlightened ideals to a dark world. The Roman orator and pundit Cicero, however, saw things differently. He wrote to his friend Atticus: "Do not obtain your slaves from Britain because they are so stupid and so utterly incapable of being taught that they are not fit to form a part of the household of Athens" (Parillo 2000, 18).

To the Romans, the Britons were a wild and unruly race. In contrast, their North African rivals across the Mediterranean in Carthage were despised not as a different race, but as imperial competitors and a domestic threat—"Hannibal was at the gates," they said, and indeed he had shown up quite uninvited with a lot of raging elephants in the Second Punic War. Africa was a province in a Mediterranean civilization, not a separate continent with a separate race. When Anthony was dallying with Cleopatra he was denounced, not for allying with an African woman (she was in fact a Macedonian descendent of one of Alexander the Great's generals), but for messing around with an Eastern hussy. People have been eager to divide humanity, but racial boundaries have always followed political expediency rather than any logic of ancestry. The divisions that we have inherited, as Cornell West contends, are the products of Europeans trying to categorize the world they were colonizing.

Yet these divisions have tremendous power to become the flashpoints of conflict: ancient hatreds from a dark past that emerge from the grave to claim new victims in the modern world. At his first inauguration, Bill Clinton spoke of how "a generation raised in the shadows of the cold war assumes new responsibilities in a world warmed by the sunshine of freedom but threatened still by ancient hatreds." However, in an essay on "Modern Hate," political scientists Susanne and Lloyd Rudolph (1993) question the antiquity of this hate:

But recent news accounts that depict the violence as an outgrowth of old animosities are misleading. Hindus and Muslims in India under the Mughal emperor Akbar, the nationalistic leadership of Mahatma Gandhi and the Congress government of Jawaharlal Nehru have gotten along more often than they have gone for each other's throats. So did Serbs, Croats and Muslims under Tito in Yugoslavia. Clinton and others too easily invoke "ancient hatreds" to explain what are really contemporary conflicts. The question, in other words, is not why old conflicts are flaring up anew, but rather why traditionally harmonious mosaics have been shattered (Rudolph and Rudolph 1993, 25).

A debate has stirred in the social sciences between attributing the all-too-common outbursts of violence to emergent "modern" hate versus primordial "ancient" hate. The primordial view looks to the effects of history, religion, and culture. Primordial hatreds do matter, if only for their ability to stir the blood and to rally the crowds. Religious fundamentalists in Israel rally Jews with accounts of the domains of David and Solomon, and a God-given right to the land. Across Jerusalem, Muslim fundamentalists rally Palestinians with similar accounts of their heritage and the holy place of Jerusalem and the land in the life of Muhammad and early Muslims. Protestants in Northern Ireland recount hundreds of years of common history in the land, Roman Catholics recount centuries of domination and exclusion. Serbs are told of the heroism of ancient struggles against Turkish invaders and the hollowed ground of those battlefields that must remain within Serbia. They are in one commentator's words, "sick with history." Assessing the claims of history is never easy: each claimant has their own history, historic wrongs are not easy to right after generations have passed, yet a people's history is precious, and most are not eager to forget, nor to relinquish, ancient claims.

A second view ties conflicts to very modern, emergent ethnicity rooted in economic competition and political manipulation (Bonacich 1972, Olzak and Nagel 1986, Olzak 1998). Newly created states with centralized control upset old balances and create new rivalries. The changing global economy and power structure erases all balances and puts groups in a bitter struggle for access to power and privilege, and for survival. Somalia has long been a land of clan alliances. These were fairly stable until a newly created central state, armed in Cold War struggles first by the Soviet Union and then the United States, suddenly held tremendous power over resources. In a country as poor as Somalia, clan control over those resources can mean survival, exclusion can mean extermination. Fighting bitter battles for control suddenly seems to make more sense.

In Rwanda and Burundi, French and Belgian colonial administrations used and manipulated ethnic divisions to their advantage. With colonial control removed and old hierarchies unseated, a bitter struggle for control ensued. In a dangerous game without rules, each side was prone to use genocide for fear that if they were not the perpetrators they would be the victims. In this setting it is very easy for extremist leaders to issue brazen calls to violence. Likewise in Yugoslavia, ancient rivalries provide the language that can be manipulated in very contemporary power struggles.

Middleman minority groups, in particular, can find themselves an easy target for those eager to draw on old animosities for political gain. Idi Amin of Uganda legitimated his violent repression by sniping at European powers, but then directed his ferocity against middleman Asians as "imperial lackeys." Sowell has noted the particular vulnerability of middleman minorities, who have enough economic assets to covet, but little political clout to provide protection:

While many kinds of minorities in many countries have faced hostility and even violence, truly historic levels of lethal violence have been directed at various middleman minorities. On more than one occasion in the history of Southeast Asia, the number of overseas

Chinese massacred within a week has exceeded all the blacks lynched in the entire history of the United States. In the twentieth century the scar of slaughter against the Armenians in the Ottoman Empire, and then against the Jews in Nazi-occupied Europe, required a new word—genocide (Sowell 1993, 32).

Riots in Jakarta in 1998 were kindled by economic hardship following the drop in the national currency. The growing protests resulted in the resignation of Indonesia's dictator of over thirty years, Suharto. Resentments against Suharto and his cronies are not surprising—in a land still struggling to meet basic needs, Suharto's six children are each estimated to be billionaires. Yet the rioting also targeted Chinese businesspeople, who tried to flee the country in search of safety. These "overseas" Chinese are only 3 percent of the national population but control most of the businesses. Most are small businesspeople in true middleman minority fashion, yet their prosperity is resented and their dealings are blamed for the national crisis just as Jewish business interests were blamed for the woes of depression-era Germany. In similar fashion the Los Angeles riots of 1992 were ignited by abuses in the police force and criminal justice system, but immediately targeted middleman minorities, the Chinese and Korean businesspeople in poor neighborhoods. Responding to the growing violence in Jakarta, a university professor decried what had come of a student-led movement for democracy: "Look at the city burning. That's not what the students wanted. That's anger, opportunism, and the old racism showing its ugly face" (*Chicago Tribune*, May 15, 1998). He could have been describing any of many social movements that have foundered on such hazards lurking just below the surface.

War Lords and Soldier Boys: The Institutionalization of Violence

Differences do not always bring violence. With time and a measure of security people find stable patterns of relations between different groups. These are rarely equitable but often quite enduring. Intergroup relations are institutionalized into a stable, functioning social order. The bloody internal conflicts of this century, from Mexico's ten-year revolution early in the twentieth century to Lebanon's twenty-five years of self-destruction, show that violence can also become institutionalized. A new social disorder is created and perpetuated: frightened people are forced to align themselves with one of many factions, if only for a measure of protection, weapons circulate and recirculate with such profusion that they become a mainstay of the economy and as much a part of the fabric of life as locks and keys. Whatever the ancient grievances, soon everyone has a very real and recent loss to grieve and revenge. Children grow up knowing only allegiances to fighting forces, and "the struggle" as the only way of life. Leaders emerge with no agenda but to rally the next round of troops, soldiers grow up with no livelihood but continuing the battles. What a generation earlier might have been unthinkable behavior now becomes the code of the streets, and new standards emerge. This could be the Middle East, it could be East Africa, it could be Central America, and it could be the inner city of many a U.S. city.

Sometimes this occurs in cycles of repression and terror. One threatened side uses the more subtle violence of state repression: razor wire, tear gas, mass arrest, and detention, bull-dozer raids that destroy homes and armored car patrols that threaten what remains. The other side uses whatever means of terror is at hand, from bombs to assassinations. These cycles have torn through Northern Ireland, South Africa, and Israel and its occupied territories. Without centralized power, institutionalized violence can simply become a tag-team free-for-all. We have recently witnessed this in Somalia, Liberia, and central Africa.

Without ready access to large professional armies, the localized warlords of the world often turn to child soldiers. Young people from poor families already traumatized by violence and turmoil are especially vulnerable. Some join willingly, answering persuasive calls to arms, others are conscripted. Either way, once they have become embroiled in the violence, and maybe killed, threatened, or maimed themselves, there are few alternatives. The right-wing resistance group Renamo in Mozambique was infamous for capturing pre-teen boys, torturing them into compliance with orders that often included being involved in torture and killings themselves. Once they had killed their villagers and even family members (or at least participated in these plans), there was no turning back. The pattern has been repeated around the world:

- A fourteen-year-old Nicaraguan joins the Contras after his own father is killed, finding the only "parents" he knows.

- A ten-year-old Ugandan is dragged away in the night and beaten until he agrees to "join" a rebel group in a two-year run of terror and fighting.

- A thirteen-year-old Liberian girl picks up arms to "free her land," not knowing that girls forced into military service often become older soldiers' sexual slaves.

Children younger than age fifteen were fighting in at least twenty-five conflicts in 1996, circling the globe: Guatemala, Colombia, and Peru in the Americas; Northern Ireland, Bosnia, and Russia in Europe; Liberia, Sudan, Angola, Somalia, Rwanda, and Burundi in Africa; Turkey, Iraq, Iran, India, Burma, and Cambodia in Asia among others (John 1997).

Watching one Liberian warlord's "troops"—strutting in the street in Nike high-tops, caps turned back, joking, cat-calling, and shooting off automatic weapons—one has the sense of being taken to some horrible, alien underworld;

or to South Los Angeles. Urban violence as well as national violence can give young people the sense that their only security is found in the best-armed gang. To not join can mean becoming a certain victim of those who have. These gangs are local, but they are also becoming national as "franchises" are taken up in neighboring cities. They are also becoming global, not just through huge Mafia-style organizations, but also through the movement of troubled people. Young Southeast Asians find the left-over weapons of war to be their only survival tools in hostile refugee camps, then transfer their techniques of extortion to the American west coast. The process can also go the other way. Street gangs in El Salvador display the symbols, habits, and methods of Los Angeles street gangs. Former members of LA gangs who were deported have returned to San Salvador with new methods of gaining power and seeking "respect." Violence, once internalized and institutionalized, is never easy to contain.

Places of institutionalized violence are often derided as "knowing no other way." "Entering its 3,000th year of fighting . . . ," Paul Harvey begins a report on the Middle East. But peace, as well as violence, is a product of enduring social relations and the resulting norms and expectations. A news story about rampaging Swedes or hordes of Norwegian terrorists (Lutheran fundamentalists perhaps) would be taken as some sort of a joke. This is just not their way. Yet at the height of Norse incursions into Europe (and probably North America), rampaging Scandinavians were no joke. Years of peace have created very different standards of normalcy, decency, and morality in these societies.

Anthropologists once vigorously debated whether human nature was naturally violent or peaceful. Ample evidence can be provided on both sides, of course. It is safer to say that human nature is extraordinarily malleable —our passions and behaviors adapt to the circumstances. The global challenge ahead is to replace cycles of terror and institutionalized violence with new institutions of peacemaking and cycles of reconciliation.

From Warsaw to Wausau: Seeking Refuge

War has always had its exiles and refugees. The complexity of conflict in the new world disorder has created complex and sometimes chaotic patterns of flight around the globe. Some locations are especially heavily burdened; other places who thought they were isolated have suddenly found the world on their doorstep.

A walk through Marathon Park suddenly places one in the midst of an ancient Asian culture that has lost none of its exuberance. Scores of Hmong children are everywhere playing *kotaw* (kickball) and a version of jacks. Older women sit in distinctive attire and offer *nab vaam* (coconut, tapioca, and ice) to men who play ball or cards (Koltyk 1998). This is neither Asia nor California; it is

Wausau, Wisconsin. Church sponsorship first brought the Hmong here, then the family-based chain migration that has characterized so many migrations to this country brought ever more to a small Midwestern city that was noted in the 1980 census as the most ethnically homogeneous in the United States. Just beyond this park scene, you can get sauerkraut on your hot dogs and the park carousel plays polkas. But this piece of traditional Midwestern Americana with a German-Polish flavor is forever changed. Not everyone is sure it is for the better.

Comments one longtime resident, "Now we're beginning to see gang violence and guns in the schools. Immigration has inspired racism here that I never thought we had." Another laments, "This was a very nice thriving community; now immigration problems have divided the town and changed it drastically. Neighborhood is pitted against neighborhood." "Is there a problem relating to racial tensions in Wausau?" the mayor asks and answers, "Emphatically yes." In an *Atlantic Monthly* article, Roy Beck (1994) calls this "The Ordeal of Immigration in Wausau."

I have heard similar worries and stories before, though sometimes with as much amusement as consternation: "Landlords are running scared—rent to one, and soon you have twenty or thirty in one little flat." "I heard of one case where they poured dirt into the attic to grow vegetables up there; destroyed the ceiling." "Walk downtown and you start to wonder what country you are in." "Where are all these Hmongs from anyway—they don't look like anybody I've ever seen." I've heard these stories because this part of the country is as close as any to what I could claim as home turf. Grampa and Grandma had their farm near here. The comments come from relatives and their neighbors, so I don't lecture on globalization. I don't show off the beautiful Hmong handiwork that I bought at a nearby outlet. I don't remind them that Grampa and Grandma were seen in their day as a mixed ethnicity couple, one from Yankee stock looking for land, the other from German immigrants who came north because they couldn't afford land in Indiana. Even while citing the sources of hostility, Beck admits that it took those German, Polish, and Yankee immigrants almost a hundred years to get used to each other.

Portraying the Hmong as New Pioneers in the Heartland, Jo Ann Koltyk (1998) challenges Beck's assertions in the Atlantic that these newcomers have brought all the problems. The Hmong, in fact, bring strong family ties, an extraordinarily resilient spirit, and an incredibly versatile means of adapting. They now have bought homes, started businesses, gone on to college, and in some cases, come back as computer programmers, businesspeople, and engineers. Their vegetable farms are productive and ready for the farmer's market. Grandma and Grampa gave up on this sandy, stony ground long ago. I'm delighted to be able to see the latest in Hmong needlework right behind the Amish quilts and the Scandinavian needlepoint in Donna's Ethnic Crafts down the road in

Norwegian Osseo. Yet I can also understand the confusion of people who proclaimed a Midwestern paradise far from the "fruits, and nuts and newcomers" on the coasts, only to find that the world has come to Wausau.

Though they are continually referred to as "immigrants," the U.N. would classify these Hmong as refugees fleeing war and persecution in their homeland. Like the Roma (gypsies) they have traveled far and have been fleeing violence for a long, long time; in fact, since about 2700 B.C. when the Chinese empire started encroaching on their land. Many Indochinese refugees came to the Midwest because of sponsorship, not initial choice. No one coming from the fall of Saigon would probably choose Fargo, North Dakota, and indeed many later moved on to more familiar terrain: the marshy, French-accented delta country of Louisiana, or the urban opportunities of California. Those who remained have often found gracious hosts until they were settled. Many have also found suspicion. In Rockford, Illinois, some unemployed residents lament the presence of other Laotian refugees: "The Vietnam vets, they get nothing, and here these people are buying rice by the sackful." "They eat dogs. They probably eat cats. I just don't like them" (FHS 1987). Employers speak highly of the Lao: they have revitalized a failing furniture industry that had been built by European immigrants and then dwindled once they found better jobs. The Lao have also changed the cultural face of Rockford, and their Buddhist temple set amidst Illinois cornfields has drawn stares as well as pipe bombs and shootings.

Refugees have tended to congregate in locales in which they can have the support of their country fellows, and have often gravitated to locations as close to home as possible, yet ties to family and sponsors mean more than proximity. Southern California has seen large numbers of Central American refugees fleeing fighting and terror in Guatemala, El Salvador, and Nicaragua. It has also seen refugees from Iran, Turkey, and points far afield. Cuban refugees were originally dispersed across the United States, but then began a process of congregating as close to Havana as possible, building a Little Havana that changed the face of Miami. Haitian refugees have struggled to gain acceptance in Florida, being suspect of bearing everything from AIDS to secret voodoo rituals, yet often come bearing little more than the ideals of the American dream, albeit with a Caribbean beat. In his aptly titled *Pride Against Prejudice*, Alex Stepick cites one young Haitian named Herve and his amateur rap:

> My name is Herb and I'm not poor
> I'm the Herbie that you're lookin' for
> Like Pepsi,
> a new generation
> of Haitian education and determination
> I'm the Herb that you're lookin' for (Stepick 1998, 1).

While Central American and Caribbean refugees garnered attention in the United States in the 1980s, larger numbers came from Poland and Eastern Europe. The role of international politics was also very evident here. So long as Poles struggled against a communist regime, they were welcomed as refugees. Once the government fell, they became merely immigrant hopefuls waiting in line with all the others. Likewise, in the closing days of the Cold War, Nicaraguans and Cubans fleeing left-wing repression found a more sympathetic reception and were far more likely to be granted refugee status than those fleeing right-wing violence in Guatemala and El Salvador. New concerns focus on disease and sheer numbers. For the first time, the United States has begun to detain and even turn back Cuban refugees. Commentator and presidential candidate Pat Buchanan has gained a lot of sympathy, along with ridicule, for his proposal to build a wall along the United States southern border.

Despite the view of some Americans that the entire world is on its way to American shores, the United States does not bear an inordinate amount of the world's refugees relative to its size. Most burdened are often locations that border trouble spots: Thailand with Indochinese refugees, Iran with Afghan refugees, Zaire with refugees from Rwanda, Malawi with refugees from Mozambique. The faces and places shift with the latest civil war, drought, or reprisals, but at any point in time over the last decade, around fifteen million people have been seeking asylum and refuge (UNHCR 1997). Many are still looking.

The U.N. High Commission on Refugees is the primary agency seeking to accommodate this tremendous flow of homeless humanity. The U.N. has produced several protocols that call on signatory states to make certain accommodations for refugees, and at the least not to return them into harm's way. Refugees don't vote and can make no claims on "civil rights"; they must trust in international recognition of fundamental human rights. Many are reluctant hosts, fearing economic drains and social turmoil. Yet as feuds rage in the global village we are finding we can't just "send them away." This is not just due to political and moral imperatives. It is because we are realizing that in an intertwined world there is no longer a "them" nor is there an "away."

Our People

The world at the turn of the third millennium is an odd assortment—mixed and remixed—of cultures, traditions, and identities thrown together with the frightening realization that our common survival depends on one other. Humanity finds itself a strange mix of characters cast together on a small island in space. Sometimes it looks like Lord of the Flies, sometimes more like Gilligan's Island. The old rules do not apply and adequate new rules have not yet been forged. Yet amidst both the fearful uncertainty and the absurdity, we are learning of our connectedness. Richard Rodriguez (1992) writes of the 1992 Los Angeles riots: "Here was a race riot that had no border, a race riot without nationality. And, for the first time, everyone in the city realized—if only in fear—that we were related to one another" (p. 16).

My People
Scott Sernau

"Aren't you ashamed of what your people have done?"
She asks as if to bite with words.
I am.
But no more for their color than their shoe size.
When her great granddad was working the plantation
Mine wasn't holding the whip.
He was, I suppose, working some old world plantation
For someone else
Who held the whip.

What is it to me if the ancestor we share
Is in a photo buried in grandma's bureau,
Or in records hidden from the census bureau,
Or in an unmarked grave on some ancient African plain?
Why argue shades of melanin
When a thumb's rub below we all share the mark of Cain?
I am ashamed of what my people have done
At Sarajevo, At Soweto,
At Auschwitz, At Nanking,
At My Lai,
And all the killing fields along our long trail of tears.

My people?
Hands raised, they shouted "We shall overcome."
Hands raised, they shouted, "Heil Hitler."
My people wrote, "All men are created equal."
My people wrote, "Separate but equal."
My people marched on Selma.
My people marched on Wounded Knee.
My people have cried, "Oh, freedom!"
My people have cried, "Crucify!"
They are all my people,

Every one.
Ones we love to honor,
Ones we long to forget.
Mine
And yours.
We are all common kin,
But it is to us to decide
Which birthright we would claim.

The world is facing riots without borders, reminding us of Martin Luther King's warning, "A riot is the language of the unheard" (Takaki 1993, 423). The U.N. convened a conference on human rights in Oslo in 1992, bringing together peace activists from Ireland and Palestine, President Havel of the Czech Republic, and former U.S. President Jimmy Carter, and many others to search for ways to respond to those riots and to those voices. The realization that these concerns had only deepened over a decade led to the 2001 World Conference Against Racism, Racial Discrimination, Xenophobia and Related Intolerance with South Africa as its location. Yet it is also at the local level, on the streets of Los Angeles, of Sarajevo, and of Dayton, where the decisions will be made. Will the response be a blend of new opportunism and old racism, or of a new generosity of spirit that can embrace difference and practice cultural hospitality?

The situation in the United States is simply a larger and newer picture of each of the world's multicultural societies, and now a portrait of the world itself. Our origins are in many places and many faces, yet this has become distorted and polarized through centuries of power struggle into racial and ethnic divides and hierarchies. The goal ahead is to restore the recognition of the multifaceted mélange—many places, their cultures and heritage embodied in many faces of many hues—coming together to forge something new. They are, each and every one, our people.

6

WORLD OF WONDERS, WORLD OF WIRES

The Reach of Global Technology

"The computer manages the store."
—McDonald's employee

The world has come together, not with hands across the water, but with wires under the water.

TRAVELING THE LESS-DEVELOPED world, a traveler no longer gets the sense of remoteness as of a world tripping over wires. Let me take you for a moment to the Mexican coast north of Puerto Escondido ("hidden") and a couple of hours south of Acapulco, where a large lagoon and a national park provide a wonderful opportunity to view coastal ecosystems. Mexico, like many places in the world, allows indigenous populations to live within their parks, so the edge of this park has a small village, primarily of Zapotec background along with a few merchants, a surfer from Mexico City, and El Italiano, an Italian traveler who liked the spot so well he married a local Zapotec woman and stayed. As we walk through the tiny stick buildings that comprise this village, however, we have to keep an eye to the ground. Don't worry about the snakes, it's the extension cords that will trip you up. Every hut seems linked to every other by long lines of extension cords plugged together into a huge net. The reason for the cords becomes apparent as we look through the walls of the huts where a familiar bluish light flickers through the walls. These dwellings have outdoor kitchens and bathing areas. The interior of many, in fact, has little more than a few hammocks strung between the stronger poles of the walls; hammocks that form an umbrella over the television. The televisions provide the greatest reason for getting plugged into this web of cords. A few years ago a school building out by the road was electrified. This provided the possibility of bringing the power down into the cluster of homes, one extension cord after another. A single village set placed in the school would be more sociable, as with theaters of just a few years ago, but this only breeds conflict. After all, some want to watch the latest *telenovela* soap opera from Mexico City, others insist on "Baywatch" and "Knots Landing," others claim "The Beverly Hillbillies" is funnier, while others scoff and want CNN. Their links to one another are now mediated by extension cords, but their links to the world have never been stronger.

An odd phenomenon occurs around the world, in that it seems the poorest places have the most wires. The corners of central Port-au-Prince, Haiti, are almost darkened by the dense net of wires overhead, a three-story tangled web that gives the impression that some great spider is going to drop on you as in the Godzilla movies showing in their theaters. This is just what street corners in New York and Chicago also looked like around the turn of the century. In time, wealthier places put their wires in buried cable. Much of the Western European landscape is blessedly wire-free (just don't dig anywhere). With more timber, the United States has opted for poles that line the landscape, but at least these consolidate the wires. Elsewhere around the world, the wires simply weave amongst each other as everyone seeks to plug in. This creates opportunity as well as confusion. Poor entrepreneurs in Latin America are famous for fashioning their own meter-free connections to local power lines and getting free electricity—at least until the whole system crashes in frequent blackouts.

Weaving the World Wide Web

"Glory to God in the Highest, peace on earth, good will to men." So Queen Victoria cabled U.S. President Buchanan in 1858 over the first transatlantic telegraph cable. Thousands of miles of cable (with faulty insulation it turned out) had been lowered to the sea floor by steam ship to connect the continents. The connection was commercial as well as political; it was hoped that messages at $5 a word would pay for the venture. Shortly after "Glory to God," the next message was "Go to Chicago," from a London merchant to his New York representative.

The weaving of the world together by wires continued and accelerated: Western Union opened a line between New York and San Francisco in 1861, putting an end to the Pony Express after only a one-year ride. In 1866 a better cable crossed the Atlantic, and then telephone quickly replaced Morse Code in crisscrossing the country with lines that themselves crossed the Atlantic in 1927, the same year experimental television was tested by Bell Laboratories. Television completed its global coverage with the space age and instantaneous satellite transmission. Wires were made not obsolete—although they may now be fiber optic rather than metal—as television embraced cable and computers were linked together in a vast global Internet. Like many communications ventures first conceived for defense purposes, the Internet quickly gained commercial importance. Internet and fax allow almost instant worldwide communication, and "to fax" and "to e-mail" have become the new active verbs of an electronic age. "Glory to God," e-mail missionaries who were once isolated in Oceania and Central Africa, as they now translate ancient texts on their laptops. "Go to Chicago," e-mail Hong Kong stock traders to their global representatives. Around the world, walls hum with electrical messages while the air itself vibrates with millions of broadcasts that encircle the globe. The reach of global technology is no more equitable than the distribution of political power and economic opportunity, but it has filled the planet from the ocean floor to the ionosphere.

The world has come together, not with hands across the water, but with wires under the water to create a world of wonders and, with it, a world of electronic-age worries. Technology provides both concentrations of power and new opportunities. The balance between these affects the rate of innovation as well as the application and distribution of its results.

Birth of the Electronic Age

My elementary-school world history book was eager to divide human history into recognizable periods, and did so in pure Eurocentric fashion. The classical period was the era of Greece and Rome—classical to seventeenth-century Europeans who saw this as the epitome of human civilization to date. When Rome fell, it was therefore the Dark Ages, inaugurating the Middle Ages that came between classical civilization and their renaissance, or revival, in Europe. This revival brought the Age of Enlightenment and the Age of Discovery. The discoveries and the enlightened thinking led to the Industrial Age. Of course these ages say little about the rest of the world. The time of the "Dark Ages" encompassed the high tide of Byzantine and Arab civilization, and the Classical period of Mesoamerican civilization. The Age of Enlightenment and Discovery enslaved and killed many of those who were "discovered."

It is also pure vanity to suppose we can accurately assess the significance of our own times, and the "ages" we define seem to be getting ever shorter. The favored term in the 1960s was "Space Age" as the moon was explored for the 1969 landing. But landing on the moon did little to change the lives of very many. As I watched, I thought that just as amazing as the human footsteps on the lunar dust was that we were watching this on television in real time, and that "we" included millions of people around the world.

What we were witnessing was not so much the dawn of the space age as the electronic age. When given the elementary school essay-writing task of naming our age, I thus opted neither for the mind-changing peace of the Age of Aquarius nor the mind-boggling power of the Space Age, but for the mouthful of the "Electromagnetic Age": a time when the power of electrons will be harnessed, not just to turn machines, but to carry information or to translate it into unseen waves. The power of lasers turned out not best suited for HG Wells-style battles—although laser-firing satellites were attempted in the Strategic Defense Initiative "Star Wars" proposals of the early 1980s—but for delicate surgery, for reading information off of universal product codes (UPC symbols), and, most significantly, off of compact disks (CDs) that can place a entire public library on my desktop. We overlooked the other life-changing wave, microwaves, altogether. In 1969, I was still unaware of the full power of electronics and how soon they would change the world. Four years later, a bold attempt by a social scientist to label the changes occurring gave us a new, if not very descriptive, term for our age in Daniel Bell's (1973) *The Coming of Post Industrial Society: A Venture in Social Forecasting.* Maybe it wasn't vanity to try to name a new age; the world was indeed changed.

While European philosophers tried to impose a certain intellectual order on their version of history, archeologists probing still earlier times found it convenient to label ages by the material of artifacts left behind in the ground. So we have inherited labels such as the Stone Age, Bronze Age, and Iron Age. By this reasoning we are in the Polymer Age and will be known by our piles of plastic trash.

A more significant criteria, however, is the core technology that shapes how a society survives. For close to five thousand years this was the agricultural techniques of agrarian societies. A flurry of innovation led to the beginnings of large agrarian societies around 2600 B.C. But then the next four thousand years saw much slower innovation. New ideas emerged, new technologies emerged, but the life of the average person changed very little. A peasant from the Middle Kingdom of Ancient Egypt could be resurrected in Medieval France or in nineteenth-century China, and go right to work knowing what to do. Lenski's (1966) hypothesis is that the system becomes one of negative feedback to innovation. Instead of innovation breeding innovation, it instead breeds a backlash. Since all surplus goes to the wealthy rulers, producers have no incentive to increase productivity, while the producers themselves are far too isolated from the productive process to understand the needs and possibilities for innovation.

Technology is born of technology in ever-accelerating cycles of innovation but only under certain social situations. For technological advance to occur it must be encouraged and rewarded. Institutions that foster and promote technology are now everywhere, but once were quite rare. In Europe, monasteries preserved and occasionally advanced learning; for instance, the founder of genetics was the monk Mendel. Out of monastic "scholasticism" came the university system that has spread around the world. Eventually beyond the university systems were broad clearinghouses such as the Royal Academy of Science, in which members debated, ridiculed, accused, competed with, and insulted each other into better refined theories and new discoveries. Some suggest that modern research institutes and universities seem to have borrowed this pattern! While we might prefer the courtly decorum of the Chinese Confucian sages to the barbs and insults and intense competition of the Royal Academy at the time of Isaac Newton (who served briefly as its president), it was the latter that fostered constant innovation.

Further, inquiry must be rewarded and seen as an appropriate means to gain. Early thinkers needed patrons, usually royal or noble patrons. Naturally they tended to mold their talents to the needs of those patrons. Imonhotep designed the first great pyramid to assist his patron pharaoh on the road to immortality, but his civil engineering genius was never tapped for public housing, roads, or other social or commercial ventures. Archimedes's brilliance went into war machines for the defense of ancient Syracuse, while Chinese engineering brilliance went into designing the Great Wall for the defense of China. Even the forward-looking Italian states were much more interested in using Galileo's improved telescopes to search the seas for clues to enemy ship movements rather than to search the skies for clues to the universe. Even at the beginning of a new age of science in the 1400s, Leonardo da Vinci designed fabulous machines, but had no engineers to build them nor patrons to pay for them.

One of the great absorbers of creative energy was astronomy and astrology. Agrarian societies needed to know the movement of the seasons and these could be traced in the stars. Mesoamericans built incredible observatories and created mathematical systems using zero to accommodate huge numbers, but this to keep track of their cosmology. Babylon, China, and India also had great astronomers and astrologers who knew the stars, but were not encouraged to bring their math and their precise observation down to earth.

Technology is not just science, but science applied to practical problems. Many early discoveries never found an application. In Alexandrian Egypt of about 100 B.C., a thinker named Hero built a steam engine: a hollow sphere that spun when heated water inside escaped through two opposing vents on opposite sides. He did nothing with it but amuse his friends. Within a few years of James Watt's 1765 steam engine, however, steam was turning factory wheels, ship's paddle wheels, and train wheels. The difference was not just in the more sophisticated design of the engine, but in a society that was eager to embrace and capitalize on any new idea for its commercial advance.

Once the commercial value of science was appreciated, patrons included not only royal sponsors but commercial competitors as well. The developing legal systems devised the patent so inventors could claim the gain on their ideas. In earlier agrarian times, this would have simply gone to the royal monopoly. A striking example is the smelting of iron, first done much more cheaply and efficiently in China in Hunan around A.D. 1000. This was done so well that production boomed, and iron implements were beginning to abound. A suspicious emperor, however, claimed all the profits, and gradually workers saw no reason to endure the smoke, soot, and back-breaking work this entailed (McNeill 1982). Inexpensive iron smelting was abandoned, later to be rediscovered by European commercial interests who soon built huge empires of steel.

The industrial revolution that transformed stable agrarian societies into ever-changing industrial entities began not so much with any key technology as with a complex of ideas, dispositions, and social arrangements that fostered innovation and production. This change is sometimes simply labeled capitalism, but full-blown capitalism emerges gradually as part of this shifting social system. Industrial society begins in Britain, and it begins with water power. Water power is not new; it had long irrigated Egyptian and Chinese fields. But in the early 1700s, the British found it could power looms. Internal colonialism provided Scottish wool and Irish flax, while overseas colonialism provided American cotton, and now machines could turn these products into the engines of progress. Of course, the competitors were on their heels. Mills sprang up on waterways in Germany, France, and—most worrisome of all—in New England. The race was on. Steam engines turned coal and water into power that could be located everywhere, and soon England was filled with the soot of the "dark Satanic mills" that churned out ever more products. Workers may have seen the face of Satan in those mills, but they created wealth and power in Britain on an unprecedented scale, and the wealthy and powerful could always escape to country estates—expensive estates no longer built on the labor of peasants but paid for by the labor of an urban proletariat.

Industrial society was built on harnessing external energy sources, turning natural power into economic and military power. With an industrial lead, Britain could rule the world. China may have had 300 million people to Britain's twelve million, but British steam-powered gunboats could churn up the Yangtze unchallenged and unleash their steel guns and mass-produced ammunition without retort, forcing China in the Opium War of 1840 to acknowledge British commercial supremacy and political domination. British imperial might was not just vast, this power was cumulative—power led to power—and accelerating. Agrarian empires led to riches that invited sacking by poor but powerful barbarians. Industrial empires amassed resources that could be turned into new machines of commerce and domination. As Hilaire Belloc boasted of Britain, "Whatever happens we have got the Maxim gun and they have not" (Isbister 1998, 68).

But technology was flourishing elsewhere as well. Japan borrowed and revised both British and German technology to become China's next foreign taskmaster.

The strength of its military technology moved Germany to the center of world power at the beginning of the twentieth century. Yet as Nazi Germany challenged the world at mid-century, the weight of industrial might was already shifting. With a huge network of industrial cities, and a vast network of universities and institutes patronizing the work of an international assemblage of scientists, the United States was a formidable opponent. At the peak of World War II, U.S. industry turned out one major ship everyday along with hundreds of aircraft, a production level that could overwhelm any counter-strategy. Ultimately, the U.S. science enterprise, ironically bolstered by exiles from Europe, produced the ultimate in technological terror and inaugurated the "nuclear age." The unleashing of nature's energy had attained unimaginable levels.

Technology is not just about unleashing energy, however, but also about controlling it. The key to the Jacquard loom of the early 1800s was not just the water power, but a punch card to precisely control the movements of the loom without skilled human hands. During World War II as much energy went into coding and decoding messages as in bombing cities. The key to the *Wehrmacht*'s blitz was not just the tank and the dive bomber, but the Enigma coded radio system that could control fast and vast movements until the opposition just collapsed in confusion. In time Jacquard cards became IBM punch cards controlling networks of wires rather than thread. The on-off switches shrank from vacuum tubes to transistors to ever tinier micro-processors. The electronic age was born.

Stolen Nights: Facing the Great Ghost

Agrarian societies were expansionistic in that rulers were eager to bring new lands under cultivation. Yet their expansion ended where fertile land gave way to inhospitable expanses. They might trade with neighbors in those lands, but also were eager to insure a boundary between within and without. If geography did not provide a natural barrier such as the mountains that isolate the Indian subcontinent, a manmade barrier could be called for, as Hadrian's wall between England and Scotland, or the colossal Great Wall of China. Early industrial societies needed a broader reach. The quest for raw materials could extend into previously remote regions. The key to control of the system was to ensure that the core industries were located in the heart of the industrial power.

With an advanced-industrial, electronic information-based society, a second shift occurs. No longer is it necessary to hold the industries themselves, but rather to retain the nodes of command and control. Power lies not in the smokestack but the boardroom. In this situation, industry can be located anywhere, just as the early imperialists transplanted their agriculture. The new cores are the centers of information flows. Since the digitalized, modulated, electronically mediated information of our age flows freely, it can reach every region. And this it has.

Deep in the Amazon, the slow tropical twilight beckons villagers to join the fire circle. Here all gather to share the news, to learn of one another's lives, to hear elders tell the old stories, entertain, and socialize the young into the right ways of living. Yet there are ever fewer young at this fire circle. The elders explain in hushed tones, "They have fallen to the ghost, the big ghost." For this jungle is haunted. As night falls, great clusters of bats swoop overhead blocking the moonlight, deep-throated frogs call, and the fleeting, flickering light of a ghost can be glimpsed in the village. The ghost prefers young people; one by one they disappear from the fire circle. Some are never seen in the circle again. Others return with a zombie-like glaze in their eyes. The elders know they have seen the Madonna—the one in strange underwear, that is. The big ghost arrives by satellite dish, and brings Madonna and MTV to the Amazon along with cartoons and a world of other offerings. The Amazon's Kayapo Indians used money from gold and mahogany on the world market to install a small but effective satellite dish. Some wish they hadn't. The chief regrets his decision, "I have been saying that people must buy useful things like knives or fishing hooks. Television does not fill the stomach. It only shows our children and grandchildren white people's things." Bemoans an elder, "The night is the time the old people teach the young people. Television has stolen the night" (Simons 1989).

The elder's comment strikes a chord with many. The evenings now consumed by television were once consumed by conversation, by passion, by intermingling in unmediated public space. In the United States, where such things are closely monitored by the sponsors, almost two million children are still watching at midnight, and they claim the average American watches thirty hours a week, a number that could only be achieved by watching television while eating and as an accompaniment to many other activities. Electronic media now do just that—mediate a vast array of social relations.

The decline of human-to-human contact is apparent around the world. Throughout the Middle East, café life—where people used to tell stories over a cup of tea—is disappearing. Bistros are going out of business in Paris; many close earlier in the day. Henri Miquel, owner of Le Dufrénoy, shuts down at 8 pm instead of midnight. Where do patrons go? "They rush off to watch television," he says (Swerdlow 1995, 6).

What they watch also has a strongly corporate-mediated conformity. California-based U.S. television has dominated since the early days. Currently one of the most popular and widely seen programs in the world is Baywatch, a scary thought if one is concerned about the intellectual content of world culture. Yet sun and swimsuits, luxury and leisure translate more readily than complex dialog. The essentials of Baywatch are apparent without dubbing. Of course, a host of attitudes about beauty, appropriate apparel, gender relations, and lifestyle are also communicated. Presumably it was the allure of wealth and glamour rather than intellectual challenge that has brought Wheel of Fortune to 100 million people in twenty-five countries, and spawned a host of imitators such as Russia's favorite, Field of Miracles (LA Times, Oct. 20, 1992). The previous global choice was also Californian, Santa Barbara. Sex, lies, and great wealth have also made Dallas and Knots Landing world favorites. Before the evening soaps, the world got another glimpse of tele-mediated American culture in an early favorite, The Beverly Hillbillies. Whether world viewers imagined that they, like Jed Clampett, would find crude oil bubbling on their hunting grounds and move to Beverly Hills, or whether they just enjoyed the silliness (I Love Lucy continues to thrive overseas), they also learned of a distant, made-in-Hollywood world.

The culture of the air depends not only on what tantalizes foreign tastes, but also on who can gain foreign dominance. Viacom not only brings Madonna and Ice T to 210 million households around the world on MTV, they also own Nickelodeon for children, the Showtime movie channel, and an array of local cable, radio, and television stations. This single conglomerate has an enormous video-enhanced voice in shaping youth culture around the world (*Business Week*, Sept. 21, 1992).

Increasingly, our perceptions of the world are shaped less by political speeches, the reports of travelers, or personal experience, and more by the immediate visual image of global news. The "you are there" feel can often mask the reality that what we see has been edited, framed, and focused for us by media interests. The Cable News Network (CNN) alone now reaches 137 countries (Roodman 1995). At the outbreak of the Gulf War, the world, including the world leaders launching the war, could watch the first bombs fall on Baghdad via CNN hookup. People could watch the war as it happened, or at least as it was shown. Managing world impressions became as important as hitting targets. Clearly, trying to manage perception is not a new trend. Casualty counts in World War I were not released until after the war to avoid demoralization. Many of the great images of World War II, a highly photographed event, were staged: the Marines joining together to raise the flagpole on Iwo Jima (they did it again with more gusto for the camera), MacArthur coming ashore in the Philippines (the cameras missed the original so he went back in the water), and the exuberant waving of the Soviet flag over the *Reichstat* in Berlin (staged by the secret police after the fact). In Vietnam, the cameras started to gain autonomy and fueled opposition to the war. Realizing this danger, President Reagan banned the media from the Grenada invasion, and only offered selected and edited glimpses after the fact. In the Gulf, the cameras were there, but their angles and topics were also edited, access being tied to cooperation. The entire Gulf War had only a few hours of actual fighting surrounded by considerable media posturing on both sides. We know world events firsthand, but that knowledge is carefully handled for both political and commercial purposes.

The developing world has long complained that both the images and the control of the media reflect First World dominance and bias. When poor nations are seen, and this rarely, it is often in the context of revolution, civil war, or natural disaster. Think for a moment of your visual images of Bangladesh, or the Congo, or Colombia for that matter. A U.N. conference in Belgrade in 1982 called for a "new world information order" that would challenge information inequity.

Upstart challenges are emerging from other continents, at least where sufficient concentrations of wealth and technology permit. The largest is Hong Kong-based STAR TV, launched by Richard Li and bankrolled by his billionaire father. STAR now reaches forty-two million homes in fifty-three countries, with its satellite broadcasts targeting a still relatively untapped audience of 2.8 billion in Asian and the Middle East. Plans call for educational broadcasting in Mandarin, Urdu, Hindi, and Arabic, but the popular programs are still largely American (Applebaum and Chambliss 1996, 393). While STAR eyes the world, Rupert Murdoch's News Corporation empire is eyeing STAR, and now holds a majority share of its stock.

Claiming to bring "information affluence" to the have-nots around the world, Ethiopian-born but Washington-based Noah Samara is promoting his WorldSpace system of satellite relayed digital radio. With financial backing from the Saudi royal family and other gulf investors, he is banking on new technologies to break into world markets making him "a household name from Lagos to La Paz: the Rupert Murdoch of the Southern hemisphere" (*Business Week*, June 30, 1997, 36).

Media technology can promote cultural conformity but also resistance and cultural flourishing. While billionaires struggle over the big systems, small-scale technology provides almost limitless alternatives. While MTV brings rock and rap to the world, the cheap and portable cassette recorder allows for the survival and dissemination of what might otherwise be lost forms: traditional women's song in Quechua in the Andes, the twangs of Wolof instruments in West Africa, the sounds of traditional instruments in India and in Indian homes around the world, the chants of Tibetan monks to Tibetans on three continents. The inexpensive reach of radio keeps local languages and cultures alive and in touch as with the pledge of Farmington, New Mexico's KNDN, "All Navaho, all the time." Desktop publishing allows inexpensive micro-printing in a host of languages and scripts. Fax and e-mail connect the diaspora of refugees, while tapes and disks allow them to preserve a common identity and culture (Weatherford 1994).

These can also introduce a curious world to new possibilities and old traditions. As I am typing this chapter on my computer, the speakers and CD player on that computer are bringing me Christmas carols in Portuguese by a Brazilian-Caribbean group from a world beat album benefitting Special Olympics International. I don't speak much Portuguese, but I can readily translate the familiar words over the drums and marimba: "Glory to God in the highest, and on earth, peace, goodwill to men." Indeed.

Wired to Kill

It's a market: this one in Abu Dhabi in the United Arab Emirates looks like a cross between a traditional Arab bazaar and the huge marketing conventions that fill cavernous halls in the world's cities. Every market has its specialty, and this one caters to mass destruction. It is a famous arms bazaar, and many of the shoppers are Middle Easterners wary of their neighbors, although anyone who can pull together enough cash is welcome. It takes a lot of cash to buy an F-16, the hottest item in the market since it proved its worth in the Gulf War. Jet fighters and strike aircraft are a must have, and this has spawned competition. The French Mirage offers a sleek new design, and the promotional material is out for the Eurofighter, the "best of a new Europe." For those who can't handle the truly big ticket items, there are bargain hand-me-downs from Russia and small arms from the Czech Republic.

Technology has always been turned to war, often at great price, and now high technology warfare claims a colossal price tag. Worldwide weapons expenditures reached a peak in the late 1980s during the heightened tensions of the final hours of the Cold War. They have declined slightly since, but total military expenditures still claim over five trillion dollars a year worldwide (Sivard 1997). There has also been an increase in U.S. dominance of the trade, with American weapons dominating markets such as this. After the budget crushing arms race between the United States and the USSR, the end of the Cold War has created new insecurities and new cycles of arms buildups. U.S. arms flooded Iran during the era of the Shah. Then as Iran and Iraq moved toward conflict, they flowed to Iraq to restore the armament balance. Then as Iraq grew increasingly aggressive, new arms had to go to Iraq's neighbors to restore this elusive balance of weaponry. The Gulf War finally erupted with American and European billion-dollar weapons ultimately triumphing over the million-dollar weapons that Iraq had secured. The lesson of that conflict seems to have been the importance of having top-shelf rather than year-old weaponry, and the races go on.

The Middle East remains the biggest buyer, but East Asia also has money and its share of tensions. New buyers such as Peru and Chile keep the market open late. With the end of the Cold War, U.S. firms find smaller domestic contracts and increasingly turn to the world market. Russia has few ready exports, but has no shortage of lethal weapons. The Czech Republic has earned a reputation for peaceful transitions, but had previously earned a reputation as arms supplier for the Eastern bloc. With many of their industries in competitive decline, Eastern Europe can garner cash from its weapons stocks. Europe is eager to prove its technology, and challenge American monopolies. Japan has avoided direct weapons production, but contributes parts and electronics to many. China sought to build its own arsenals, and now exports missiles across Asia. This global trade has become a bizarre dance of death that no one seems able to stop.

The world's bestseller is not one of the big ticket items, however, but one of the cheapest, and Russian at that. The AK-47 automatic rifle has probably killed more people than all the aircraft combined, and continues a lively, or deadly, trade around the world. By some estimates, it is the most widely produced and distributed machine ever built. It is cheap and places a powerful wallop in untrained hands, and has been the mainstay of civil revolts and internal conflicts around the world. The most eager shoppers are not in Abu Dhabi, for they are not governments but independent traders, rebels, and militia moguls. They won't get an invitation to Abu Dhabi, but if they have money, they will get a hearty welcome in the towns that sit along the legendary gate of invaders, the Khyber Pass. Here on the Pakistani-Afghan border AK-47s go for a mere $75. Something deadlier only requires some looking: "You could mistake it for a Weedwacker, this green fiberglass tube weighing just 35 pounds, yet with it a man is a god wielding a meteor—a man who truly owns the sky" (Duffy 1997, 73).

Light and lethal, the heat-seeking Stinger missile helped bring down Soviet ambitions in Afghanistan. Unleashed on the black market, inspectors worry it could have brought down TWA Flight 800 in the Atlantic. Its heat-seeking electronics make the Stinger the match of those high-priced aircraft and so the choice of revolutionaries; it is also a match for the jumbo jet and could become the choice of terrorists. Controversy circled around supplying these to diverse groups of Afghan rebels and their Pakistani suppliers, yet in Cold War logic, this was an easy way to sting and bleed the Soviet army, just as the AK-47 and the wired booby trap had bled the United States in Vietnam.

With the close of the Cold War, the "nuclear clock" that ticked minutes to an eternal midnight has been set back and missiles no longer target U.S. and Russian cities. This was none too soon, for faster, deadlier weapons with ever more precise electronics had created a hair-trigger world in which a superpower leader would have less than twenty minutes to decide on a response to an attack warning, to decide, in effect, the fate of the planet. With hindsight, it is apparent that one reason Kennedy and Khruschev were able to avoid nuclear disaster over the Cuban missile crisis was that they had days to talk through the entanglements; they might not have done as well with twenty minutes. The magnitude of the destructive force has also increased phenomenally, so that one Trident submarine carries the multiple warhead destructive force to obliterate the planet. The entire future of humanity hung on the hope that these death boats had sound commanders and responsible crews.

Such lethal technology may have kept the superpowers apart for forty years but also threatened to make a slip in the balance of terror irreversible. Yet the relaxation—we hope it is the end—of the Cold War has brought its own terrors. Russian and American nuclear material is missing and new nations join the nuclear club every year. Indian underground nuclear tests shook the already troubled Indian-Pakistani border in the spring of 1998, setting off political aftershock across Asia. Pakistan responded quickly with tests of its own to restore the "balance of terror." These programs are sources of great national pride, although they remain embedded in geopolitics: Pakistan has developed its nuclear and missile programs with Chinese assistance, while India receives technical assistance from Russia.

"Now the world must take notice of us," proudly announced an Indian engineer. It is ironic, and tragic, that the countries of the Indian subcontinent with over a fifth of the world's population, increasingly skilled and educated, and a legacy of some of the world's most ancient and enduring civilizations, feel they have not "arrived" and will not command global attention and respect until they set off nuclear bombs. It is clear that the one and one-quarter billion people of India, Pakistan, and Bangladesh will be important actors on the world stage in the new century. What is less clear is whether they will be inspired by the spirit of Mahatma Gandhi, who was killed for his willingness to seek justice and reconciliation between Hindus and Muslims, or haunted by the spirits of wars past, present, and future, now robed in nuclear terror.

Nuclear weapons can completely alter old ideas of a balance of power. The answer to guns has always been more guns and bigger guns. But if Saddam Hussein had nuclear weapons, it would have completely altered the situation in the Gulf, regardless of the fact that the allies would have had thousands more, and many times more powerful, weapons. Iran and Iraq scorched each other's capitals with imported ballistic missiles. If they had succeeded in attaching nuclear, or chemical or biological, warheads to those missiles, the tragedy would have been multiplied many times over. Chemical weapons, the "poor man's atom bomb," pose added terrors, seen in World War I, in Iraqi attacks on Iran and its own Kurdish population, and in terrorist attacks in Tokyo's subways. Biological weapons pose an even greater potential for terror, unleashing custom-designed plagues on whole populations.

While global-scale devastation remains the stuff of speculation and spy movies, smaller-scale devastation is the everyday reality of trouble spots around the world. Years of war, with ever deadlier weapons, have brought Afghanistan to the bottom of the world's measures of well-being. The global arms assembly line includes young boys in Darra, Pakistan, loading ammunition into long belts for Russian antiaircraft guns to compound and extend this misery. The tale of unaccounted-for weapons includes as many as two hundred of the one thousand Stingers shipped by the CIA, as yet unrecovered.

. . . Existing as she does at the top of the terror food chain, Stinger remains a major threat to civilian aircraft. At the same time, she's our New Age Medusa, symptom of a binge-and-purge world consumed by wars and awash with arms—arms for sale by people so angry, desperate or casually greedy that, frankly, it's a miracle we've seen as little terror as we have" (Duffy 1997, 74).

Like the portable cassette, the portable missile shifts the balance of power, but now to any threatened group who hopes to keep a culture, a way of life, or an idea in the public mind, not with a song but with a deadly sting—terror to the people. Terrorism is as old as the dagger, but the magnitude of mayhem now available to a few has been vastly multiplied by technology.

The guns of Afghanistan are a reminder that the wires of war cannot be promptly switched off, or even defused. In Cambodia and across Southeast Asia, the land beneath their feet is also wired—wired to kill. Long after the original conflict has passed, buried land mines continue to kill and maim hundreds of curious children, desperate farmers, and whoever else happens their way. While international organizations struggle field by field to remove these menaces, the worldwide movement to remove them from the world's arsenals received the 1997 Nobel Peace Prize. Countries around the world have agreed to stop manufacturing and deploying the mines. The United States is not among them. Claiming to need their protection against North Korea's reputed million-man army, the United States balked at signing. Meanwhile, around the world, unexploded bombs and uncontrolled arms shipments remain the "gift" that keeps on killing.

The Call to Conversion

The collapse of East-West rivalries brought hope for what was to be a "peace dividend." That dividend has proved elusive, in part because new small-scale conflicts have consumed energies and money, and in part because weapons manufacturing, like the weapons themselves, tends to endure. C. Wright Mills (1956) spoke of the American military-industrial complex and how it was interwoven in the national life. Still today, military base closings bring bitter opposition, even though the Pentagon has determined that the millions of acres in military hands has become a drain rather than a benefit for national defense. The bases bring in dollars, as do weapons plants and defense contractors, to local economies in what has been termed military Keynesianism—government spending to bolster economic demand. Yet at the same time, domestic Keynesianism is being rejected as wasteful, and the IMF is demanding lower levels of government spending from its client states around the world.

Leaders in the United States also often cite a shortage of technically trained people, yet the sole justification for some defense projects seems to be to keep these people employed producing deadly products no longer needed. Places where this expertise might be better applied abound. The United States has also resisted the call to conversion of its vast military on the ground that it is still "a dangerous world." Yet one wonders if this industry is lessening or compounding the dangers. Justification for a new generation of deadlier fighter-strike aircraft was provided in that the world's arsenals of current top-of-the-line military aircraft is growing explosively. Yet most of these planes were built by the United States, and are held by U.S. allies. The cycle is as bizarre as any during the Cold War: deficits produce the need to sell arms, these arms find their way into dangerous hands and must be countermanded by superior arms, and the production of these arms generates new deficits. The United States, like much of the world, seems addicted to a debilitating spiral. Despite gradual reductions, the United States in 1994 still spent more on "defense" than the next nine biggest spenders combined (Rourke 1997). Is there any hope for a break in this addiction to dangerous substances, a global armaments anonymous?

We are starting to realize that both the United States and Russia lost the Cold War as the spending wreaked havoc on their economies. Ironically, the dismantling of Cold War weapons is also expensive. With four trillion dollars of public debt in the United States alone, our grandchildren will still be paying for the binge-and-purge arms gluttony of the 1980s. This realization that military winners can find themselves economic losers could lead to greater restraint in future military spending, but the advanced industrial nations who lead the new race and produce most of the world's weapons will have to lead the way in getting off the treadmill. The possibilities for conversion are as staggering as the weapon costs themselves. The price of a single Stealth bomber, over two billion dollars, would vaccinate one billion children in developing countries against measles, tuberculosis, diphtheria, whooping cough, polio, and tetanus, possibly preventing the deaths of six to seven million children per year (Brown et al. 1995). Taken together, one wonders if the five trillion dollars of arms expenditure, if applied to addressing human need, might not go a long way in creating a world in which massive armament was unnecessary.

The Health of Nations

The Kiss of Death

Technology can both heal and harm. Jet airliners and container ships not only move people and products quickly and easily around the globe, they are also wonderful carriers for infectious disease. Global encounters have as often provided the vector of deadly disease as they have the vector of healing interventions. Agrarian society brought larger food supplies but also provided fabulous hothouses for disease. Large, dense populations in close proximity to one another and one another's wastes, to disease-carrying livestock, and to exploding populations of grain-eating rodents provided an incubator for disease like never before. Poor sanitation and poor nutrition kept the great agrarian empires always on the edge of disease-borne disaster.

Interactions between societies were sufficient to carry new diseases across vast distances. The black death of bubonic plague developed in Asia, then swept across the central Asian steppe and into Europe, carried by warriors, herders, and traders and their flea-infested caravans. Populations fled afflicted cities and carried the plague into the countryside until between one-quarter and one-third of the European population was dead. The population collapse utterly rewrote the fourteenth century, and maybe much of European history. Mighty Constantinople soon fell to invaders, while elsewhere in Europe urban labor shortages gave new opportunities to peasants fleeing the land, and helped to undermine rural feudalism. The truly tragic losers in the global disease exchange were the peoples of the Americas. Across the Americas, populations crashed, sometimes losing three-quarters of their population, and abandoned urban centers as whole civilizations unraveled.

The global spread of disease has continued raging into this century. The world's deadliest single epidemic may well be not the black death plagues but the simple flu. The influenza pandemic of 1918, the "Spanish" or "Black Lady" flu, swept around a war-weary world and claimed twenty-two million people, almost 1 percent of the world's population and twice as many people as World War I itself. Each year new influenzas emerge, many—as in 1918—in the densely populated regions of East Asia where humans are in close contact with livestock and one another, and an upstart virus can make the genetic leap to infecting human populations and travel the world in a matter of months.

HIV, the AIDS virus, similarly seemed to make the leap from infecting animals to humans in central Africa. HIV traveled around the world before it was identified. AIDS continues to ravage Africa, where in some locations between one-quarter and one-third of the population is infected. It also continues to expand rapidly around the world. East Asia has the most new cases. Thailand, in part due to a globally sponsored sex trade, was hard hit first, but now China is experiencing a surge in cases, even while remaining reluctant to admit the full extent of the spread of the disease (*New York Times*, April 5, 2000). Meanwhile, new possibilities for global infection incubate in remote regions and in the cauldrons of biological weapons experimenters, keeping the threat of global infectious disease alive.

Sanitation and Nutrition

With the growth of industrial societies the spread of global disease travelled at the speed of steamships, but it was countered by worldwide efforts in sanitation, nutrition, and medical technology, largely in that order. These three efforts continue around the world. The first reductions in mortality came not from medical intervention (antibiotics were first effectively introduced around World War II), but from improved sanitation. In one famous incident a London cholera epidemic was stopped by a careful observer who traced the source to a single contaminated pump and broke the pump handle. Cholera and other water-borne disease are still major killers worldwide.

Until only several years ago, the world's single deadliest cause of death was the dehydration of lowly diarrhea from cholera, dysentery, and simple gastroenteritis (essentially "stomach flu"). This is particularly dangerous to small children, whose bodies cannot afford massive fluid loss. Oral rehydration therapy, giving a simple mixture of sugar and salt water, has helped enormously, but the big long-term gains are still to be found in sanitation, especially covering sewage systems and providing covered clean water supplies. While some big gains have been made, pollution—both chemical and biological—threatens ever more water supplies, and rapid urbanization stresses over-taxed sanitation infrastructure.

The next prime target is nutrition. Malnutrition kills directly, and it weakens its victims who fall to other diseases. Here too, the role of new technologies is both hopeful and disheartening. The green revolutions of new higher yielding plants have continued to increase global food production beyond expectations. New agribusinesses have arisen to package, store, ship, and distribute these higher yields. Yet a quarter of the world is still hungry, very hungry. Some of the "basket cases" of three decades ago that seemed as if they could never feed themselves are now veritable bread-baskets. India exports food. Yet should it—India still has many malnourished people. The world is still stalked by famine due in large measure to absolute poverty—the food has been grown somewhere, but the poor cannot afford to secure it. This is not a new phenomenon: ships carried grain out of Ireland during the great potato famine; ultimately more food left than was provided in aid.

Agribusiness can compound the problem. Small farmers cannot afford the expensive fertilizers and equipment that new production demands, and they cannot compete with those who can afford them. Subsistence crops are replaced by profitable export crops: in Brazil black beans give way to soybeans ready for the oil press, in West Africa corn and cassava give way to peanuts, also to be turned into oil and manufactured export products.

Rapid transportation and improved storage and spoilage prevention has meant that food exports need not be limited to more durable products such as grains and dried beans, but now can include a wide array of fruits and vegetables. Take a walk through one of the very large mega-markets that are replacing the smaller, no-longer-so-super "supermarkets" that once replaced the still smaller corner grocery. These mega-markets have products that would have been thoroughly exotic only a few years ago, including a wide range of tropical fruit. Even the more familiar products may have distant origins. Here too you can get a geography refresher by noting the "fresh from" signs and stickers.

Chile has become a major agricultural exporter, taking advantage in part of its southern hemisphere location that gives it winter during our summer, and offers grapes, oranges, nuts, broccoli, and many other products exactly when they are not available from places such as California. Northern Mexico shares a similar climate to Southern California but has cheaper labor for labor-intensive harvesting: melons, tomatoes, citrus, and more. On the way out grab a guava from Guyana or a star fruit, and get the right coffee from South America, the Pacific, or Kenya. Even the all-American orange juice notes "concentrate from the United States, Brazil, or Belize." The further expansion of Minute Maid into Belize was only slowed, not by protests from Florida growers, but by European Green Party activists who threatened to protest the resulting destruction of the Belizean rain forest by boycotting the soft drinks of the parent company, Coca Cola.

This diversity of imported products means new profit-making possibilities in select areas of the world. Access to fertilizer, irrigation, and transportation is often as important as climate in being one of the chosen, which is why the Northern Mexican desert is the most productive region of that country. It can also mean that fewer fruit and vegetable crops stay in the country to feed the local population.

Exports can, of course, buy imports, and Mexico, the birthplace of corn domestication, now imports U.S. corn, while many developing countries have also become importers of basic grains that can be planted and harvested cheaply in mass mechanized operations in the United States, Canada, Australia, and Argentina. The United States is a major rice exporter, finally moving into even the reluctant Japanese market. Twenty percent of the United States corn crop is exported. Most of the remainder is fed to animals or turned into manufactured products. This is why the mid-American countryside is filled with corn from horizon to horizon, yet corn is only occasionally featured on American dinner tables, where many would just as soon have Chilean-grown broccoli.

The problem with the export-import equation is not so much lack of food as lack of quality. The high-vitamin, high-protein products are exported to foreign markets, leaving the local population dependent on the cheapest imports, often bulk grains with limited and non-diversified nutritional value. New productive, storage, and transport technologies can be used to alleviate hunger and malnutrition, or misapplied, can contribute to both.

While dramatic breakthroughs in high technology intervention have captured attention and world imagination, most of the real gains in child survival and community health have come from simple but effective measures such as oral rehydration therapy. Even more effective is to protect water and food supplies from contamination in the first place. Inexpensive immunizations also hold great promise at modest cost, yet often do not reach remote or poor populations. UNICEF has calculated that it would take about twenty-five billion dollars a year to completely turn the tide on child malnutrition and childhood diseases, and ensure that all communities have safe water and adequate sanitation. This is half the amount Europeans spend annually on cigarettes, and six million less than Americans pay for beer. Priorities of developing countries would also need to shift, however. With an infant death rate of 137 per 1,000, one of the highest in Asia, Pakistan still spends a whopping 31 percent of its budget on the armed forces, and only 1 percent on health care (UNICEF and WHO, cited in Dahlberg 1997).

New Medical Technology

The last technological intervention to battle global disease has been direct medical technology. Medical intervention only became decisive, consistently doing more good than harm, with the rise of immunization and safe surgery in this century, and the use of antibiotics around mid-century. By this time death rates in wealthier countries were already falling dramatically due to advances in nutrition and sanitation.

Immunization has completely eradicated some global killers. Smallpox is the first such disease to be officially declared extinct—it has no hosts but humans and no one in the world is infected, although concern remains about remaining Cold War vials of the virus and who else might try to harbor a supply for weapons purposes. Measles, a disease that sickens otherwise healthy children but can develop complications and kill vulnerable, weakened, or malnourished children and adults, is in decline as long as vaccination rates continue to increase, but started to increase in the United States once vaccination rates declined. Antibiotics have proven powerful weapons against bacterial infections such as pneumonia, one of the world's top killers, but ever-evolving strains of bacteria threaten to bring back antibiotic-resistant strains of old killers such as tuberculosis. Worldwide overuse of antibiotics, including in livestock and the food-supply, continues to compound this problem.

The other important medical intervention has improved surgical techniques for birth defects, chronic illness, and maternity problems. Until recently, maternal complications were life threatening in as many as one in ten births—a real risk to mothers, especially in times and places where women frequently had eight to ten pregnancies. History and literature is filled with references to women dying while giving birth or from protracted bleeding, often due to miscarriage and other maternal risks. Risks were even greater to the infants, with as many as 20 to 50 percent dying in infancy. Risks may have been even greater for the poor in high-fertility, low-nutrition agrarian societies than they were in simpler societies. Today, as surgical techniques become safer and more routine, concern in the advanced industrial world has shifted to overuse of techniques such as Cesarean section.

This points to a debate and dilemma throughout global health care: "high end" interventions using high technology for dramatic cures often at high costs, versus "low end" interventions using simple technologies to prevent illness. How to pay the bills for medical technology continues to vex national governments. Despite attempts at reform, the United States continues with a fee-for-service system of private providers and private insurers that leaves many without insurance or the way to privately pay for big medical bills. The United States has much of the world's finest medical technology yet also pays a big price. Americans pay more for their health care than anywhere else in the world, without evidence of having the best outcomes. Canada has gone with a single payer system, essentially a single national insurer that covers all Canadians. The system is well regarded by most Canadians, but limited funding can mean older technology and longer waits for some interventions. Russia, China, and Scandinavia use a more thoroughly socialized system in which health care professionals are salaried government employees. They command less income and less prestige than American physicians, but provide services to a wide range of people regardless of income. China's "barefoot doctors," trained in essential preventative care, became the cornerstone of its attempt to extend health care to all. The Chinese system was also one of the first attempts to establish a self-sufficient system not heavily dependent on foreign professionals and technology. Still, in much of the world, more is spent on intensive critical care than on broad-based preventative care. In the United States, half of all expenditures go to persons in their last six months of life: that is, diagnosing, monitoring, and treating the critically ill rather than into wide-ranging prevention.

New technology brings new health risks: "man-made" famines, exposure to radiation, dangerous chemicals, and air and water pollution. At the same time it offers new opportunities for prevention and intervention. Around the world, people are living longer. Whether they will also live better, with healthy active lives, will depend on the applications, priorities, and management of health technology in the next century. Health care epitomizes the local-global connection that we have so often encountered. While health care regimes are often organized at the national level, the most effective interventions have often been local initiatives involving the active participation of local residents, personal trust between providers and the population, and local initiatives to improve community environments. At the same time disease is, and has long been, a global concern. A sick pig in Fujian, China, in June may be an influenza pandemic in New York by January. An exotic condition in tropical Africa could be mutating into the next global scourge. Local efforts must therefore be integrated internationally into global efforts to monitor disease and share solutions.

Electronic Surveillance and Resistance

The "neolithic revolution" that created agrarian societies brought cities and potential food surpluses. The price was drudgery and despotism. Drudgery resulted as the hazardous and unpredictable collective pursuit of wild foods in wild lands gave way to the ardors of the plow and back-breaking hand harvesting. Despotism came as powerful rulers monitored the produce and demanded their share, while keeping the producers isolated from the possibility of collective action. History is filled with peasant revolts against this drudgery and despotism.

The industrial revolution promised freedom from the drudgery and a new autonomy for workers. Machines would swiftly complete the routine tasks of harvesting and threshing as well as spinning and weaving. The industrial age did replace some back-breaking tedium and provide greater autonomy and power to at least certain groups such as organized labor and skilled middle classes. Yet it also introduced drudgery and domination of its own: the stopwatch-monitored assembly line and the supervisor-stalked sweatshop. Many hoped that the electronic revolution would be a purer liberator. Computers would handle tedious calculations and recordkeeping, robotics would tackle the most routine assembly, and workers would be freed to develop and apply new skills involving creativity, analysis, and technical knowledge.

Some of this has happened. Most college students hope for careers that include autonomy, creativity, and challenge, and the current array of careers with this promise has grown. Yet not nearly as much as was hoped. For every computer systems analyst needed, there are many more data entry clerks with routine tasks. In some cases, we have merely created a new routinized, supervised, time-driven tedium, what Barbara Garson (1988) calls *The Electronic Sweatshop*. This includes fast food enterprise:

"They called us the Green Machine," says Jason Pratt, recently retired McDonald's griddleman, "'cause the crew had green uniforms then. And that's what it is, a machine. You don't have to know how to cook, you don't have to know how to think. There's a procedure for everything and you just follow the procedures (Garson 1988, 17).

Every ounce and every second is accounted for and prescribed by policies and built into "idiot proof" machines. "There is no such thing as a McDonald's manager," claims Jason, "The computer manages the store" (Garson 1988, 39). Garson goes on to describe the "automated" social worker, the "programmed" airline attendant, and the routinization of everything from conversation to medical care. With electronically controlled routines also comes electronic surveillance. Already by 1984 (bringing to mind Orwell's classic vision of Big Brother) the U.S. Department of Labor estimated that nearly two-thirds of workers using video terminals were monitored by their employers—consistently, precisely, and inexpensively—and often without their knowledge or consent.

Some worry that new electronic technologies, especially once all linked into large networks, could be the eyes and ears of authoritarian Big Brother. Supercomputers can be used to track criminals such as with the Interpol international police information clearinghouse. They can also be used to keep track of dissidents, political enemies, or entire populations. People in fearful societies once had to worry about who was listening through the wall, now many wonder about what actions are videotaped, what phone calls are recorded, what financial transactions are recorded and monitored, and what this could mean to their private lives. Where are the electronic "radar traps" on this information super-highway?

Elaborate conspiracy theories spread as electronic gossip, while the reality in most of the world is that governments are just as confused as everyone else in how to harness ever-changing technologies and manage mass data flows. The difficulty in consistently tracking down those who fail to pay child support, fail to repay student loans, or just write bad checks, seems to indicate that the time when everyone's every move is monitored is not yet here. There is also an opposite side to the spread of technology.

The reach of technology can foster resistance and even revolution. Many reformers and rebels had challenged the Roman Catholic Church before Luther, but they did not have the printing press, and the monasteries controlled the scribing of books. With Gutenberg's development of moveable type in the 1450s, the challenges of reformers from Luther to Calvin could reach all of Europe and the Reformation took hold. Years later, inexpensive pamphlets from cheap local presses allowed Thomas Paine to call his fellow American colonists to "Common Sense," and revolution. Around the world new technologies can play this role.

The fall of authoritarian—some once claimed totalitarian—regimes in Eastern Europe was due in part to the difficulty of controlling rapid electronic communication. Satellite television leaped over iron curtains and media censors with reports from around the world, and most importantly, in neighboring regions. Dissidents could communicate by e-mail and fax with one another and with interested parties around the world. The flow of information was so vast with so many sources, that it could not be fully censored or contained. The power of this information flow is not lost on resistance movements around the world: Chiapan rebels e-mail communiqués from the jungle to sympathizers around the world, Kayapo tribal defenders videotape illegal oil company incursions on their land, rural Nepalese and Tibetans applaud Nelson Mandela's appearances on village television sets and demand their own rights. Videos were distributed so widely in Eastern Europe to circumvent government-controlled broadcasting that Lech Walesa pointed to one key element in the fall of Eastern European socialism: television (*Los Angeles Times*, Oct. 20, 1992). Chinese authorities wonder about this as ever more prosperous Chinese take delight in the satellite dish that can capture television waves from around the world—as well as the latest waves of political thought and discontent.

Some media development analysts credit ever expanding media information sources—cheaper newspapers, as well as more available radio and television—with a movement from authoritarian to democratic regimes. Like so many applications of technology, however, this is not inevitable. Technology can increase the power to control, and can create new opportunities to resist. It can generate new routinized, alienating work environments, or it can empower creative individuals to launch their own independent ventures. The controls, and ultimately the choices, remain in human hands.

Rehumanize Yourself

Technology is a prime mover in every aspect of the modern globe. This is not to assert technological determinism: that technology is all that matters. Technology is embedded in a social fabric that creates and directs its use. But unlike most other forces, technological change is constant, one-directional, and exponentially accelerating. This is true of few other social and economic phenomena, which tend to wax and wane: times of peace and violence alternate, democracy and authoritarianism each seem on the assent in some decades, and so forth. Yet technological advance continues and accelerates.

The only comparable phenomenon is population growth, which in recent times has also been one-directional (populations do not usually decline) and exponential. Yet while the rate of population growth appears to be abating, technological expansion only continues to accelerate. Barring scenarios in which technology would be its own undoing—nuclear, chemical, or biological holo-caust, or environment collapse—the pattern can only be expected to continue. To some this is a doorway to the best of times: *technophiles*, the technology lovers, assure us that everything will be easier and better with the next genera-tion of products. *Technophobes*, the technology haters, can only see harmful effects for humanity and the planet. The manifesto of the Unabomber reflects the deep-seated fears of many that technology itself is the root of evil. History suggests a middle position: technology is power—power to create horrendous weapons or miraculous cures—and the choice is ours. Technology does create new possibilities, new opportunities, but what is not determined by technology itself is how these will be used and who they will reach.

Cellular phones have become our latest infatuation with technology on the move. They can be a status symbol for the upwardly mobile, or a life-saver for a stranded motorist. Cellular phone technology is also encompassing the world. In major cities of Latin America it is not uncommon to see young successful professionals driving imported sports cars, wearing imported open-finger driv-ing gloves, and talking on their cellular phones. They appear oblivious to the impoverished hawkers, street vendors, and homeless children as they navigate the city by car and by phone simultaneously, in apparent imitation of New York techno-fashion (real New Yorkers know they had better keep both hands on the wheel in self-defense).

At the same time, cellular phones are penetrating Bangladesh, not the cities but the countryside. The Grameen Bank, famous for its successful micro-lending programs that capitalize the poor in general and poor rural women in particular, is offering loans to buy cellular phones. This is not the boondoggle of some aid agency that has never been to the field, but a clever capitalization scheme. In a country with a very limited and very poor telephone system, the rural poor can only send messages by time-consuming travel or endless waits for a few malfunctioning pay phones. Women who buy a cellular phone on credit immediately become an important node of communication in their village. Villagers pay about six cents a minute, much cheaper than overland travel, to send messages to friends, relatives, and suppliers. This is not idle socializing, for the message may be a cry for help in an emergency, or an important contact. One intriguing side-benefit is that some farmers are now able to gain higher prices for their crops. In the past, they were utterly isolated and dependent on middlemen to offer and pay the prevailing price for their products. Now they can call urban markets directly, and with a one-minute cellular phone call, determine real price fluctuations and demand market prices for their products. Information is power, and both the women entrepreneurs and the small farmers gain new contacts and new power for positive change. The benefits, however, are not an inevitable result of new technology, which just as easily could have left villagers more isolated and excluded, but between a new technology and an innovative program to seize the opportunity and use the technology to capitalize and empower the poor.

The same double-edge to technology is apparent at the personal level. Technology interrupts traditional meeting places and contacts and creates new cadres of lonely, isolated, alienated people. At the same time, elderly shut-ins make new friends over the Internet and establish an electronically mediated but nonetheless meaningful circle of new friends who can offer support and understanding, and even help in emergencies.

Karl Marx wrote of the alienation of the modern worker in industrial capitalism. The irony is that some of the most alienated workers of this century have been in societies that adopted some of Marx's economic principles but failed to capture his underlying concern for the human spirit. The industrial process, whether under capitalism or state socialism, seems to have a terrible potential to de-humanize and alienate. In a rock rendition of Marx's idea of worker alienation, the rock band The Police sang the woes of spending every day in the factory building a machine that was "not for me." The chorus reminded listeners to "rehumanize yourself." This will be a challenge for us all as we assess our personal priorities, our national priorities, and ultimately our global priorities.

7

METRO-SPRAWL

The Making of the Global City

Queen of the Valley! Thou art beautiful!
Thy walls, like silver, sparkle in the sun.
                    —Robert Southey, Mexico City, early 1800s

When I think of New York, I think of people with an unearthly pallor, dressed all in black; of black jackets and white ties; black limos and white lies.
                    —Pico Iyer

HIKING BRINGS TO MIND treks through the wild, but let me suggest you consider cultivating the art of urban walking: exploring urban areas on foot with a careful eye to the socioscape. Possibilities for great urban walks abound, even in smaller or mid-sized cities—a walk through Wausau's Marathon Park, noted earlier, brings you into contact with ancient cultures and global forces of change. Some great urban walks are rightfully famous: San Francisco's Fisherman's Wharf, New York's Fifth Avenue, Toronto's downtown and waterfront, and San Antonio's Riverwalk. The chance to observe the urban intermingling of the world's cultures and economies is not limited to well-known and well-regarded attractions, however, so let me take you for a moment on an urban walk in downtown Los Angeles. I realize some skeptics might object, "But no one walks in Los Angeles," while others might add, "Besides, Los Angeles doesn't have a downtown to walk in." There is an element of truth behind both stereotypes, yet hidden behind these images is a very revealing socioscape waiting to be encountered.

Nowhere is the compression of social and ethnic communities seen more dramatically than in downtown Los Angeles. Two blocks from the gleaming high-rise downtown hotels begins a narrow strip occupied primarily by very low-income and transient African-American residents. A steep descent downhill from the glass towers and atriums of 1990s urban architecture are the brick bastions of an earlier era. Here urban power and powerlessness share the sidewalk: one of the country's largest and most extensive homeless centers occupied a space right down the street from the Ronald Reagan government building until it was moved to a newer, and less obvious, location amidst abandoned buildings. Even the newer facility is not large enough or accommodating for all, and the sidewalks here have scattered cardboard box dwellings tucked under stairwells. Most on the street are men—many of those inside the new shelter are women with children. Some drink, some greet one another as they return from temporary jobs as day laborers, many just sit and watch. There is no need to be fearful: the daytime atmosphere is sociable, almost friendly, and this strip of poverty is only two blocks wide.

Two blocks further, the signs change to Spanish in a cluster of small businesses and working-class Mexican-American residences also only several blocks wide. If you step into one of the big discount stores you will be more often greeted by a scowling security guard than a happy hostess or "personal shopper," but the bargains are real, and the emphasis everywhere seems to be on hard work and managing life's necessities.

Walk on one block further, and the bargains are on more expensive merchandise. Electronics stores are advertised in English, Spanish, and Japanese, announcing the transition to Little Tokyo. Here, high-rise Japanese banks, a Japanese-owned luxury hotel, and the Japanese cultural center anchor a small business district specializing in electronics, cosmetics, specialty items, and travel. The stores and streets are filled with Japanese clientele, but the only Japanese residents live in a nearby senior facility. Most shoppers come from outlying areas and communities, or are tourists. The suburbanites pick up brochures about flights to Kyoto, while the Japanese tourists give themselves away by the Disneyland logos on the hats and shirts of the children as they seek brochures on local attractions.

Step across the street, and the language and the attractions again abruptly change. A single block separates Little Tokyo from the plaza that introduces the Mexican commercial district of Olvera Street. Suddenly the sights and sounds, and a majority of the visitors, are Mexican and Mexican-American. Again, however, few live here. Olvera Street provides a weekend diversion for the residents of the Hispanic neighborhood immediately to the south, as well as those in East Los Angeles and beyond. The oldest building in Los Angeles and a Mexican-style plaza evoke the time before 1848, when this was the Mexican frontier.

Crossing Cesar Chavez Boulevard, the look of old Guadalajara gives way to a look more reminiscent of Singapore or Hong Kong. Mexican music and Spanish are promptly replaced by signs in both English and Chinese that indicate the start of Chinatown. While almost close enough to Olvera for the smells of salsa to mingle with the scent of ginger, the clientele is suddenly predominantly Chinese. Businesses display whole butchered ducks and pigs and other distinctive specialties, but also a wide range of apparel and general merchandise. Vendors beckon buyers in both Mandarin and English, stores are small but busy, and change for purchases is more likely to come from a vendor's pocket than a cash register.

The clustering of ethnic groups is further seen in Saigon Plaza, an enclave within an enclave. Although situated in the heart of Chinatown, within the rambling walkways of this plaza the signs, music, and language of choice is Vietnamese. In the larger businesses, however, the names on the business cards frequently indicate proprietors who are Vietnamese Chinese.

If you still have energy after this miniature circuit of the Pacific Rim, venture a bit further west of downtown on Olympic Boulevard toward Koreatown. This was a major locus of looting and struggle during the riots of 1992, but it is also quite safe. This is also a prime location to observe an encounter of both sides of the Pacific Rim. Despite the signs, Koreatown is far from a small slice of Korea, it is a slice of the Pacific: an Asian label over a Hispanic-built product. A simple green sign welcomes you, in English, to Koreatown. More strip than town, hundreds of Korean businesses cluster along Olympic Boulevard between Vermont and Western Avenues. With signs in both English and Korean, they offer specialized products and seem to specialize in travel to Korea. A single turn off the strip onto a side street in either direction, however, reveals not a Korean but a Hispanic neighborhood. Well-worn apartments advertise "No Deposito," and clusters of Latino men dot the sidewalks talking and occasionally shooting dice or selling lottery tickets. That many of the workers in Koreatown businesses are Latino, therefore, should come as no surprise; many can walk to work. Others walk the strip looking for work. To the south and west, just beyond the Hispanic neighborhoods that sandwich Olympic Boulevard, are larger, predominantly black neighborhoods. The largest businesses in the heart of Koreatown serve a largely Korean clientele, but those on the periphery of the area are middlemen, serving their Hispanic and black neighbors. Most live scattered across the city, but a few Koreans live nearby in a well-groomed pocket of Spanish-colonial houses set back from the commercial bustle of Koreatown in a middle-class neighborhood that stretches north to Wilshire Boulevard. Sunday morning finds them in suits and dresses, greeting one another on their way to the nearby brown adobe Korean Presbyterian church. Most of the rest of the week finds them at work.

You can walk on, of course. Westward will take you to the more famous star-studded sidewalks of Hollywood, or the roller blade-streaked walkways of Venice beach. The real heartbeat of this city, however, is not blonde nor bikini-clad, but a world at work.

The truth is that, in time, California will turn the Mexican and Chinese teenagers into rock stars and surfers. But I think the immigrants also will change California—their gift to us—reminding us of what our German and Italian ancestors knew when they came, hopeful, to the brick tenement blocks of the East Coast. Life is work (Rodriguez 1991, 147).

The working neighborhoods stretch on into the hazy distance, far further than we can walk. Filipinos and Armenians share Montebello, which here forms a wedge between the largely Asian dominated Monterey Park to the north, and the largely Spanish-speaking "barrio" area of East Los Angeles to the south and west. The Pomona expressway serves as both lifeline and boundary, carrying Filipino workers to municipal and clerical jobs downtown, and marking the beginning of Monterey Park. The winding streets and cul de sacs of Monterey Park attract few tourists—no loud Chinese New Year parades are going to attempt to climb the hills here—but attract a continual stream of middle-class Asian immigrants, most particularly Taiwanese. After all, notes an accountant and newcomer from Hong Kong, the restaurants here are cleaner than in Chinatown.

This urban excursion can be repeated with various twists and turns, in urban centers everywhere where local and global converge: an urban world meeting one another in the global city. It is also a good picture of the world itself. Writes Pico Iyer, "The place we reassuringly call a global village looks already a lot like a blown-up version of Los Angeles, its freeways choked, its skies polluted, its tribes settled into discontinuous pattern—the flames of South Central rising above the gated communities of Bel Air" (Iyer 2000).

Cities without Limits

A landmark was passed somewhere about the turn of this millennium: for the first time the world holds more urban dwellers than rural people. The home of humanity is now primarily an urban center. Just how urban varies with the definition of city limits, a difficult definition as cities increasingly burst old boundaries and spread into sprawling metropolitan regions. Is the American small town dweller who now drives thirty miles to work in a neighboring city urban or rural? What of the Latin American worker who rises to the call of chickens only to walk several miles to the highway, ride a swaying old bus to the edge of a massive metropolis, switch to a new bus to the city center where work waits—is such a life urban or rural? The urban world at the end of the beginning of the twenty-first century is not the triumph of the compact, imposing city on the hill, but of a sprawling metropolis that climbs hills, fills valleys, and sends urban tentacles far into what had been the countryside.

The world's first cities may have been trade centers and religious centers, holding both market and temple, *agora* and *acropolis*. Such centers were essentially multinational, in the old sense of the word, drawing people from many nationalities, many tribes, to exchange ideas and offerings. The centers that became dominant were the centers of empire that commanded the trade routes: Babylon, Carthage, Rome, Constantinople, Beijing and its predecessors, Tenochtitlan and its predecessors in the Valley of Mexico, Madrid, Amsterdam, Paris, London. Trade, not industrialization, defined these cities right into the twentieth century. Early factories could be located in the countryside and often were, often near water power, but bankers and brokers like to keep an eye on one another.

As industry came to be tied to a steady supply of coal, meaning urban dockyards and rail yards, the industrial city wrapped around the older trade centers and populations surged. Ideally, growing industry reduced the need for rural workers, while simultaneously creating new work for them in urban industry. Often migrations were forced, sometimes by direct action to clear the countryside and to provide the captains of industry with an army of laborers (as in Japan, England, and Pennsylvania in the 1800s), sometimes simply by the exhaustion of agricultural lands and incomes (as in Ireland and the southern United States).

The movement from the land to the city continues. In the United States at the turn of twentieth century, one-third of the population was still farm families and farm laborers, at the turn of the twenty-first century it is less than 3 percent and declining. This trend continues irrespective of U.S. Census measures of movements to and from the city. Small towns lost population to the city rapidly in the 1970s. Some regained population in the 1980s as weary urbanites moved further out. These urbanites did not become farmers, however; they moved into what had been farm market towns as telecommuters and long-distance commuters with jobs tied to urban areas, bringing these towns into a growing metropolitan orb of exurbia.

The United States, most of Europe, and the major Latin American countries are all 70 to 80 percent urban. Many of the new, sprawling megacities are in East Asia. Only sub-Saharan Africa and South Asia are primarily rural. Here a pattern of dispersed villages has become ever more dense until in some places village runs into village creating dense population agglomerations without a viable urban center. Of course, some might contend this also aptly describes Los Angeles and southern California. The world's megacities can now be found on all continents, with an ever-increasing share in the developing world.

The rank ordering of cities is always tentative, especially given the difficulty of establishing the urban limit. Numbers that focus on the city proper differ from those that emphasize the metropolitan region. Driving from New York City, when

Table 7.1   The World's Ten Largest Urban Areas

Urban Area	Population (in millions)
1980	
New York, United States	16.5
Tokyo-Yokohama, Japan	14.4
Mexico City, Mexico	14.0
Los Angeles, United States	10.6
Shanghai, China	10.0
Buenos Aires, Argentina	9.7
Paris, France	8.5
Moscow, USSR	8.0
Beijing, China	8.0
Chicago, United States	7.7
2000	
Tokyo-Yokohama, Japan	28.0
Seoul, South Korea	19.1
Mexico City, Mexico	18.1
Mombai (Bombay), India	18.0
Sao Paulo, Brazil	17.7
New York, United States	16.6
Shanghai, China	14.2
Lagos, Nigeria	13.5
Los Angeles, United States	13.1
Beijing, China	12.4

Data from: U.S. Bureau of the Census 1997; Brown et al. 1999.

does one leave the metropolitan region: Portland, Maine; Arlington, Virginia; Harrisburg, Pennsylvania? In metropolitan terms, Germany's largest city is neither Berlin nor Frankfurt, but Essen, standing at the node of a sprawling network of crowded industrial river valleys. Depending on how one does the counting, the largest continuous metropolis in the world has between fifteen and thirty million people, and is either Tokyo-Yokohama, New York-New Jersey, or Mexico City and its environs in the state of Mexico. A brief look at these three gives a good glimpse into the new urban home of humanity, the metro-sprawl.

New York: The Big Apple Turns Sour

In its urban development, the United States has been fortunate that forces of history and geography have kept it from developing a single seat of political and economic power, one dominant magnate city that dwarfs all the others. The

United States has no real equivalent to London, Paris, Tokyo, Mexico City, or other locations that combine political, commercial, financial, and industrial power in a single location. Politics brings foundations, think-tanks, and assorted associations to Washington, D.C. Chicago anchors the industrial and agricultural core of the Midwest. Industry follows the rivers, rail lines, and Great Lakes across a network of cities. The electronic media is dominated by the West Coast, and the print media by the East. Yet since the early 1800s, the harbors of New York and its environs have formed the commercial heart of the country.

Swelled by immigration at the beginning of the twentieth century, New York, now reaching well into Connecticut and New Jersey, remains one of the world's dominant cities and the buckle of the great population belt that runs from Boston to Arlington, Virginia. For a time this was the world's largest city with the world's busiest harbors and tallest buildings. Shipping may route elsewhere, the title of the tallest building was lost to Chicago and then to Malaysia, and the Big Apple itself is no longer the leader in world population—but if the world has a capital, this is it.

The closest thing to international government, the United Nations, stands here despite frequent objections from both residents and global diplomats. Fifty-nine of the world's five hundred largest corporations are headquartered in New York, far more than in any other city—Tokyo has thirty-seven, Mexico City has one. The New York stock exchange remains the world's largest (followed by London and Tokyo, respectively), and the financial and investment might concentrated in the city is still unmatched anywhere else. Visitors from around the world flock to New York, called by business demands, attracted by the lights and the mystique, the brashness and the power, the promised excitement, or maybe just pulled in by its sheer gravitational pull. Visitors from a lovely town in Scandinavia stand in awe of Times Square's newly refurbished glitter, "It is so beautiful, all our friends will want to see this." At Rockefeller Center busloads of international visitors come to have their picture taken in front of the leaping, dancing fountains that wash over a golden mermaid. They seem to feel they have arrived at the center of the world, as people standing on the capital plaza of some gilded ancient empire. Encircling this spot are the museums and library that would awe Alexandria. This is the Empire State indeed.

New York also stands as the city Americans most love to hate. A city of unmet promises and passionate conflict, it has vied for the title of murder capital of the world for almost two hundred years. It offers the extraordinary congestion of Midtown Manhattan and the abandoned desolation of the South Bronx and portions of Brooklyn and Harlem, sitting within easy view of the great centers of power. A place to visit but no place to live has become the cliched assessment of New York. The popular American image of New York is akin to Batman's Gotham City, a dark, grimy, dangerous, and somewhat surreal setting. Pico Iyer refers to it as a city in black and white:

The lighting is harsh, the contrasts are stark, and the effects are as loud as the tabloid headline in your face. When I think of New York, I think of people with an unearthly pallor, dressed all in black; of black jackets and white ties; black limos and white lies (Iyer 1997, 80).

I shared those lines with a black-suited limousine driver parked between the black carriages of Central Park. Yeah," he smiled and spread his arms, "Ain't it great?"

Mexico: Montezuma's Misery

Seven thousand feet atop the great plateau that separates Mexico's two mountain ranges and situated at the foot of two enormous snow-draped volcanoes, Mexico City has been an imposing place for centuries. On his march inland, Hernan Cortez moved his troops up to the high saddle between the two volcanoes and looked down on the magnificence of Aztec Tenochtitlan. Bernal Diaz, one of Cortez's men who chronicled the event, described the awe that took their breath away as they beheld the gleaming city with its vividly painted palaces and pyramids gleaming in the sun. The city rivaled the largest in Europe in size, but evoked something more like the glories of ancient Babylon in the simple grandeur of its architecture and grand canals.

The Spanish eventually destroyed Tenochtitlan by protracted seize and subsequent vengeance, but used the stones of the ruins to build a new Mexico City in grand style with great buildings and broad avenues that could still evoke awe. When Fanny Calderon de la Barca came within view of the city in 1839, she looked out from her coach and remembered the lines of Robert Southey's tribute:

Thou art beautiful.
Queen of the Valley! Thou art beautiful!
Thy walls, like silver, sparkle in the sun.

She wrote a friend, "At length we arrived at the heights on which we look down upon the superb Valley of Mexico, celebrated in all parts of the world, with its framework of magnificent mountains, its snow-capped peaks, great lakes, and fertile plains" (both quotations in Fisher and Fisher 1966, 87).

Mexico City continues to evoke awe, but it is no longer always in such poetic cadences or praise-filled phrases. Former president de la Madrid warned: "If we become careless, Mexico City can become uninhabitable. Catastrophe is not out of the range of possibility" (Vasquez 1983).

The center of what has long been a highly centralized power system, Mexico

City continues to push, and burst, the limits of geography and engineering. The original compact city spread to encompass neighboring hills and woods and adjoining towns until it was pressing against mountains and wetlands. Filling of the lakes had begun with the Aztecs, and accompanied by natural drying, has completely buried them. Mexico City is a city built on fill. The great cathedral that stands across from the ruins of the great Aztec pyramid both impresses and perplexes. Visitors often stare at it oddly for a moment—yes, it really does tilt, the victim of earthquakes and the weight of a huge stone structure perched on landfill. With a fragile skin of soil laid over the sleeping dragons of Mexico's valley of fire, the quake-prone city dare not build upward, and so it sprawls like an impoverished Phoenix or Los Angeles.

The city has entirely filled the original Federal District and continues to spill outward. To the east, former lake bed and wetland is now lined with seemingly unending concrete structures of a vast "proletarian colony"—some would just say slum although these are working poor—of three million people. Named for an indigenous poet king, Ciudad Netzahuacoyotl ("Netza" for short), considered independently it would be Mexico's second largest city. Colonies also climb the rugged, eroded mountainsides, far above the reach of water and sewer and other city services, but clinging to the hope that these mud and clay slopes will provide the foothold into the city's promised prosperity. Squeezed into narrow valleys and up steep slopes, these new communities of the hopeful again explode into sprawling agglomerations wherever the terrain opens enough to permit it like some great urban amoeba consuming the countryside in a manner reminiscent of those horror films (usually set in Tokyo or New York) about the unstoppable blob.

The challenges poised by such huddled masses yearning to breathe free of want, or increasingly just to breathe, is intimidating. Providing housing for mounting millions that won't crumble with the next seismic tremor is a massive task. Engineers scour the neighboring mountains for new sources of water. Rivers of open sewage, "black waters," swirl around inadequate facilities that cannot contain them, even though half the human waste in the city never even makes it to the sewer, but dries in open latrines to blow in the air with the dust and smog. An impressive subway system still cannot reach the city limits, so commuters are left to continue by minibus and on foot. Commuting across this vast expanse can consume up to five hours a day. Old buses and old cars clog old roads and new highways, pouring pollutants into the thin mountain air. The toxic smog soup contains enough lead and hazardous chemicals to cause brain damage, and enough tars that just breathing each day is equivalent to smoking two packs of cigarettes (Davis 1994). Mexican novelist Carlos Fuentes mused "that jammed city of toxic air and leafless trees may be the first to know the asphyxiation of progress" (quoted in Gardels and Snell 1989, 15).

Why would anyone come here? For all its misery, Mexico City remains a fascinating place. Cheap and usually reliable French-style subways, the Metro, whisk daily workers through the maze of neighborhoods to ever-insecure but nonetheless diverse jobs throughout the city. The wealthy retreat into secluded, walled neighborhoods on rolling high ground with spectacular views. On weekends, old and new rich converge on nightspots such as those that fill the upscale Zona Rosa. Families fill the city's great central park, Chapultapec, and its amusements. World-class museums, world-class cultural performances, and world-class business opportunities continue to make this a place of awe and opportunity. Like the elderly patient with dozens of interconnected chronic and acute illnesses who nonetheless continues to defy the doctor's premature prognosis that all systems will soon give out, the city goes on, gasping and groaning, yet working, struggling, and enduring.

Tokyo: Searching for Fuji

The Japanese islands are a mountain range pushed from the sea. The only flat, fertile land hugs the coast of the main island of Honshu from Kobe-Osaka to Tokyo Bay. This strip, the East Road, is quickly becoming one long metropolitan agglomeration like the Boston-to-Washington strip of the U.S. East Coast. It already contains upward of sixty million people, half of Japan's population on just over 1 percent of its land. The financial and industrial might of this beltway reaches around the world, but its territorial reach is severely constrained by its own mountains and ocean into one of the most congested, most expensive swaths of land on earth. Most congested and prized of all is the land between Mount Fuji and Tokyo Bay, the Tokyo-Yokohama strip that now contains almost half this population, thirty million people.

Like the Valley of Mexico, this has long been an important congregating point. The pre-Tokyo city of Edo may have reached one million people by early in the eighteenth century. Centralization during the Meiji restoration of the late nineteenth century added further growth, and subsequent international industrialization led to extraordinary growth, so that Tokyo, like Mexico City, now adds one thousand residents a day in a neck-to-neck race to be the world's largest urban center. Like Mexico, this growth spurt continues on loose, alluvial land set at the foot of volcanoes and known for its earthquakes. Unlike the heavy masonry dwellings of Mexico, Tokyo's flexible frame structures are not likely to crumple, but if set ablaze by broken utility lines, nothing but the ocean could stop the fire storm.

Day to day, Tokyo-Yokohama residents worry about more immediate matters—like getting to work. Even Tokyo's famous array of trains and subways cannot accommodate the millions who converge on the city center each day, beginning early in the morning as professional "pushers" cram them onto overcrowded railcars to be jostled and jammed into the city center and then pulled up into the "vertical city" of high-rise offices. A car is no relief, even with half the population using public transportation, the center city streets are locked in a perpetual traffic jam. They also do not breathe much easier than those in Mexico City. Concentrated industry once made Tokyo Bay the world's most polluted. A huge public investment effort has reduced the toxins, yet ever more people and vehicles has made the urban air even fouler than in the early 1970s when Tokyo movie-goers cheered as Godzilla battled the Smog Monster. Often the smog obscures beloved Mt. Fuji, just as Mexico's smog obscures its volcanic guardians, and residents must climb to see the national symbol. The erasure of the sacred mountain by the airborne by-products of commercial and industrial success stands as a symbol and warning to many that Japan's unique heritage may also be in danger of being erased, or at least obscured, by the fumes of commerce.

Godzilla, that great mutant lizard, a creation of nuclear fallout who none-theless helped his people fight the horrors of the nuclear-industrial world they had created, is making a comeback in Hollywood but is seldom heard from in Tokyo these days. Maybe he couldn't afford the rent. The other daily concern of residents is paying the bills in what may be the most expensive location on earth. Apartments routinely rent for five to ten thousand dollars a month, houses of half a million dollars are not labeled mansions but affordable housing. The last square meters of open space command extraordinary prices. A single gov-ernment-owned former rail yard was appraised at forty-seven billion dollars. One fanciful estimate of the value of the Emperor's royal estate in the heart of Tokyo at 1990s inflated prices was higher than the combined real estate in all of California. Even with falling prices accompanying economic recession, the value of the emperor's property—he is of course neither planning on listing nor leas-ing it—would still total to all the real estate in Indiana. Such astronomical prices severely strain even the most prosperous residents and firms as they try to stake their claim on the Japanese dream.

Those old enough to remember the long postwar recession realize just how far they have come. Yet it is these who have experienced, and in some sense created, the Japanese economic miracle, who are often the first to strain to see Mt. Fuji, and wonder about the price that has been paid.

Urban Divides: The New Global City

The term "world city" has been applied to the most important centers of world trade and power: New York, Chicago, Los Angeles, Tokyo, London, Paris, Amsterdam, and others. None of these are third-world cities. Yet the third world is urbanizing explosively, in part from global forces. The major impetus is not the pull of industry, but the wilting of small-scale farming and the lure of service sector jobs. Globalized economies find their ties to the land, at least the local land, reduced. When food comes from the neighboring countryside, the best place to find fresh, affordable, appealing produce is at the village markets that have dotted the globe since the dawn of agriculture. When food comes as cheaply by container ship as by farm basket, however, this tie is severed. The urban market, close to major nodes of transportation, quickly dominates. As cheap transportation proliferates and as ever more people are drawn into a cash economy, the varieties of light industrial trinkets—which transport cheaply anywhere—proliferate as well. The sprawling urban marketplace offers a multitude of specialized niches for the eager—or desperate—entrepreneur.

The glitter and might of the new megacities is far too thin a facade to be the foundation of much optimism, yet the predictions of doom and collapse have also continually proven premature. After several years of hearing the competing predictions of first world prosperity and glory versus absolute calamity and collapse for the "urban leviathan" (Davis 1994) of Mexico City, I continued to return to a city that is both energetic and emphysemic, rich and poor, hopeful and desperate, and leave with the conclusion that contradictions are likely to continue side by side, even if on an ever grander scale.

We have glimpses of a new world economic order. I suspect the best glimpses will not be found primarily in the high rises of Tokyo and Manhattan, nor in the desolation of Mogadishu, Somalia and Kinshasa, Zaire. A more likely glimpse of the future can be seen in Bangkok, Thailand, where economic miracles and social nightmares coexist daily. We might include Juárez and Tijuana in Mexico, São Paulo and Rio de Janeiro in Brazil, Kuala Lumpur and Jakarta in Southeast Asia, perhaps Lagos and Nairobi in Africa, probably Los Angeles and Miami in the United States—all those hot, noisy, hazy mixtures of hope and despair. They provide the products and services for a growing global middle class, along with the prospect of a door into that class for the otherwise excluded. Without fundamental changes, however, for many it will be a rapidly revolving door, offering an invitation, a quick glimpse of air conditioned affluence, and a rapid return to the street (Sernau 1994, 137).

The Non-Industrial City

The developing world's megacities are often not choked with industrial smoke as much as with throngs of vendors, the smoke of charcoal cooking fires mixing with the diesel fumes of old delivery trucks. The traditional merchandise of the markets such as fruits and vegetables, fish, flowers, and crafts can still be found but these are becoming secondary to newer wares. Cassette tapes are always found (usually even in small-town markets), along with manufactured clothes and accessories (especially jewelry and belts), radios, watches, and other manufactured goods: domestic, imported, or pirated. Often these markets sprawl on for crowded block after crowded block beyond their official confines, snarling traffic and confounding wayward tourists.

Informal marketing provides a vast sink for labor absorption. The level of underemployment is only apparent in the duplication of offerings, the high ratio of vendors to buyers, and the low incomes. To the outsider, the prospect of great metropolises built largely on the prospect of ever more people coming to try to find their niche serving the needs of ever more people, mostly just as poor as themselves, may seem a house built of cards. Yet this is the urban "growth machine" (Logan and Molotch 1987) that churns day and night in much of the world.

The shifting course of the Nile and the shifting courses of history have moved the capital of Egypt about the fertile delta before settling on what is now Cairo. As the core of country with limited fertile land, the city has grown phenomenally: 3.5 million in 1960, surpassing 10 million by 1990. Its greater metropolitan area now holds over one-third of the total population of Egypt. Families cluster into tall, narrow apartment buildings, adding rooms and stories as they grow. The city is no anonymous mass, but is organized around clusters of family and clan that give its residents a sense of place and grounding in the explosive growth. These do not, however, guarantee employment. People come because the land cannot sustain their growing numbers, but the city offers little industrial growth to fill the void. Development theorists have referred to Egypt as a classic example of "overurbanization" (Palen 1997). More urbanized than France or Sweden, it has little heavy industry to suggest the need for such urban agglomerations. Yet as insistent as the Sahara sands the multitudes arrive, filling the only arable strip of productive land in a country of sixty million that adds a million persons a year.

Lagos, Nigeria, is one of the world's many overcrowded urban islands, separated from the mainland by a polluted lagoon that gives the city its name. Established and named by the Portuguese to serve their fleets, seized by the British to serve theirs, it continues to add population: from just under two million in 1972 to over four million by 1985. Oil revenues fund the city and keep international businesspeople in its hotels, but only generates a handful jobs on the platforms or in those hotels. Already in 1974, it was the epitome of the non-industrial, informal-sector dominated city.

Lagos was unlike anything I had seen before in Africa; it was more like an overcrowded city in India . . . people are jammed into this area, almost all of them selling something to someone . . . Whole sections of the town are devoted to headscarves, and women walk nonchalantly down the street with two- or even three-foot piles of these scarves on their heads . . . All night the city is alluring: candle flames flickering in the small shops or on stalls by the roadside, green or pink electric light bulbs casting eerie shadows in beer parlors (Baker 1974, 16).

This allure continues to draw thousands of migrants into the nerve center of west Africa. Yet the accompanying problems also continue to mount: housing shortages, traffic jams, crime, pollution, inner city blight, fragile and often overwhelmed institutional and physical infrastructure. Like many of the third world's great cities, it totters between an intriguing and enduring cosmopolitan chaos and the utter collapse into an urban abyss of dysfunction and despair.

The image of urban despair that has often gripped Westerners has been that of Calcutta, India: the city of Mother Theresa and the Sisters of Charity pulling the dying poor from the streets. Neither the largest nor the poorest of the world's cities, Calcutta is now indelibly associated with human misery. Calcutta is largely the creation of British colonialism, built for ready port access like Lagos, and has continued to grow. Paul Harrison described his encounter with Calcutta:

I had seen a good deal of India and of the Third World before I visited Calcutta. But it was still a culture shock to arrive there, in a hot and damp rush hour, as dusk fell. It is the nearest thing to an ant heap, a dense sea of people washing over roads hopelessly jammed as taxis swerve round hand pulled rickshaws, buses run into hand-carts, pony stagecoaches and private cars and even flocks of goats fight it out for the limited space (Harrison 1984, 165–66).

Harrison concludes that "hell is a city." Yet Calcutta and places like it are also streets of hope for rural villages who feel they have nothing to lose. It has a growing, albeit fragile, middle class, and remains one of India's windows on the world as the country moves from attempts at self-sufficiency to cautious yet growing involvement in the global economy.

The New Industrial City

Watching the informal economy-driven cities add layer upon layer to their colossal house of cards, one can be left to wonder who manufactures the cardboard? Where is the industry to be found?

Some of it can be found in micro-manufacturing scattered throughout the city, where global materials are hammered into local products. Welders, dye casters, painters, tool cutters, and others work behind garage doors to craft what cannot be imported. Informal manufacturing further fills the need for employment as young "apprentices," often family members, join in the micro-production. Safety standards, hours, and wages are largely unregulated, and the often-toxic effluence trickles into gutters and streams, or vaporizes into the unventilated air. These places survive with low costs and enormous flexibility while much of the old brick-smokestack industry stands vacant. The decline of central city industry is as true in Mexico City as in Michigan City. Where then did the industry go? Increasingly, the pull of industry is often a pull to the periphery, and to the border.

Modern global industry seeks large, often pre-fabricated and replicable plants on large industrial campuses that can accommodate a huge, one-floor metal-skinned shop floor fronted by a glass-skinned front office. In an era of massive mechanization, single floors with cruising forklifts are preferred to the old urban multi-story factory, and demand less expensive suburban land. In an era of containerization, railways are often less important than a good highway. In Mexico, automobile plants and new industry avoid the central city for new highway corridors: Volkswagen along the highway corridor from Mexico City to Pueblo, Nissan along the highway near Cuernavaca, and new plants—German, Swedish, Japanese, and U.S.—sprawling along the highways to the northwest. This also describes the new automotive plants along the Kokomo-Indianapolis corridor and the Detroit-Ann Arbor corridor, as well as the "technology corridor" between Chicago and Rockford, while the old industrial cores of Rockford, Chicago, Detroit, and Indiana stand largely vacant and crumbling. The new face of industry is seen in the new Chrysler technology center in Auburn Hills, Michigan, with three million square feet on 503 acres, including a wind tunnel, test track, design studios, and pilot factory for computerized production equipment. It is also seen in the Ford plants that make the "world car" in identical factory-clones in the United States, Britain, Germany, Austria, and Mexico, assembling parts from fourteen different countries (McMichael 2000).

The pressures of global production have pushed industry not only to the urban periphery but also to the national periphery: to the border and the coast. Export processing zones beckon across the sea from the shores of the Philippines on the outskirts of Manila, from Haitian shores on the edge of Port-au-Prince, from the Malaysian coast on the urban fringe in Penang State and island-bound George Town, and from dozens of other regions well situated to receive components, assemble them cheaply, and reexport them to the world market. While informal manufacturing and services dominate the old urban core of Manila, Port-au-Prince, and Penang, the textile and electronics firms curl out from the periphery in long arms of development pointing to world markets.

Border regions likewise offer profitable possibilities. No city has grown more expansively by working the border than has Hong Kong. Spilling over an island and an irregular peninsula along the broad bay at the mouth of the Pearl River, a setting typical of many export-oriented locations, the site was chosen by the British as a means of controlling the trade that had long been carried on from the city of Guangzhou, which Westerners called Canton. Hong Kong grew as a middleman between Guangzhou and London. When newly communist China closed to the outside world, Hong Kong grew explosively, taking in refugees from the communist regime, and putting their capital and labor to work in a dense pack of high-rise housing and offices, and close-quarters industry. Just as it was becoming too expensive to continue intense global manufacturing in Hong Kong proper, China opened its doors to world trade. The corridor between Guangzhou and Hong Kong quickly became filled with million-person cities in what was really one vast manufacturing metropolis that filled the Pearl River Delta: Guangzhou, Hong Kong, the old Portuguese colony of Macau, the special economic zones of Zhuhai and Shenzhen, and at least five other neighboring cities, each with a population over one million. A permeable border meant that Hong Kong's special status and international capital could readily be combined with China's abundant labor to fuel an export dynamo that by 1997 was channeling over 100 billion dollars worth of export products (Edwards 1997). The same year, Hong Kong returned to China and there is no longer an international border between Guangdong Province and Hong Kong, but no one seems too eager to interfere with what has been so profitable a growth machine.

Likewise, border status has transformed what might be a sparsely populated desert into Mexico's greatest growth corridor. A line of twin cities clamps to each other like opposing magnets along the border from San Diego-Tijuana through El Paso-Juarez to Brownsville-Matamoros. Old Tijuana is dominated by the service economy of hawkers seeking U.S. tourists and serving Tijuana's sprawling population. Industrial Tijuana stretches east toward Mexicali in sprawling industrial parks lined with *maquiladora* industry. Similarly, the economic heart of Juarez is not its core but the industrial campuses with factories not of dirty brick but painted metal warehouses with glass office fronts. These do not pour black smoke into the air in great plumes but rather leak toxic trickles of unknown composition quietly out the back toward the Rio Grande.

Sprawling developments, part suburb and part shantytown, house workers who cram the buses that take them to their plants. The urban core contains mostly amusements and inducements for the workers to quickly part with their minimum wages, wages that are a fraction of those just across the border, but higher than in the rest of Mexico. Meanwhile, San Diego and El Paso grow research institutes, consulting, engineering, and accounting firms, high-priced housing developments, and golf courses for those whose livelihood is tied to a factory that they may never see, just across the border.

The Post-Industrial City

The counterpoint to the new industrial zone is the postindustrial city. The first generation of industrial cities were built on the promise of water power and rarely grew much larger than the streams that turned the water wheels of mills. The next generation grew on steam: steamboats and steam-engine trains delivered coal to power their own steamy industries. Factories clustered along rail yards and dockyards—great brick fortresses flanked by the tenements, row houses and frame shacks of their workers in Baltimore, Pittsburgh, Buffalo, Cleveland, Gary, Milwaukee, and Chicago in a great swath across the U.S. industrial heartland. The scene repeated in the dockyards of London, the mills of Manchester and Liverpool in England, Glasgow in Scotland, and the first factories of the Ruhr and the Rhine in Germany. Many of these places eventually became famous for economic hard times, and many are equally proud of their comeback. They have come back, however, as something quite different from what they were.

I am writing this in a new office building in South Bend, Indiana, that sits on a site where two years ago my son and I watched Japanese-made machinery munch through the brick walls and topple the smokestack of an old bottling plant. I take guests for lunch at a restaurant that now occupies an old brick building situated between the river and the old industrial "race" or channel for water power, with potted plants hanging from industrial-strength steel rafters. Across the river, upscale apartments occupy the site of a shirt-waist factory that once employed hundreds of immigrant women using locally made Singer sewing machines. South Bend was one of the first cities to experience de-industrialization when Studebaker closed in the early 1960s. At the time all the major employers were manufacturing firms: Studebaker, Uniroyal, South Bend Lathe, Singer Sewing Machines, and Bendix Automotive. After hard times, city boosters now proudly boast of low unemployment rates, but the largest employers are the hospitals, the universities, and the city schools. Bendix is now part of the multinational Allied Signal, which is still hiring engineers and technicians to design and test products that will be made elsewhere. The last surviving local industry, now part of American Motors General, holds a lucrative defense contract to build army Humvee all-terrain vehicles. Even as an old Uniroyal plant is being demolished to make room for riverside condominiums and many Bendix and Studebaker facilities stand empty, they are seeking to demolish older homes on the edge of town to build a sprawling single-story plant to make a civilian sport utility vehicle version of the "Hummer." The other surviving industry is small and flexible: recreational vehicles and van conversions in neighboring Elkhart, orthopedic surgical devices further on in small-city Warsaw, and the like. The old brick industries stand as fossilized shells of a species that thrived only fifty years ago but in a different climate and another age, and the neighborhoods that surround them are the city's poorest.

Elsewhere the story has been repeated on a larger scale. Cleveland was once the industrial boomtown of the Midwest, the symbol of mid-American industrial might and progress. Quickly the air and water pollution that accompanied the might sooted this reputation, and Cleveland became the "mistake by the lake." Cleveland is back in a new and cleaner form, not because the industry cleaned up, but because they cleared out. The old dock fronts are now lined with refurbished piers such as the Nautica complex. The site of the White Sewing Machine Company now offers stately apartment units with "impressive amenity packages." The old sugar warehouse houses nightclubs. The powerhouse now only powers restaurants, entertainment, and "specialty retail." Similar changes have transformed Pittsburgh's waterfront, where the meeting of rail and water transport is now the meeting of malls. Baltimore's old industrial waterfront is now back as a collection of upscale entertainment and shopping, anchored by the Harborplace mall complex. Upscale Waterside stands amidst the Norfolk shipyards, and luxury residences are replacing London's dockyards.

Each of these places presents an attractive new facade over the old industrial city. Yet who is attracted? Most of the dining and entertainment is "upscale," geared to prosperous urbanites who earn good incomes elsewhere. For several generations, industrial work was the crucial step on the ladder from poverty to the middle class. With those rungs now severed, the urban poor can be left without a way up or a way out (Wilson 1997). The new renaissance cities are in many ways cleaner and more appealing than their sooty predecessors, but they are also divided cities.

The Commercial Service-Sector City

Some cities have grown as centers of education, government, commerce, tourism, and administrative services without having ever depended heavily on industrial output. Such cities have little image problem, yet the daily realities of life for their working-class residents may not match the allure of their reputations. This is the story of San Francisco, New Orleans, central Paris and Rome, Washington D.C., and Guadalajara, Mexico. Examining Mexico, John Walton contrasted the dirt, smog, and worker shanties of industrial Monterrey to the old colonial charm of Guadalajara. Yet it is service-oriented Guadalajara that has the greatest numbers of poor struggling in the informal economy (Sernau 1994). Likewise, the ultimate international service-sector city, Washington D.C., has grown hometown woes of drugs, crime, and urban decay on a colossal scale, ahead of grimier Baltimore to the north. So too in Brazil, where it is not the industrial grime of São Paulo but the tourist and finance gleam of Rio de Janeiro that has spawned the most dramatic *favela* slums and the most painfully obvious gap between rich and poor. From Birmingham, England, to Birmingham, Alabama, the old industrial cities seek to overcome their reputation for ugliness and to find a new industrial base, often in electronics. Yet it is the white-collar cities, the centers of government, tourism, and trade that often hold the most excluded and the most desperate: from the muggers of Amsterdam to the street children of Rio de Janeiro to the mean streets of Miami.

When turning to smaller cities, the service-sector cities of the United States have been the rising stars of the American urban landscape in contrast to the old mid-size industrial cities: Princeton gleams while Camden struggles, Albany continues to grow while neighboring Schenectady grapples with industrial decline, and Seattle surges while neighboring Bremerton rusts. Madison, Wisconsin, garnered Money magazine's 1996 top ranking for U.S. cities with government, university, and high technology spin-off employment while old industrial Rockford, Illinois, just across the border, came in absolute last. Yet for the urban poor, the two types of cities may be equivalent: one has no jobs, the other has no jobs for them; one has dwindling numbers of stores, the other has dwindling numbers of stores in which they can afford to shop. The focus on these places as entirely separate entities can be misleading, however. Albany-Schenectady are part of a single divided urban cluster, Princeton and Camden anchor opposite sides of a single sprawling metropolis, and even Madison-Rockford are becoming threaded together by development-lined highways. These pairings are no longer tales of two cities, but tales of two worlds within a common globalized metropolitan region.

The New Frontier: Edge Cities

The skyscrapers of the great world cities have been likened to vertical cities in themselves. They became the symbol of urban power: the Empire State Building, long the world's tallest and symbol of New York's power; the twin World Trade Towers that shifted the center of power from midtown Manhattan to a site closer to Wall Street; the black needle of the Sears Tower that surpassed them all and proved that Chicago, Sandburg's city of hog butchers and broad shoulders, was also the city of tall dreams and service-sector sophistication. Now the global sky is pierced by the twin Petronas towers of Kuala Lampur, Malaysia, standing like hybrids between a pagoda and New York's Chrysler Building, joined at the waist by a lofty skyway, and a few feet taller than the Sears Tower—a brash claim to the economic power moving southeast. With a falling currency, some wonder how this economic upstart will pay for such towering extravagance. The title of tallest could go south in part because many in the north have abandoned the race to the skies in favor of a suburban space race. The soaring floors of the Chrysler Building reflect an earlier statement of power; today it is made by the three million largely horizontal square feet of robots and platform teams in their new technology building.

The Sears Tower still dominates the Chicago skyline as a virtual vertical city. You can find almost anything in its 110 floors; anything except Sears, that is. There never was a Sears store anywhere in the tower—those were built in the new suburban malls. Now there are no longer Sears offices in the tower for they have also moved to more spacious land on the city's periphery. The new site is accessible by beltway highways and sports a new corporate campus with the requisite glass and concrete facade set amidst two hundred acres of ponds, wet-lands, fountains, and a few geese on a former soybean field in suburban Hoffman Estates. As Sears stores have fled the city—and abandoned the big book catalog that famously served the rural countryside—in favor of new suburban locations that call to both urbanites and exurbanites, it is perhaps fitting that the head-quarters has shed its place in the clouds for one on the edge.

Joel Garreau (1991) dubbed these growing commercial urban rims "Edge Cities." They are clearly much more than suburbs, a name that evokes quiet residential "bedroom communities." The new edge city is filled with enterprise: huge malls with long mall districts that stretch for blocks beyond the enclosed space, new corporate campuses and glistening office buildings. The favored sites line the beltway highways that were ironically built to carry traffic around ur-ban congestion. Places where the beltway draws close to major airports are especially favored sites. Many commuters no longer move in and out of the city proper, but live in a suburban configuration of Einstein's curved space, commut-ing—often longer than ever before—around the city from a suburban home to an edge city office, fighting rush hour traffic that is just as dense in either direc-tion. The size and economic power of these edge cities is colossal: northern New Jersey has more office space than Manhattan while outer Dallas has three times the office space of the central business district (Palen 1997). One single edge city next to Dallas, the once-quiet suburb of Plano, is now home to the corporate headquarters of five multinational corporations, more than most countries in the world can boast.

The explosion of edge cities reflects changing national and global econom-ics. The price of lofty urban space has grown, and yet for some it has become less strategic. What used to matter most to the big corporations was proximity to one another and to their bankers. Now it is proximity to their airport and ready flight across the country or across the world.

Will globalization then make cities more or less central? The forces work both ways. Air travel concentrates headquarters at major hubs, but even Cincin-nati, Ohio, or Shannon, Ireland, can become a hub. Dependence on electronic technology can free commercial conglomerates from dependence on nearby city services, so that Lands' End can manage a global network from Dodgeville, Wisconsin (population 3,883), L.L. Bean from Freeport, Maine (population 6,905), Wal-Mart can build its assets in Bentonville, Arkansas (population 11,257), and Nike can "just do it" in Beaverton, Oregon (population 53,310).

At the same time, the lines between city and country are becoming ever more blurred. The rural New Englanders in Marlow, New Hampshire, (pop. 650) are less likely to work the electric milking machine as to work on software and peripherals at PC Connections, Inc. Rural Midwesterners in Elk Point, South Dakota, (pop. 1,423) are less likely to slop hogs than to seek Taiwanese components for Gateway Computers. Whether the Census Bureau counts them as rural or urban, they are linked to the world by fax lines, airlines, and turnpikes in a network of vast metropolitan regions.

Conference in Cairo: Population and Limits

It was fitting that the 1994 U.N. Conference on population was held in one of the burgeoning metropolises of the third world. Population pressures are felt most compellingly in these new megacities. Jostling through the traffic of the crowded streets, the delegates had ample opportunity to wonder: where will all the jobs come from, as well as the health care, the food, the housing, the water? How far can the bounty of the Nile be stretched, how many people can a poor country support?

These questions have led to furious debates since the Club of Rome began talk of limits to growth in the 1970s, and Paul Ehrlich (1968) wrote of the impending "population bomb." Years earlier the gloomy economist Thomas Malthus predicted that the gap between a geometrically increasing population (a rising exponential arc) and an arithmetically rising food supply (at best a straight line increase) must eventually be brought down—by famine, war, and disease. The bleak, violent overcrowded earth of the future became the stuff of science fiction scenarios. Yet a billion people later the grim reaper has yet to ride across the globe. Famine remains regional, confined largely to poor people in poor places (of which there are, of course, no shortage). Food supplies have kept up, life expectancies have increased, and disaster has been averted, at least so far.

Some argued at the conference that all this attention to population was misguided. Conservative Muslims and Roman Catholics argued that children were a gift from God, certainly not to be aborted, but maybe also not to be limited. The only remaining socialist attenders were China with its official one-child policy and Cuba with low birth rates due, in part, to highly educated working women and a dismal urban economy. A generation earlier the socialists would likewise have argued that people were a source of strength, creativity, productivity, and progress, not to be limited. Mao had seen the great numbers as China's strength, not its problem. Today, France is actively encouraging women to have children as did Napoleon as part of increasing national strength. The French birthrate, as in other parts of Europe, is below replacement level, and France is no more eager than most other European nations to fill this decline with large numbers of immigrants. Others have argued that growing populations lead directly to growing economies.

A simple correlation between people and prosperity is difficult. Burgeoning populations strain services, infrastructure, and labor markets around the world. But more people does not always mean fewer jobs to go around, since more people are also more consumers and more entrepreneurs. If this were not the case, the last job would have been taken long ago. Nor is population density a reliable measure. Places with weak economies and very high population densities such as Bangladesh face enormous hurdles. Yet some of the world's most prosperous and productive places have the highest population densities: central Japan, central Germany, Hong Kong, and Singapore. Some of the world's poorest places are African nations with fairly low population densities. People come to crowded Cairo, in fact, to seek prosperity and escape rural poverty.

Nonetheless, one warning signal of problems is often a very high rate of population growth. Localities and economies cannot quickly accommodate such a rapid expansion of the population: schools cannot keep up with all the children and labor markets cannot make space for all the young job-seekers. This problem is especially acute if a centralized government is a major controller of the economy and supplier of goods and services. Policies and planning are overwhelmed by ever-expanding numbers. Often the people must provide for their own needs through informal economic activity and squatter settlements and occasionally political mobilization, trying to turn their numbers into a resource.

The demands of an ever-increasing population can be seen in an interesting question: why after twelve thousand years of invention and innovation, is the average person on our planet little better off, and in some ways worse off, than the average hunter-gatherer? Inequality "used up" much of the gains of humanity's collective genius, but so did population. The soaring exponential arc of technological innovation is matched by a suspiciously similarly soaring arc, that of human population. Agriculture brought much denser human populations, most notably to the multi-crop rice cultures of southern Asia. Recent decades have brought still greater rates of population increase. What we have gained by applying technology to our planet is more people, many more people. By some estimates, one-quarter of the people who have ever lived are alive right now. More are on the way. This can be seen as a gain: if they are leading good and rewarding lives, more people can be seen as a value in itself. Yet we look at the world's megacities with limitless poverty and wonder.

How many billions the earth can support we just cannot know, but we may not want to find out. Population growth continues to "use up" gains in technology. We build automobiles that run 25 percent cleaner, but then add 25 percent to the number of cars on the road, and our air gets no cleaner. We tap new food and water resources, but only manage to keep pace with ever more hungry and thirsty mouths. Those who have thirsted for a long time remain as parched and impoverished as ever.

We also keep pace with growing populations at enormous cost to the planet. Indonesia ships its homeless and jobless throngs from crowded Java to remote Irian Jaya, where they slash settlements out of the rain forest. Brazil likewise sends its surplus population to the Amazon where they deplete the natural resources and the indigenous inhabitants at a fearful rate. Europe, of course, did much the same for four centuries as its surplus populations stormed the forests and plains of the Americas, at terrible cost to anything and anyone who was already there. Countries without a primeval forest in their backyards send the "surplus" into the cities, places like Cairo and Calcutta. Haiti already has so many people on such badly deforested and denuded land that the only hope seems to put ever more of them to work in the export factories. India feeds itself but only with huge projects that flood some lands while deforesting and desertifying others.

Some look at this and see impending catastrophe, and this is still possible. Given our history, a more likely scenario is not catastrophe but growing misery: more pollution, more displaced persons, more bleak, crowded conditions—not a last gasp, but lives of grasping, gasping drudgery. As our numbers grow we are diminished. We are using up not only the riches of our own creative innovation but the riches of the planet. If the last tiger in India or the last lemur in Madagascar falls to encroaching populations, we will keep them alive somewhere in zoos, but a planet of urban cages is not a planet of wildlife. If the nutrient-rich soils of India continue to wash and blow away, they will spread the output of new chemical plants on the land to keep the production coming, but at great cost—economic, social, and environmental. We may avoid catastrophe, but we have not proven adept at avoiding tragedy.

Globalization has served to both contain and compound the problem of population growth. The spread of certain global technologies—pesticides, antibiotics and vaccines, health and sanitation regimes—have significantly lowered death rates in most parts of the globe. At the same time, local populations have more often been mere recipients of these interventions and campaigns, rather than active participants in reshaping their economies and communities. At the same time that global technology and politics have made the length of poor people's lives more secure, they have often made the prospects for those lives ever more tenuous. Thus in much of the world, the poor still seek security in large numbers of children who can work with them and later provide for them. Families, and especially women, with few educational and career prospects have little incentive to reduce family size and little power to resist older expectations of their role as bountiful mothers.

At the same time, third-world urbanization has been a force for lower fertility rates. Urbanites may feel less support from kin and clan, but also tend to feel less pressure to conform to older family models. Raising children, and especially large numbers of children, in an urban environment in which children can be economic liabilities rather than assets, and an environment that can seem hostile to children in particular, can be an intimidating prospect. People gradually begin to limit their family size, sometimes in hope of joining the middle classes, sometimes out of fear and dislocation.

Which will prevail: pressures to maintain high fertility, or pressures to lower fertility? Once again, this is not a matter of global determinism but a matter of priorities and choices in a global context. The more culturally acceptable means of contraception are made available and understandable, the more the poor and working classes see that foregoing large families will actually mean better lives for themselves and their children, and the more women are included in opportunities for education and advancement, the more likely people will freely choose to limit their family size. Women in Western Europe with the power to limit their fertility and the opportunities to invest their energies in other areas sometimes actually need incentives to have even the replacement fertility level of two children. The world's women with the least power and least opportunity are the least likely to limit their fertility. Says Dr. Nafis Sadik, a Pakistani woman who heads U.N. efforts on population control, "Give women more choices and they will have fewer children" (Ashford 1995). The opportunities we offer to this generation will, in large measure, determine the size, and thus the opportunities, of the next.

A Slum with a View

Cities of Refuge

Large urban areas have been places of refuge, of last resort, for the poorest and the displaced for centuries, perhaps as long as there have been large urban areas. Lenski (1966) estimates that the population of London in the 1500s of about 80,000 included as many as 12,000 beggars and "expendables," from 10 to 15 percent of the total. Agrarian societies everywhere produced such expendables and they tended to gather in the great cities: the landless, the disabled, unskilled and disfranchised artisans, socially unmarriageable women confined to prostitution, peasants fleeing starvation or brutal lords, beggars of all kinds, organized brigands and petty criminals. They survived by informal activity and illegal activity, and often died young to disease, malnutrition, and violence.

The great cities of the current global system have continued to acquire "expendables," only on a still larger scale. Mechanization and high population growth rates have made ever more people ever more excluded from the formal economy and ever more "expendable." Around the world they gather in squatter communities encircling and threaded through the major cities: the *favelas* of Brazil, the *kampongs* of Indonesia, the *colonias proletarias* of Mexico. Homes are pieced together out of the scrap and refuse of the urban economy, as the often-illegal homesteaders attempt to piece together livelihoods out of the fringes and leftovers of that economy. Mexican anthropologist Larissa Lomnitz Adler calls them "the hunters and gatherers of the new urban jungle" (Lomnitz 1977).

The particular settlement pattern has varied with culture and conditions: social, economic, and geographic. The kampongs of Southeast Asia frequently perch over waterfront areas prone to flooding and too unstable for formal settlement. Residents wash with, bath in, and drink from polluted waters that lap at their doorstep or possibly course through the living space. A similar pattern can be found on the flood-prone fringe of Brazil's Amazonian cities. The most famous favelas of Brazil, however, are not bobbing over the backwaters, but clinging to the mountainsides.

Latin American settlements frequently perch high above valley and coastal cities, occupying land too high, too steep, and too unstable for easy access and basic services such as water lines. Settlers come from the surrounding countryside, often rugged highland communities, and find their space on the urban fringe in places where rugged terrain has halted formal urban development. Like the Biblical account of Moses, their hopes lead them to the mountain's edge, able to see, but not fully enter, the promised land. From the heights they look down on Lima, Peru, on Caracas, Venezuela, on Mexico City, and out across the glittering, celebrated mountain-ringed bay of Rio de Janeiro. They are truly slums with a view. Yet for many, the bright night lights of the city might as well come from distant galaxies. The wages of informal and occasional work— vending, handicrafts, and, ironically, construction work—are quickly spent on purchasing necessities, such as water, that must be hauled up the mountainside. Many know as well that their homes may endure only as long as the authorities cannot figure out how to get a bulldozer up the mountain.

The North American shantytown at first resembled those of Latin America. Early Irish immigrants lived in poorly drained and ill-served clusters of homemade shanties on the edge of Manhattan's midtown. This land soon became valuable, and the "shanty Irish" were displaced. Yet Anglo-Americans have often been more eager to escape the city than Latin Americans. Ancient Greeks and Romans both glorified the city and were suspicious of it. The elites often retreated to the purer countryside. The Spanish, often in harsh and rugged terrain, continued the pattern of glorying in the city and finding their retreats internally inside walled patios. This pattern was thoroughly grafted onto Latin America. Elites placed themselves in the city center, near the plaza and the cathedral, and found seclusion behind walls.

The English preferred to imitate the Greek and Roman gentleman farmers and flee the grimy glories of London for "purer" country estates. Their colonial elites also continued the pattern: this is Washington's Mount Vernon and Jefferson's Monticello. The first wealthy American industrialists built their castle-like mansions on prominent urban streets, but soon were eager to escape the mounting noise and pollution that their factories and products were unleashing on the city. As a result, North American slums have often been wedged between the urban core and elite suburban retreats, and "inner city" has come to denote poverty. In Latin America, elites and the middle classes held to the urban center longer, and "the marginals" were indeed relegated to the urban margins. The distinction is diminishing as some prosperous North Americans return to gentrified urban enclaves to avoid the misery of long commutes, and some prosperous Latin Americans seek to escape the growing congestion and pollution of the urban center. In both places, gentle highlands have come to denote luxury and privilege: all the secluded urban and suburban "Heights" of U.S. cities, and the prestigious "Lomas" neighborhoods of Latin America.

For the marginals and the expendibles, the United States has its own "kampongs" such as the East St. Louis waterfront where the urban poor swelter in a chemical stew dumped upon them from above by industries who probably will not hire them, and face authorities more likely to close bridges to contain them than to build bridges to integrate them. Children try to play, caught between the asthmatic haze that hangs in the air and the sewage-filled chemical soup that leeches up from the ground (Kozol 1991). The United States also has its "favelas" in clusters of shacks and trailers that lean against the slopes of mountain hollers in Appalachia. Much of the new "rural" poverty in the United States is no longer the remote location, but the trailer park and the substandard housing on the urban edge (Fitchen 1991, Harvey 1993).

Along with these, the United States has its own unique form of urban poverty: the new American ghetto with boarded up buildings and vacant lots in places too dangerous for any but the most desperate squatters (Vergara 1995). The remaining buildings are occupied by often jobless families who owe their soul to absentee landlords and relinquish their streets to very present would-be druglords (Wilson 1996). As fires and bulldozers claim old dwellings, vacant lots become the norm so that U.S. ghettoized underclasses often have no shortage of "green-space," albeit untended and often unusable. In parts of inner-city Detroit an adventurous visitor can flush pheasant out of the brush of abandoned lots. These places are considered too dangerous and undesirable for banks and developers to risk their dollars; abandoned strips in an urban conflict zone like Lebanon's infamous Green Line. Jonathan Kozol describes the school "fire drill" in such a zone in the South Bronx:

"What are these holes in our window?" asks a fourth grade teacher at P.S. 65 in a rapid drill that, I imagine, few of those who read this will recall from their own days in school.

"Bullet shots!" the children chant in unison.

"How do police patrol our neighborhood?" the teacher asks.

"By helicopter!" say the children.
"What do we do when we hear shooting?"
"Lie down on the floor!" (Kozol 1995)

Localized economies and rural society also hold their terrors: exploited peasants, degraded castes, sequestered and brutalized women. Yet as globalized economies and metropolitan society have expanded they have created new terrors. Old livelihoods become obsolete and new ones inaccessible. Those caught in between become excluded from the economic, political, and cultural life of the new society (Bhalla and Lapeyre 1999; Sernau 1996).

Cities of Refuse

Have you ever complained "my home is a dump"? What if it really was? One of the most extraordinary examples of human degradation and human resilience must be the garbage dump dwellers of the global cities. Amid the flies and wind-blown stench of one of Brazil's largest dumps, children stoop over collecting garbage that can be sold, fighting over the arrival of the next truck. Toddlers too young to work race barefoot over the trash chasing vultures in an amazing expression of childhood exuberance (Berger 1977). In Manila, the great dump has spawned its mini-city of trash pickers, working in the stinging haze and fumes—and sometimes taking time out for a game of basketball with a hoop extracted from the trash and set on a pole. Behind them the fires of "Smokey Mountain" burn incessantly, fed by garbage-generated methane. Out of the foul haze, a young girl emerges in a fresh dress, smiles, and goes out to play.

A vast dump outside of Tijuana has filled a 150-foot canyon, turning it into a forty-foot mound of toxic, oozing yellow mud that is home to an entire community of trash pickers who live their lives in competition with a canopy of circling gulls. The dump, the community, and the adjacent cemetary—filled with the trash covered graves of children—look down on the bright lights of San Diego, just beyond the distant fence. Some go crazy and wave for passing planes to take them away, others hold on to hope, and talk of planting roses (Urrea 1996).

Outside of Cairo, the trash of fifteen million people piles in great mountains, fills the air with eye-watering stench and burns in sporadic fires. Around the fires the trash-pickers gather for warmth and camaraderie and then set to work seeking saleable treasures. They are poor Coptic Christians, banned from much other employment in the Muslim nation. They are dirty and desperate, but hardly defeated. These dump-dwellers eventually organized their work into an officially sanctioned recycling center. They have used loans from the World Bank to mechanize their recycling center and to build a large apartment complex with water and electricity (Macionis 1997).

Don't Dump on Us

It is clearly a mistake to suggest that the excluded and degraded of the world metropolises are too defeated or too isolated to organize and take action. Poor communities are often rich in informal networks of exchange and self-help (see Stack 1974; Lomnitz 1977). With the right opportunities and leadership, this can be translated into concerted, coordinated, and political action. This is the story of the Dudley Street neighborhood in Boston's poorest sector:

Beginning in the 1950s, disinvestment, abandonment and arson turned Dudley homes, yards and businesses into wasteland. By 1981, one-third of Dudley's land lay vacant. It became a dumping ground for trash from the city and state. The dumping wasn't legal, but the violators came and went without fear of the law, blighting the neighborhood with toxic chemicals, auto carcasses, old refrigerators, rotten meat and other refuse (Medoff and Sklar 1994, 2).

Yet out of this abandonment, a multi-racial mix of residents both new and old came together.

For years, Dudley has looked as if an earthquake had struck, leveling whole sections. Streets crisscross blocks of vacant lots where homes and shops used to be. In the summer, the lots bloom with violet wildflowers, nature's gift to a community working to rebuild against great odds (Medoff and Sklar 1994, 1).

Beginning with a campaign that demanded "Don't dump on us," the resident-led Dudley Street Neighborhood Initiative eliminated illegal dumping, won grudging city support, gained outside financing, used eminent domain laws to regain control of the land, and began building a viable "urban village."

Similar efforts on an even grander scale have transformed the Villa El Salvador shantytown above Lima, Peru, into a poor but thriving community of over one-half million. Residents gained land rights and grudging political recognition, then secured development loans and invested in housing and infrastructure with an emphasis on employing resident labor throughout the building process.

In rare cases entire cities have participated in community-based revitalization. Like other Brazilian cities, Curitiba has seen explosive growth—an elevenfold increase in fifty years to almost two million—and grinding poverty with average family incomes below $100 per week.

Nonetheless, Curitiba is a green, clean, and very livable city. It began twenty-five years ago when the mayor, rather than building highway overpasses and shopping centers as was occurring elsewhere in Brazil, instead advocated pedestrian malls and recycled buildings. Crime is minimal. People come into the center on a system of express buses running in separate high-speed bus lanes (Palen 1997, 463).

Old buses have been converted in mobile vocational classrooms and street children, rather than stealing and becoming the targets of death squads, can enter apprenticeship programs where they work half-time in exchange for food, a living stipend, and their school expenses. The shantytowns in the hillsides are unreachable by garbage trucks but remain clean since the poor can bring their garbage down to the trucks and exchange garbage for basic food supplies.

Curitiba isn't a miracle, but it does show that even without substantial funding, ingenuity and common sense can do a great deal to turn around urban problems. There is hope (Palen 1997, 464).

Seeking a Community of the Soul

Urban theorists have long posited the city as a place of rootlessness and alienation, a place where people experience what Emile Durkheim called "anomie": a normless state cut off from the community solidarity of the village. Toennies spoke of the inexorable movement from personal community (*gemeinschaft*) to impersonal society (*gazelleschaft*). Yet urban dwellers have continually found ways to create face-to-face community within the larger cosmopolitan society, to bring the village into the city and become what Herbert Gans (1962) termed *Urban Villagers*. For all its appearances of utter chaos, the global city continues to be built upon institutions of soulful locality and familiarity that offer a sense of place, a sense of community belonging.

Cities of God: The Not-So-Secular City

Examining the changing social landscape of the day, Harvey Cox (1965) wrote of the "secular city." Readers who thought he was predicting the demise of religion would be astounded at today's cities with the streets of shoulder-to-shoulder churches, synagogues, temples, shrines, and mosques. What is new is that increasingly these are on the same street. Diana Eck (1996) notes that along New Hampshire Avenue, just beyond the Beltway of Washington, D.C., there is a stretch of road a few miles long that passes the new Cambodian Buddhist temple, the Ukrainian Orthodox Church, the Muslim Community Center with its new copper-domed mosque, and the new Gujarati Hindu temple as well as the new dimensions of America's Christian landscape: Hispanic Pentecostal, Vietnamese Catholic, and Korean evangelical congregations sharing facilities with more traditional English-speaking "mainline" churches.

Religion can function as world culture, giving identity to global civilizations that are no longer anchored to a single locality (Huntington 1996). Religious groups can be one way of resisting the homogenization of modernity, and reestablishing one's roots, heritage, and a distinctive identity that cannot be reduced to the digits encoded on a credit card. These enduring identities converge in major cities. The world's great religions have finally come together, not in spirit, but in Chicago:

Today, the Islamic world is no longer somewhere else, in some other part of the world; instead Chicago, with its 50 mosques and nearly half a million Muslims, is part of the Islamic World . . . The map of the world in which we now live cannot be color-coded as to its Christian, Muslim, or Hindu identity, but each part of the world is marbled with the colors and textures of the whole" (Eck 1996, 44).

Durkheim believed that people turned to religious celebrations to celebrate and solidify their common community; today many turn to religious celebration to find and create an intentional community that is not absorbed by urban anonymity. For many, the metropolis is not where they finally shed the faith of the fathers, but the one place they are free to express the faith of their fathers and mothers, to find a critical mass of fellow believers, and to create a community of faith.

The Last Great, Good Places

Cafes, whether wood-paneled in Vienna or on French sidewalks; pubs, whether with dart-throwing in London or barb-throwing in Dublin; the German lager beer garden, whether in Munich or Milwaukee; and other gathering places have also preserved community and locality in the urban setting. Ray Oldenburg (1997) describes these informal gathering spots as "third places" after home and work, and contends they serve community best to the extent that they are local and inclusive when so much of our lives is neither. Robinson and Keen (1997) note this quality in the traditional coffeehouse culture of Vienna:

In the midst of our noisy consumerism, the Viennese cafe shows us the need for a space of relaxation as well as encounter, a space of contemplation and questioning, in touch with the world and yet distant from it, a space that is both public and private. Framed by an impersonal mass society and private closure, we need a place of public hospitality . . . Perhaps the resurgence of coffeehouses all over the world is not just a trendy fad, but an indication of that need (p. 32).

Awareness of the global and love of that which is local are entirely compatible. A place remains for the idiosyncratic neighborhood coffeehouse with Internet connections (as in "cyberbars" in Seattle, San Francisco, and Minneapolis) or with newspapers in twelve languages: "think globally, drink locally."

Yet one might argue that the café keeps in close touch with the world and serves as a sounding board for new ideas. In its heyday the Central [in Vienna] had more than 250 newspapers, and today all the traditional cafes carry papers in many languages, for a coffeehouse is judged as much by its newspaper collection as by its coffee (p. 25).

Neighborhood organizations also reestablish awareness and neighborly concern. In my own community, the South Bend Heritage Foundation combines historic preservation with community activism and a well-managed community development corporation. Older homes are restored rather than bull-dozed, then sold at affordable prices. Deteriorating store blocks are restored for local business and community centers, or replaced with newer facilities that still fit the historic neighborhood feel. Not everyone agrees on each agenda but this draws a diversity of people into dialogue with one another. Historic preservation does not remain the domain of "gray-haired ladies," and affordable housing does not remain the domain of the bulldozer and the prefabricated unit. Some great old buildings are restored, but more importantly the sense of neighborhood is retained and restored. Such a sense of place is often vital to ongoing community mobilization and to activism that extends beyond an immediate crisis.

Increasingly, we are seeing global networks of local activists willing to learn the lessons of Boston, Lima, and Curitiba. Those who do are often reassured of both the distinctiveness of place and the commonality of the human condition. Such activities are a long way from creating the City Beautiful, but they are a force in balancing the mall sprawl and intense individualism of World Mart, and in keeping a sense of place in the spinning globe.

8

TENDING COMMON GROUND

The Global Environment and the Future of Humanity

The right to breathe free is the most basic human right of all.
—Jesse Jackson

Justice and ecology are linked indissolubly.
—Desmond Tutu

EL NIÑO, THE LITTLE BOY, is a strange name for a great mass of warm water that sloshes about in the Western Pacific like a disturbed bathtub. So named because it is often first noted at Christmas, this great reservoir of heat can affect the entire globe in a strong El Niño year, and provide a powerful reminder of how closely interconnected our global environment is. El Niño has brought floods to California and, with the help of real estate developers insistent on tacking houses onto steep, unstable slopes, great mudslides. It has brought warm breezes to the Dakotas and snow to Mississippi. It has doubled the price of rice in Tokyo, increased the price of coffee in New York, and brought drought to sub-Saharan Africa. El Niño shifts the course of south Asian monsoons, and brings dry winds that drop Sahara sand on the Indian subcontinent. It shifts the course of the upper air jet streams, not only changing weather flows, but forcing airlines to alter their flight patterns. It has brought unceasing rain outside my window, rain that falls with the warmth of the Pacific, the ash of a Philippine volcano, the soot of raging central Mexican forest fires, the dust of a Nevada strip mine, the silt of a prematurely plowed expanse of Iowa, and the acid of coal fires along Chicago's southern rim.

Al Gore once proposed placing a satellite in space to relay continuous video coverage of the planet as a whole to our televisions. He hoped to create a reminder like that provided by the Apollo astronauts of the earth as a blue-white gem, seeming small and fragile, floating in a vast expanse of blackness. That image helped spark the environmental movement of the 1970s. For now the reminder is offered by the slosh of warm water in the Pacific whose oscillations can dramatically alter the flow of wind, water, aircraft, and financial transactions around the globe. We are part of an egg-shell-thin layer of interconnected life that encircles a small planet, and a disturbance anywhere soon affects the whole. We must take great care before we trouble the waters.

Global Pillage

The embrace of globalization continues: enfolding and nurturing some while suffocating and stifling others, creating a world of world-class winners and global losers. As we enter a new century, the greatest loser may be the globe itself. Dreaming of a prosperous global village, we have woken to the nightmare of the magnitude of global pillage. The attacks on the global environment come from each quarter we have considered. Cultural globalization has weakened the power of cultures with long ties to sustainable relationships with the earth, replacing their teachings with the messages of mass consumption.

Global manufacturing and marketing has left a planet awash in refuse. A trek through subtropical forest in the Mexican state of Michoacán leads to the beautiful falls. The water seems to leap from the forest, crashing over volcanic rock, cascading amidst ferns and flowers into a deep pool ringed with the bright colors of hundreds of white, pink and aqua plastic bottles that bob with the current. The local population has ready access to a wide variety of detergents and laundry agents, but not to any reliable laundry facilities. They use the pool where the bottles remain while the chemicals join the downstream surge. In nearby Uruapan, signs in a national park of natural springs and manmade fountains advise people to take their laundry somewhere else. The signs are often ignored by people who find daily necessities more pressing than aesthetic niceties. Further south in otherwise beautiful Cuernavaca, signs call on people to keep their trash from the gorges and waterfalls that in some other locale, wealthier in currency and poorer in scenery, would surely themselves be major parks. The signs are largely ignored, obvious trash tumbles down the gorges, while the less obvious toxic chemicals from micro-enterprises swill in the streams below, surging on to mix with the toxic wastes of the larger industries beyond.

The trashing of paradise is not a uniquely Mexican trouble. The rims of lovely tropical lagoons in the South Pacific are often filled with great banks of trash: colored plastic and shiny metal gleaming in the tropical sun. Years ago this trash would have been mostly shells and husks that would have been washed away unnoticed. The forces of World Mart have brought new products and new packaging, but not the means to recycle and reuse them. Global mass production has filled the world with products of synthetic materials that have limited duration of utility and almost endless duration in the dump.

The new world of work has compounded the problems. Traditional livelihoods are displaced. New livelihoods on the global assembly line take women from traditional tasks of providing food, clothing, and shelter from local resources to working long hours in frequently toxic conditions. They, in turn, become dependent on industrial products to fill personal and family needs for which they no longer have any time. The manufacturing plants themselves may well have come to the export processing zone not only for lower wages but for laxer environmental regulations. The levels of toxic output allowed in the burgeoning east Asian nations are many times what could be spewed into European or North American air and water. At times the deadly potential is catastrophic as in the Bhopal chemical plant disaster, killing three thousand people in a great toxic cloud, and forcing many more to abandon homes and livelihoods. More often the effects are quiet deaths and lingering disability from cancers and respiratory illness.

Wars have long scarred the earth as well as its inhabitants, and the unrest of the new world disorder continues to take a terrible toll on the planet. Attacks on the land have long been part of human conflict: the ancients sowed salt in the soil of defeated enemies, warring Medieval armies trampled and burned crops and forest, Britain deforested its landscape in search of timber and charcoal for ships and cannon, and U.S. forces slaughtered bison to compel Plains Indians to surrender. Modern wars increased the assault with the poisons of World War I and the great incendiary infernos and ultimately nuclear attacks of World War II. The black billows of the burning oil wells of Kuwait created a vast shroud of Hades-like gloom lit only by fiery torches as crude oil and chemicals streamed into the gulf. The defoliant Agent Orange debilitated land, villagers, and soldiers alike in Vietnam. Both wars saw the landscape cratered by carpet bombing. For decades now we have lived with the realization that full-scale nuclear war could reduce the earth to a great radioactive fossil of the life that was. Even the preparation for that doomsday war brought devastation to Pacific islands, parts of the American Great Basin, and parts of the Russian Caucasus. Yet it has been the "small" conflicts of the world that have taken the greatest toll. Desperate refugees flee into previously secluded or protected regions, they clear trees for homes and firewood, and slaughter wildlife for food or from frustration. Government regulations break down, and well-armed bands of guerrillas and displaced insurgents become the ultimate poachers.

New technologies are only rarely applied to the causes of conservation and local control, and often add to the demands for more: more paper, more energy, more chemicals. The soot and smoke of the old coal fires is replaced by subtler threats: the invisible slow burn of radioactive waste, of acid rains, of dioxide contamination in soil and water, and of pesticide residues in groundwater, fish, birds, and human livers. The deceptive clean shine of electronics plants and products covers the myriads of toxic by-products generated in their manufacture. The radioactive wind from Chernobyl silently crippled local populations, then drifted across Europe and ultimately circled the globe, leaving the planet to wonder about the global reach of toxic technologies.

The strain of global population is compounded by its concentration in ill-prepared cities. The new urbanites create lifestyles that require diesel transportation, electrical production, and ever greater energy demands, and that pour pollutants into the air, land, and water. Their hopes are no longer grounded in the promises of the bounty of the land, but in the promised lifestyle of the billboards. The resulting demands for energy and materials can lead to frenzies of giant dam projects, yawning open pit mines, and great "development" projects that consume the land and displace even more villagers who in turn become new urbanites.

The combination provides a grim picture of the planet's future. Will this global pillage strip the planet of its ability to support life? Will the global embrace of humanity become a stranglehold that chokes the globe itself? Disasters such as Bhopal remind us of the potential for catastrophe. Disasters such as Chernobyl demonstrate the international dimensions of environmental catastrophe. Warnings of global warming are a reminder that catastrophe need not come with a spectacular fireball but with a slow simmer. Pick your doom: to go out in a blaze of nuclear fire or drown in the meltwater of polar ice caps. Perhaps the most likely prospect we face is of a global Chernobyl: local regions of devastation interconnected by vast regions facing risks and rumors of spreading poisons. Our past mistakes have not always led to catastrophe but often simply greater misery. We could face more of the same: a pillaged planet each day offering less bounty and less beauty, fewer options, and more misery for more people. The price of environmental neglect is often miserable people living a miserable existence in a miserable relic of a better time. A different future will require a different mind set.

Facing a World without Frontiers

Americans moving west in the middle of the nineteenth century to claim their "manifest destiny" were led by the Angel of Progress, or so they dreamed. A classic frontpiece illustration of the time shows the settlers below, eyes fixed on the flowing robes of Progress as she soars above, always looking west. Ahead of her is the wilderness in retreat: jagged, inhospitable mountains, unplowed plains, snarling grizzly bears, wooly bison, sneering native hunters. Behind her, the sun breaks forth on a new land and a new vision: rolling hills, plowed fields, guns, trains, steamships, and telegraph bringing enlightenment, prosperity, and above all, progress. This is the frontier myth we created and perpetuated: the glimmer of civilization, the ever-moving line of the frontier, and beyond the beckoning, though threatening, wilderness. The myth is so powerful that we continue to look for "last frontiers": Alaska, Antarctica, the realms of the ocean, or the realms of outer space. We have wilderness areas—zones closed to roads and development—but sense that a wilderness with borders and rangers is quite different than the boundless beyond. That wilderness seems to be gone.

The truth is, it never was—at least not for thousands of years. Perhaps the first paleolithic hunters who crossed the Bering Strait in the Americas encountered a true wilderness free of human impact. What this wilderness looked like we don't really know, but it did not look like what white settlers found as they moved west. The great north-central swath of the continent probably looked more like a northern Serengeti Plain: a great savanna of grass interspersed with massive sprawling trees (oak instead of baobab), and home to wandering elephants (mammoths and mastodons), woolly rhinoceros, predatory cats and wolves, and vast thundering herds. For the years that the first adventurous hunter-gatherers ventured ever southward along the Panama isthmus, across the equator, and on to Patagonia there was a true moving frontier.

Those humans settled the land—and changed it. The largest animals disappeared, maybe in part from climatic change, maybe because they did not have the long millennia their Afro-Eurasian cousins had to adapt to human predation; instead they faced a sudden incursion of hungry, deadly hunters. With the great herds reduced, humans set to work cultivating a more sustainable existence. They cleared the underbrush-laden Eastern woodlands and crisscrossed the great virgin forest with trails. They burnt the savanna and steppe-lands to keep it in grass rather than brush. They used selective burning to keep the Western dry country in acorn-yielding oaks rather than chaparral (Diamond 1997).

Eventually they cultivated the small seed-cluster bearing plant that most of the world calls maize. To European American settlers it was so indispensable it was simply "corn," or "the grain." The Amerindian people also cultivated squash and beans, growing them in a wonderful symbiotic planting in a single hole: beans climbing the corn stalks, aggressive squash spreading out to overcome weeds. The corn and beans were a complementary protein, and the squash provided needed vitamins. In the mountains they also found the possibilities of the potato and the tomato, in the Amazon basin fish were complemented by starchy manioc ("tapioca") and a myriad fruits.

This was the land the new European Americans found: not a densely crowded continent of many great cities, but hardly a wilderness. Progress was nothing more than the displacement of one set of hunter-farmers with a new set of hunter-farmers with steel tools and weapons. A much less poetic prospect, so this displacement instead became the taming of the frontier, the winning of the West, and the conquest of the wilderness. European immigrants in Brazil and Argentina created similar myths to justify and glorify their own struggles. Lest we cast them unfairly, it should be noted that Native American alliances often used similar justifications of superior organization and courage when they displaced one another (Bordewich 1996). They lacked, however, the utterly determined extermination that came with the progress myth.

Dismayed at what they had done to their home continent, and what was happening to their adopted continent, some Europeans created a new myth: the noble savage of Rousseau and fellow romantics. We echo this myth when we extol native Americans as ever-wise ecologists who lived in harmony with the land (Bordewich 1996). Native Americans changed the land to suit their purposes, sometimes destructively as in the extinctions, sometimes productively and sustainably as they learned to cultivate the forest and plains in ways that preserved their bounty and favored wildlife.

The new plains lifestyle that came to Native Americans, first with European horses and then guns, was also unsustainable. The bison herds, who now could no longer retreat into the great human-uninhabited reaches of the inner plains, were declining before Buffalo Bill ever fired his first shot. European Americans, in an orgy of slaughter, brought the bison down in about two decades while native hunters could have gone on for perhaps two centuries, but then they would have had to limit their hunting, return to greater dependence on farming, or try to herd bison as Eurasians had done with cattle. People have always changed the land. In oft-quoted, and frequently misquoted words, Chief Seattle speaks of the brother beasts, and articulates beautifully an ancient sentiment we are now starting to recover. Yet in the closest we have to his original statements, he laments much more the loss of his ancestral home and lands—the loss of his people—than he does the loss of the "buffalo," which in fact did not even inhabit his Puget Sound home. Seattle saw clearly the displacement of one people, his own, by another, and believed neither the progress myth nor the noble savage myth.

The other favorite locale for Europeans in search of noble savages and lost Eden was the South Pacific. Here nineteenth-century impressionist painter Paul Gauguin hoped to escape the society-fouled world of Europe and find a remnant of paradise. What he and compatriots actually found was a very sophisticated Polynesian society that extended for thousands of miles across the Pacific. The land was exotic to a European, but not nearly as exotic as before the Polynesian sailors had landed, bringing pigs and chickens and exterminating the giant Moa of New Zealand and scores of native bird species. The islands were bountiful, but only because they had already seen centuries of careful human cultivation, largely with plants that had been brought thousands of miles, island by island, from southeast Asia. This was neither Eden nor wilderness, nor a vast

Pacific frontier, but a complex society that was fighting for survival, eager for material gain (to Gauguin's disgust) and lamenting the loss of their land to new-comers with bigger boats and deadlier guns and germs.

With nineteenth-century industrialism, the human transformation of the land accelerated: more production, more intense cultivation, more and quicker extinctions, more deforestation. The Angel of Progress was proving to be an insatiable demon. It was time that someone explained to both the engineers of progress and the seekers of noble savages that, in fact, there were no natives—only old-timers and newcomers—no wilderness and no frontier, and hence no true "pioneers," only new demands for productivity and plunder.

Yet myths, unlike people and wildlife, are hard to exterminate. From the orgy of colonization that divided Africa in the nineteenth century through the great wars of the twentieth century, the myth of the Angel of Progress lived on. McMichael (2000) calls the post–World War II version of this "the development project." The assurance was that prosperity would inevitably follow in the wake of the fates: "Progress" and her sisters "Modernization" and "Take-Off" (see Rostow 1960). The call of these lovely sirens drew many onto what would prove to be disastrous shores, just as that shameless hussy, "Manifest Destiny," had earlier drawn many European Americans into a westward rush of domination and extermination.

The "development project" is giving way, but now replaced by "the global-ization project" (McMichael 2000), which only promises expanded plunder, unless we bravely reconsider our role. Of his native India, Ravi Bhagwat writes:

One hundred and fifty years of colonial rule left us a legacy not only of denuded forests and dammed rivers, but also of a belief that this was progress. In the half century since independence, we ourselves have not only done precious little to challenge this belief, but have on the contrary pursued that same model of so-called "development" with a ven-geance. The irony is that while in many Western countries today ecologists are coming round to believe in the truth of Mahatma Gandhi's world view, in his own country, as in many other Third World countries, he seems to have been forgotten. There are, however, signs that we may be on the way to some genuine rethinking about development in the days to come (Quoted in Porritt 1991, 135).

By the 1960s, just as many African nations were becoming independent, an alternate perspective, that the Angel of Progress is really the demon of Western capitalism, was growing in acceptance. New national leaders called for a return to a lost nobility, such as the *ujaama* "village democracy" of Tanzania's Nyerere. Those who rejected big schemes for a return to the land often have unleashed unsustainable populations on ill-suited land, and have created their own deadly cycles of deforestation, erosion, and desertification. The Angel of Progress and the Angel of Primordial Nobility were both running a scam, perpetrating an unattainable mythical future.

We can no longer be blinded by the bright promise of Progress, nor can we return to Eden. The reality is not as moving as either of the myths. People, of all colors, cultures, and backgrounds, of all religions and both genders, have seized new opportunities, and many of those have been destructive to the planet. Greater social and technological power has accelerated this process, and unless redirected, stands poised to wreak even greater destruction. We can learn from the wisdom of the past, but we must also craft new solutions, for great ecological visionaries have always been rare, and each has spoken to a time with changing problems and constraints.

America was never the story of pioneers, adventurers, and frontiersmen overcoming "simple savages." By and large, it was the story of careful cultivators falling to a growing tide of European exiles, desperate people who had no place in the land, economy, or society of their home country. The indigenous peoples of the Amazon and of Irian Jayan forests are not simple savages romping in Eden, but careful cultivators who need options and opportunities if they are going to survive into the next century. The Spanish-speaking Brazilians and Javanese Indonesians who are displacing them are only rarely rugged adventurers and frontiersmen; they are more often exiles from lands and economies that have found no place for them. In each of these encounters, people thought they saw exotic strangers; they were, in fact, only meeting long-lost cousins. We have more in common than we have realized. Said Seattle: "No man is exempt from the common destiny. What befalls the earth befalls all the sons of the earth."

Sacrifice Zones: Wasted Faces, Wasted Places

Environmental conservation has often been a concern of the prosperous. Urban middle classes in the United States, Europe, Japan, and now around the world, are often the ones who try to preserve an attractive landscape to visit when escaping the city. The world's poor are often initially too concerned about survival to care about grand schemes of natural preservation. Yet increasingly, poor people and poor nations are realizing that they are the ones most at risk from environmental degradation and that the struggle for a good life must be rooted in a good environment. Prosperous urbanites are disappointed when the land is spoiled, yet they can always vacation somewhere else, in some new "unspoiled" land. They can escape the smog in air conditioned homes and offices, dine on food carefully cleaned and prepared and culled from distant places, and drink bottled mineral water if need be. It is the poor who are most bound to the land: breathing and drinking the pollution, tilling the eroded soil, depending on local resources for daily sustenance. They have the most at stake and the most to lose. The wealthy can claim the spoils of many lands, the poor must live on the spoiled land. The well-off can drive past the desolation to the game park, the nature preserve, or the conservatory. For the poor to have access to both beauty and bounty, all the land—and all the air and water—must be protected from plunder and spoilage.

Jessie Jackson, civil rights veteran and leader of the Rainbow Coalition that has reached out to rural white farmers, poor urban blacks, and rural and urban Latinos, contends:

The promise of the new world order is threatened by the twin injustices of poverty and environmental destruction. Environmental destruction falls most heavily on the shoulders of the disadvantaged, and this is a threat to democracy itself. What is democracy, after all, if your air is too polluted to breathe? What is economic development if your land is too poisoned to farm? What is international law if rich countries dump their toxic wastes on the shores of poorer nations? Environmental justice is fundamental to the new world order. The United States is proud of Liberty's promise to the world: "give me your tired, your poor, your huddled masses, who yearn to breathe free." We must now extend the right to breathe free to every nation and every individual, for the right to breathe free is the most basic human right of all (Quoted in Porritt 1991, 38).

Many of the world's most devastated places have been national "sacrifice" zones in the pursuit of economic growth and progress. The people living in or near such zones have rarely benefitted much from that progress, but often appear as if they have been sacrificed themselves. Some church and policy groups have started to speak of "environmental racism" in that the most devastated, dangerous environments are often those occupied by racial and ethnic minorities with little political power. Just as accurate would be to term this "environmental classism" for it is invariably the poor who are in these locations. Whether defined by race or class, the underlying issue is the lack of power to protect one's home and to lobby for change, along with the lack of opportunity to move on to more privileged locations and enjoy the fruits of the plunder.

Darkness at Noon

All across Eastern Europe, the urban working classes have been subjected to the effects of old, inefficient, and unregulated industry. Skies are perpetually blackened by the acidic soot from burning soft coal. People walk from home to work in perpetually blackened haze. Clothes hung out to dry come back in dirty and soot-streaked. Nothing is immune from the caustic air: metal corrodes, stone dissolves, and human lungs are blackened and eaten away. This horrific environment is one of the worst legacies of decades of repression regimes. Czech president Havel describes emerging from the triumphs of peaceful revolution into the realization that what the reformers were inheriting was the most polluted land in Europe.

The problems are not limited to the formerly socialist nations. One of the greatest objections to holding the Olympic games in Athens as a symbolic return to Greece has been the terrible Athenian smog. This acid haze dissolves the ancient marble statues of the famous Acropolis, eating ears and noses off of ancient faces, while just as surely damaging the lungs and bodies of the still-living. The wealthy can escape to the fresh breeze of nearby islands, but the working classes remain in a haze that dissolves the past and imperils the future. Across Europe, it is getting harder to get away from it all: the favorite seaside escapes are threatened by a polluted Mediterranean Sea, while the Alpine slopes are marred by the brown slow-burn of acid rain on once-evergreen forests, assaulted by pollutants from both East and West.

The Eastern European air is likely to get cleaner, but this only because more and more of its industries are closing in the face of global competition. What will take their place? Some in Western Europe already seem eager to use the Eastern European countries for the dumping of industrial waste, and the low-wage, high-risk manufacture that has previously been exported off the continent. Eastern Europe's factories were fueled by the mines of the vast former Soviet domain: mines also largely without environmental or safety regulation, now pitting a landscape occupied by Russian miners never sure of getting paid, people who were part of a national sacrifice effort that seems to hold no rewards for them.

The United States has experienced similar sacrifice zones of land and people. Great stretches of the otherwise beautiful Appalachian range are stripped, scoured, scarred, and pitted with the remains of decades of environmentally indifferent mining. New restrictions on the burning of soft, high-sulfur coal have meant a limited future for many of the mines. The decades of extracting black wealth from the ground have not left the miners wealthy, but often in debt, racked with lung diseases, and now unemployed with very uncertain futures. Ironically, the places that are booming are those least scarred by mining, those whose natural beauty now attracts residents and new firms to the sunbelt. In many ways, the unemployed miners could offer a more sobering warning to Western loggers of old-growth forests than can the voices of Eastern environmentalists, yet many of the old-timers do not have much voice left. Together with their Russian comrades, if they would allow such a term, they offer a grim warning to those struggling in the great human anthills of South Africa's vast mines, to Bolivian miners picking at the mountains, and to Brazilian gold miners dumping mercury into the Amazon: in time the lure of better wages gives way to the reality of poverty and desperation in a desolate land.

The coal of Appalachia fed many furnaces, but none hungrier than the great steel blast furnaces of Gary, Indiana. These turned a land of sand dunes and lakeside forest into a great simmering industrial cauldron. For a few decades that cauldron fed the industries of Chicago and supplied car plants of Detroit, and offered readily available jobs, especially to poor newcomers, many of them Black and Latino. The forest of blackened smokestacks remains, but with few jobs. Gary now struggles with some of the countries highest unemployment rates, highest crimes rates, highest segregation indices, and highest poverty rates. New convention facilities and floating casinos have been procured to help turn the economic tide, yet the greatest obstruction to change remains the devastated urban landscape, and the devastated lives of so many of its residents. Gary may well fight its way back, but the environmental sacrifice has meant not the assurance of prosperity, but the entrenchment of poverty.

Towering Tombstones

Sacrifices can be offered to water as well as to fire. The combined desire for endless irrigation to increase commercial farm production and for inexpensive electrical energy to propel industrial expansion has led to huge hydroelectric dam projects. Dam building has accompanied industrialization from the early days of its dependence on the water wheel, but these were largely small local projects. The great concrete colossi that are being poured across the world's great rivers are founded heavily on global capital and global markets. For many years the World Bank was the premier dam builder, lending for huge schemes that promised great strides in national economic development. The World Bank has backed off from the big dam business, in part as it has become more environmentally aware, and in part because many of the projects never met their economic development promises. New sources of funding have filled the void, in the form of private international venture capital, or in the case of China, channeling profits from international exports.

For the first postwar decades of what Philip McMichael (2000) calls the "development project," great, powerful countries build great, powerful dams. The World Bank capitalists built big dams, so the Communists built bigger ones. Soviet engineers built the Aswan High Dam for Egypt, bringing greater irrigation and productivity, while destroying the soil, spreading debilitating waterborne disease, and interrupting the flood cycles of the Nile that had sustained the region for eight thousand years. The high rate of evaporation from the huge manmade desert lake leaves behind high-salt brackish water that leaves a salt trail on the land when used for irrigation. The Romans salted the sight of conquered Carthage to make the land infertile; the Egyptians are unintentionally doing the same to some of the world's most fertile soils. Land that is always wet can be in perpetual production, but it is also ideal for the reproduction of a parasite-carrying snail. As workers wade through the snail-laden muck, they contract schistosomiasis, a debilitating disease that gradually drains all the energy and stamina from its victims. Production, most notably export production, reached an all-time high, but the High Dam is leeching the ancient vitality from both the land and the people who work the land, leaving Egypt with a future as uncertain as ever.

The Egyptians might have done well to look closer at the superpower experience. Towering Hoover Dam provides electrical power to light the twenty-four-hour glitter of Las Vegas, it provides Lake Mead to boaters, and it irrigates the Imperial Valley of California. It has become a national symbol of engineering might and national progress. Yet it has problems similar to Aswan. The Colorado is also a silty river, at flood stage it ran "too thick to drink, too thin to plow." The Colorado now runs mostly blue, and certainly Lake Mead, like its upstream cousin Lake Powell, are perpetually a deep cobalt blue. The silt has not left, in fact, with evermore upstream construction and loss of forest cover it carries more silt than ever, but the silt settles to the bottom of the great man-made lakes, slowly decreasing their capacity and efficiency. Meanwhile, a desert sun evaporates water quickly from the broad shallow reservoirs, and the Imperial Valley is faced with ever saltier soil from the brackish water. High intensity production continues but farmers look north to the great salt deserts of California, Nevada, and Utah and wonder about the future. In the meantime, they maintain the production of grapes, strawberries, and vegetables with high levels of chemical inputs. Their workers, many of them Mexican-American laborers who were organized into the United Farmworkers Union by Cesar Chavez in the 1960s, complain of debilitating chronic health problems.

Across the Mexican border, the once mighty Colorado is reduced to a salty trickle that often never reaches the Gulf of California. The once-great wetlands and their wildlife are disappearing, and the water left to Mexican farmers is often minimal and all but unusable. Two pictures side by side in the *Boston Globe* showed the stark contrast of the new Desert Springs Marriott Resort with an artificial lake and indoor waterfalls, requiring fifty million gallons of water, while a Cocopa Indian stands on the dry, cracked riverbed of the former Colorado delta. "When the mighty river was dammed in 1935, the Cocopa Indians of Mexico were damned" (Grossfeld 1997, 18).

Few talk these days, as they did in the 1950s, about using nuclear and conventional explosives to blast a canal from the Great Lakes to the dry plains, or of diverting Canada's Mackenzie River so it flowed south into the U.S. plains rather than north to the Canadian tundra. Yet the great projects continue around the world. The province of Quebec has proposed and embarked on what they billed as the world's greatest hydroelectric project, damming their vast northern water resources, flooding millions of acres of wildlife habitat and native Cree territory, while producing hydropower for Montreal, and power that could be sold at premium to New York (Mitchell 1993). Cree objections to Québécois sovereignty come largely from concerns about what "national development" of this type would mean for their own sovereignty.

Poor sub-Saharan African nations wonder if water projects on the other great rivers of Africa could float their own national development, and big projects have been proposed for both the Zambezi and the Congo rivers, flowing east and west respectively from Africa's rainforest interior. India is building enormous dams for both irrigation and electrical power. The projects sometimes employ hundreds or even thousands of workers; they also displace tens of thousands who live along the river banks. The great western river banks of the United States were sparsely populated, at least at the time of the dam projects, but European and Asian dam projects often inundate scores of villages and towns, displacing millions. Dam projects in Poland buried dozens of long-time villages, their residents "transplanted" to drab government housing in bleak, hastily-planned relocation towns.

The greatest project of them all, with the greatest mass relocation, is being built on China's longtime lifeline, the Yangtze River, in a multistage operation known as Three Gorges. The World Bank and international lenders have backed out of the project, citing the environmental, financial, and social problems, but the Chinese government continues to press ahead, citing irrigation, flood control, and power production. They call Three Gorges "a glorious monument to progress," a new Great Wall that will announce to the world that China has become a truly great power—ironically just as many of the world's great powers are finally learning the lessons of Aswan and Hoover. Lost to the rising water at Three Gorges will be some of China's most spectacular scenery of towering canyon walls and raging rapids, habitat for endangered creatures such as the Chinese river dolphin, millennia-old archeological sites that hold clues to the origins of Chinese civilization, and the homes of two million people (Zich 1997). The people are already being relocated, also taken to drab government housing in bleak, hastily planned relocation towns. The greatest beneficiaries seem to be the export cities and zones to the east, and their growing production plants, who will have a huge new source of power, by some measures the equivalent of eighteen nuclear power plants. The price is the loss of some of the most distinctive elements of China's environment, history, and village life.

The Desert Next Door

Las Vegas is one of America's fastest growing cities. Sunshine and jobs, the magic combination of the Sunbelt, are in abundance, and many are eager to gamble their life chances on continued growth. New subdivisions sprawl in great arms from the commercial strips. The stucco-look houses are surrounded by bright green lawns, thanks to Hoover Dam and Lake Mead, and by stucco-look walls. Behind the walls is a startling sight—bright green turf immediately gives way to an unending expanse of stark, barren, brittle desert. A simple fence would never suffice, the wall is needed to keep the desert from drifting across the lots on windy days. This striking image is a microcosm of the satellite-view of the planet: well watered and walled oases, with the desert next door. Golfers, like American homeowners, love sunny days and green grass, and like homeowners, seem to see no contradiction in having these two elements perpetually side by side, the green fairways snaking through the sun-baked desert, with the sprinkler systems spitting reservoir water with a nightly hiss.

We are now facing the reality in that watering our private gardens and our favorite fairways, we are expanding the desert; in seeking greener pastures of all kinds we are leaving behind deserted, desertified wastes. The term "desertification" is fairly recent, but the realization of our human impact has been a long time coming; wrote Marquis, "What man calls civilization always results in deserts." One of the things that strikes students of Middle Eastern civilization is why the arc of land from the Mediterranean to the Euphrates is called "the fertile crescent." Visitors to Israel, veterans of the Gulf war, and anyone else who has been to the region knows it as the land of deserts—the only fertility is where Israeli irrigation schemes have watered the land. Was this change the caprice of nature, the result of an unfortunate slosh of El Niño, or was the weight of civilization too great for a fragile land? We do know that the sunny islands and highlands of Greece are so sunny only because of centuries of deforestation and over-grazing. The scrubland of rocks and goats was once lush Mediterranean evergreen forest. Athenians such as Plato and his amateur naturalist student Aristotle already noted then that the land of Olympus was being depleted and scoured by hungry empires and their hungry herds.

The Sahara desert has been expanding southward for centuries. Once North Africa was the granary of the Roman empire, and elephants and hippos roamed in its forests and rivers. Now the same region is an almost unbroken expanse of shifting, swirling, biting sand. How much of this change was due to natural climatic fluctuations and how much due to human overuse is not known, but the people who live on the desert's southern edge have no time for scientists to decide; they watch the sand dunes moving towards them daily like an army of relentless, thirsty giants. "The Sahara desert is expanding southward, engulfing degraded grasslands, at a rate of thirty miles (fifty kilometers) every year" (Hall and Scurlock 1991, 59). Entire villages are buried under the great dunes, while surviving villages scoop holes in the sand to attempt to plant millet.

The Sahel belt of scrub land cuts across Niger, Mali, Burkina Faso, Sudan, and into Ethiopia and Somalia, some of the world's poorest, most fragile, most drought- and famine-prone societies. With nothing but stripped trees and a few clumps of planted millet to hold down the earth, one stirring of El Niño in the Pacific can bring the dry winds that spell disaster. The sands of the Sahara seem insatiable, blowing across the vast expanse of north Africa, merging with great deserts in Saudi Arabia, and riding on global air currents to land in India, where the margin between flood and drought, fertility and desert, has always been precarious. It is a land where the fate of a billion people now hangs in the balance.

The growing global dust bowl has many sources. Irrigation demands have so depleted the Aral Sea, once one of the earth's greatest lakes, that it is now less than half its original size, its exposed salt flats and sand beds now blowing across central Asia. Among the groups analyzing the mysteries of the disappearing sea is the CIA in Kazakhstan. No longer worried about communist infiltrators, the agents now wonder about the infiltration of salt and sand, and whether environmental collapse will bring instability and revolt.

American farmers believing that "rain followed the plow" harrowed the fine, dry plains soil into loose dust that billowed in sky-blackening clouds for the dry decade of the 1930s, deepening the Great Depression. That dust bowl was subdued largely by deep-well irrigation. Flying east to west, the entry into the west is announced not by the St. Louis arch or similar symbols but by a change from squares to circles. At about the 100th parallel (roughly the point at which the Gulf of Mexico and its moist air meets the dry Mexican coast), the squares thin out into scattered green circles. This is not a change in geometric fashion, but a shift in farming strategy. In the moister east, much planting is done "fence row to fence row" with only the regularly spaced country roads dividing the land. Further west, great sprinkler arms draw water from a deep underground aquifer and spray the land as they pivot in giant circles. That multistate aquifer, the Ogallala, along with its neighbors, is being drained into a smaller, harder to reach pool all the time. If the wells can no longer reach the water, plains farmers may realize that they have not truly tamed the dust bowl but only watered it down. With perhaps as little as one-third of the continent's rich prairie topsoil still on the ground, we can ill afford another "great blow."

Farmland in the southern Americas is even more tenuous. Clear-cut rain forests in Central and South America provide a few years of planting or grazing, but the nutrient poor soil soon bakes in the sun to brick-hard pavement. Native shifting cultivation avoided this by only opening small areas and continually moving on. Under the demands of poverty and commercial markets, the land is now often used until nothing is left but a crumbling red clay whose dust silts the air and water. In Panama, the massive erosion from deforestation threatens to silt in the great canal. Once fully deforested the soil will no longer support forest, crop land, or pasture, and the rainfall, much of which is generated by evaporation from the forest itself, diminishes. The entire regional climate is altered, threatening yet more forest, and now many suspect that the global climate may be at stake.

Logging for global markets is a major culprit, clearing grazing land for beef, "jungleburgers," for the global fast-food market is a bigger culprit, but the biggest culprit of all is simply the strains placed on the land by displaced people. With no alternative, the poor in Mali climb into the last isolated trees to break off branches for firewood. Displaced settlers in Indonesia and Brazil stake tenuous claims on forested land, only to have to move on again once the land is depleted. The poor of Madagascar are climbing into the last forested highlands, depleting forest cover that supports some of the most unique creatures on the planet. Maybe nowhere is the scraping of the land so horrific as in poverty and violence-plagued Haiti. Flying over the divided island of Hispaniola, a traveler can note deforestation on the side of the island that is the Dominican Republic, much of it committed by U.S.-owned sugar companies. Yet no one need announce when you fly over the border into Haiti; the national boundary is scraped onto the landscape. The trees are gone, leaving nothing but gutted, eroded barren hills.

To save the world's remaining forests and to hold back the deserts, we must curb our appetites for exotic wood and "jungleburgers," but we must also address the needs of the poor and displaced. At the twilight of apartheid, South African Anglican Archbishop Desmond Tutu wrote:

The injustice and exploitation of apartheid have horrible ecological consequences. In our rural areas, pylons carry electric power all over the country, but not to the farms where Africans live. So they have to cut down trees for firewood, and that has encouraged soil erosion. Justice and ecology are linked indissolubly" (Quoted in Porritt 1991, 135).

People have lived on fragile land without disturbing its essential character. Hunter-gatherers such as the San people have harvested the thorn-crusted resources of the Kalahari for as long as anyone knows. A handful continue to do so even as they are engulfed in the regional and geopolitical battles that have rocked southern Africa. The Sahara region long supported oasis farmers and wide-ranging desert herders who had come to terms with the conditions imposed by a harsh land. Only as these patterns were disrupted by colonial and nationalistic powers did the system collapse. Even as the deserts encroach, hopeful strategies are stemming the tide in local experiments. Some of the Haitian hills are being reforested—with non-native trees admittedly—but fast growing trees whose commercial value may induce Haiti's poor to protect and cultivate them.

In the Sahel, local people are using community-managed windbreaks of hardy shrubs, hand-built stone walls to hold back the sand and shelter carefully situated drought-resistant plants, carefully terraced water-catching basins, small inexpensive pumps, and a new balance between livestock and farming. These have shown that the desert is not unstoppable and led Paul Harrison (1987) to proclaim the possible "greening of Africa."

Having deforested much of its highlands, Costa Rica now protects much of the remainder in national parks that have drawn a global stream of ecotourists (Budowski 1992). Even as cheap airfares now threaten much of the tropical coast land of the Indian ocean with tourist development and resulting deforestation (after all, what is a beach but a linear desert), the unique natural riches of lands such as Madagascar hold the promise of ecotourism dollars to preserve the remaining forest.

We stand at a crucial moment in the balance between forest and desert. Comeback stories are always inspiring, but some land will not come back. One of the great comebacks of all time is the reforestation of the eastern United States. The vast forest that stretched in a great green quilt from the Atlantic to the Mississippi was decimated by farmers and loggers. Only small, scattered pockets of "virgin timber" remain, but much of the land is again in forest cover. New parks and public forests, both state and national stand where recently almost treeless and depleted farmland could no longer remain productive and competitive. Exterminated wildlife is being reintroduced, and the East is "wilder" than it has been in one hundred years (McKibben 1995).

The change is so remarkable that some developing nations want to argue "You stripped your forests for economic progress and now that you are rich the forests return; we'll do the same." They are correct on the first count, but the second is a dangerous gamble. The eastern United States is being reforested in large measure because intensive grain farming has shifted westward onto the Great Plains where the soil was deeper, and once watered by the great aquifers, could produce more intensive and profitable harvests. And U.S. conservationists are able to reintroduce eliminated species only because the temperate soils can still support native tree species, and because the species lost found refuge in Canada and the Rockies, from which they can be transplanted. If the rain forest goes, the tropical soils may not recover. At the same time, instead of a few species widely distributed, tropical rain forests have many localized species that have no where to run and will simply be lost forever. The decisions to change the course of our desert-making civilizations must come quickly. The forests have fallen to the luxuries of global winners and the desperation of global losers, yet if the sands keep blowing we will all be ultimate losers. "What befalls the earth befalls all the sons of the earth."

The Road from Rio

A new global awareness by sons and daughters of the despoilers can still change the global course. A major effort to change that course occurred in spectacular but troubled Rio De Janeiro, Brazil in 1992 at the U.N. Conference on the Global Environment. Twenty years earlier, as the environmental movement first gained broad recognition, world leaders met in Stockholm to define a global agenda on the environment, especially looking at common air and water resources. Events since 1972—from the specter of Chernobyl to the debates about ozone depletion and global warming—brought a new urgency to the Rio conference. Environmental risks do not respect national boundaries, and in terms of the exchange of pollutants, toxins, and hazards the world is already a vast free trade zone.

The speech that drew the most attention at the conference—Al Gore called it the best—came not from a government official but from a twelve-year-old Canadian girl, Severn Suzuki:

You don't know how to fix holes in our ozone layer. You don't know how to bring salmon back up a dead stream. You don't know how to bring back an animal now extinct. And you can't bring back the forests that once grew where there is now a desert. If you don't know how to fix it, please stop breaking it! . . . I am only a child, yet I know we are all in this together and should act as one single world toward one single goal. At school, even in kindergarten, you teach us to behave in the world. You teach us not to fight with others, to work things out, to respect others, to clean up our mess, not to hurt other creatures, to share and not be greedy. Then why do you go out and do the things you tell us not to do? . . . I challenge you, please make your actions reflect your words (Rogers 1993, 106).

Gore contended that the world needed to be as concerned about the road from Rio as it was with the road to Rio. He outlined what he saw as U.S. priorities: energy efficiency, shifts to renewable resources, preservation of land and wildlife, and emissions reductions. Yet he resisted putting all the blame on any one country (presumably the United States) and contended:

Our governments can only do so much. It is up to the people of every nation to realize their connection to the Earth and to each other. To recognize the responsibility that comes with that connection to a global civilization and to the natural system that sustains it (Rogers 1993, 303).

The road from Rio is not likely to be a smooth one. What were once local problems have developed disturbing international dimensions, yet policy and enforcement has often not gone beyond the national level.

Air and water pollution have been with us at least since Hercules cleaned the Aegean stables with the help of a river, yet the magnitude has moved relentlessly to the global level. Cities endure the hazardous haze of urban air pollution, but these pollutants do not remain fixed over the urban center. Sulphur compounds re-mix in the atmosphere and wash down on remote mountain and forest regions. Ozone depletion in the upper atmosphere is most evident in a great hole over remote Antarctica, and the increase in UV (ultraviolet) radiation from global ozone depletion would most threaten people who spend time out of doors in distant mountain and desert regions, as well as sunbathing vacationers everywhere. The auto exhausts of U.S. cities and the deforestation of Brazil may all contribute to the accumulation of carbon dioxide that threatens to create global warming, affecting low-lying coasts and agricultural production around the world. Water pollutants seep across international boundaries and accumulate in the world's oceans.

We cannot know the full extent of some of the global risks: ozone depletion and global warming are still hotly debated. Yet we can see a pattern to guide our actions: assaults on the environment have both local and global ramifications, with the latter often a compounding of the former. The actions needed to prevent long-term global warming are exactly those that will have immediate local benefits: reducing fossil fuel consumption, seeking lower emissions and cleaner air, and preserving forests.

The past century and a half has seen a historical trend toward a greater conservation ethic. The creation of Yellowstone, the world's first national park, created a storm of controversy, yet this "national boondoggle" of the 1870s is now regarded as a national treasure. The "radical" conservation ideas of the past are part of today's conservative consensus. We can infer only that our children, in a more crowded and more strained world, can only be more not less environmentally conscious than we ourselves. Choices that may seem extreme now are likely to be lauded as visionary by a generation that will surely have more technological options but fewer undisturbed natural resources than we ourselves. Preservation of the environment is ultimately the conservation of choice: a future generation with too many forests and too few shopping malls will have no difficulty bulldozing a few more acres (if they have the fossil fuel to run the bulldozers), but a generation with too many malls and too few forests (a more likely scenario) cannot simply tear up the pavement and install old-growth redwoods nor old-growth mahogany. Said underwater visionary Jacques Cousteau, "Unless we do something radical today, we will be unable to do anything tomorrow" (Rogers 1993, 20).

The road from Rio does have a few signs of hope. At least in a few test hectares we have seen the taming of the desert and the greening of Africa, Haiti, and Central America. We have also seen the greening of politics. In Germany and across northern Europe the Green party has become a significant voice in national and international politics. A new environmental interest has reached Japan with the launching of its one-hundred-year environmental plan, New Earth

21, that begins with the elimination of ozone-depleting chemicals and moves on by staged plans for alternative energy sources.

The first faltering steps in what could become great strides in international environmental protection have been attempted. Worldwide commercial whaling has gone from the romance of Moby Dick to the scorn of the world, and fewer harpoons fly each year. Laws of the sea are still regularly debated and poorly enforced, but the first steps have been made in preventing the pillage of the land from moving off-shore, unchecked and unregulated. In an environmental peace dividend, the leaders of the Central American nations have moved from negotiations with rebels to negotiating among themselves to create natural corridors that span Central America, preserving a rich heritage that spills over the boundaries of small nations. Surely they were encouraged by the international attention, and financing, that has gone to Costa Rica for its fledgling but innovative conservation efforts.

National environmental movements have gone global: making contacts, trying new forms of agreements, and learning from mistakes, in ways that might form not only a truly global environmental movement but also a model for women's movements, labor movements, children's movements, and other social action that can no longer limit its efforts to national boundaries. One of the fastest growing conservation groups has been the World Wildlife Fund, focusing on international wildlife issues. All wildlife conservation groups, including those with long traditions, such as Audubon and the National Wildlife Federation, have widened the angle on their binoculars to encompass ecosystems and issues that span national boundaries. The Nature Conservancy has chapters that work on local development issues while the organization as whole increases its involvement in acquiring and preserving strategic corridors around the world. In Costa Rica they are working with local partners, most notably the indigenous population and black Caribbean villagers, to preserve a corridor from the tropical coast to the cloud forests of the interior (Wille 1995). Global connections are nothing new to migratory birds, and the vast spans of the migratory routes are helping to create interesting new partnerships: joint research by bird enthusiasts from Michigan and the Bahamas on birds that once frequented both places, and a "bird partnership" between a preserve in the Appalachians and a conservation area in Belize that protects 530 species of birds who move readily between the two locales without passports.

Embracing Diversity: Let a Thousand Potatoes Bud

In the natural world variation and diversity is the foundation of stability and sustainability. The most stable ecosystems are those that are the most diverse. The most reliable food regimes are based on a wide range of foods, and a wide variety of each. Unlike the image of being at the mercy of nature, hunter-gatherers have often been more resistant to the forces of drought, famine, and natural disaster than their peasant counterparts. As long as they had many foods they could adapt. With the great fields of a single grain, the world also faced its first great famines. Poor farmers in the Andes survived on hundreds of varieties of potatoes. When the poor Irish countryman became dependent on a single variety, the potential for famine was greatly increased. The hundreds of varieties of corn grown in the America's is diminishing to just a few used around the world, placing millions at risk should a blight target them. National monocropping has led to national disaster and famine, global monocropping could lead to global disaster and famine with no escape.

Nature stores its accumulated wisdom in DNA. To preserve this multitude of responses to environmental challenges we must work to preserve the full biodiversity of the tropical rainforest, of the coral reef, and of all other land and water environments rich in the diversity of species. We do well to preserve the genetic diversity in our own domesticated plants and animals, which stores the accumulated wisdom of intertwined human and natural responses to challenges.

Humanity, however, primarily stores its accumulated wisdom in culture. We do just as well to preserve the diversity of human cultural responses: in language, lifestyle, and survival knowledge. Any single cultural response, no matter how productive can fail and collapse just like any single food resource, no matter how productive, can fail. Mao Zedong proclaimed a welcome to a diversity of ideas and approaches in his phrase "let a thousand flowers bloom," an ideal often ignored in reality. We do well to take up the cry: let a thousand different flowers bloom in the forest and on the prairie, let a thousand different potatoes bud in the garden, let thousands of different cultures thrive and contribute their wisdom to the global sociosystem.

Economies of Detail

Global economics has taught us the importance of economies of scale. We must also relearn the importance of economies of detail, where time and space are on a human scale, and care can be taken to protect and preserve. E. F. Schumacher (1973) issued his famous cry for an alternative economics in *Small Is Beautiful*. Indeed, small is often beautiful except when applied to minds and vision. Small includes the mill pond instead of the towering dam. It includes the diverse family farm in place of miles of uninterrupted monocropping swept over by corporate owned and leveraged forty-ton tractors. Small-scale is not the answer to all environmental and human problems, but it can at times allow the diversity and the detail to preserve a measure of natural balance. The viability of small operations, however, is dependent on the availability of appropriate technology, appropriate financing, and appropriate public policy.

Factory farms with mass production and routinized workers has already dominated the poultry industry in the United States. Increasingly hog farming is becoming a factory operation: ten thousand or more hogs huddled together in great warehouses, fed on industrial by-products and corporate-grown grain, rivers of wastes poured into huge black lagoons. The results are increased yields but also the displacement of family farms and the towns they supported, the trampling and denuding of surrounding land, and the massive leaching of bacterial ooze into ground and surface water. Creative alternatives include inexpensive mobile hog housing that allows foraging on corn stalks and the dispersion of waste to replace chemical fertilizer. The same choice between massive economies of scale and human-scale economies of detail confronts us around the world. Coffee can be shade-grown under the canopy of sheltering rain forest or it can be mass produced with massive chemical protectors. Rubber can come from the rainforest or from monoculture plantations that replace the rainforest. Likewise, these products can be cultivated by drawing on local knowledge or the dictates of global agribusiness.

Grand scale schemes often displace many local communities and place those that remain at the mercy of fluctuating international markets. Diverse economies of detail draw on the expertise of local communities and have the flexibility to provide both products for export and for subsistence, and shift emphases with shifting market needs. One image of the promise of global production is ever greater economies of scale: one great American monoculture from the Mississippi to the Rockies consumed by a rotor-to-rotor line of huge harvesters from Texas to Saskatchewan, pulverized and packaged to feed the world and the Chicago Board of Trade. An alternate view is a world economy with enough diverse and far-flung linkages to support thousands of economies of detail, each honed to suit local environments and cultures, and to meet our human longing for variety.

In fact, we currently have both economies operating side by side. U.S. petroleum engineers fly Mexicana airlines to off-shore oil fields, sipping Azteca Gold coffee, organically shade-grown by campesinos too poor to use chemicals. We know the oil fields cannot last and must soon be replaced by more sustainable energy sources. Whether human and natural diversity can endure will be decided largely in the next decade. Many endangered species, and many endangered livelihoods, are held in the balance.

A Community Garden

Community gardens, some official and some unofficial, have sprouted in a number of U.S. cities. Residents come together and turn vacant lots that invite dumping and drug dealing into a place of flowers and play structures that invite walking and chatting while watching children. Sometimes they become vegetable patches, bringing a bit of the countryside into the lives of urban dwellings, along with fresh, organic produce. Often the camaraderie of working together and reestablishing a sense of community and neighborhood is as important as the food. Still it is more than a "block party," for there is hard work and a feeling of accomplishment at a plot of ground transformed and reclaimed.

In one such community garden in Seattle, the urban farmers are refugees from Laos, Vietnam, Cambodia, and Somalia, along with American-born blacks, Latinos, Asian-Americans, European-Americans, and descendants of the Puget Sound tribes. Somehow amidst the whirl of different languages, cultures, and gardening styles is created a bountiful collection of gardens that transforms the feel of the neighborhood. People come together to laugh at differences and find new commonalities. And they do a lot of work. Some new crops are tried, new friendships created, and probably some very interesting recipes emerge from the chilies, watercress, asparagus, and collard greens. One resident says in halting yet eloquent English, "This is how it should be, we are working together to create a thing of beauty. People can understand that, they respect that."

In this intriguing microcosm I find an appealing vision of the global encounters that could be: the world's cultural diversity leaving behind a global tangle of violence to tend common ground. The gardeners are nurturing something beautiful for their neighborhood and their children, a common goal and bond that brings them together. I'm sure they argue about when to plant and how much to water but their common care for common ground has given them a common purpose. The greatest potential for worldwide environmental consciousness would be if tending the planet and reclaiming its beauty became our common ground, with soil rich enough to provide a bit for everyone, and rich enough to nourish a halting but fruitful dialog about our common future.

Common Ground
Scott Sernau

Context matters.
Location is everything.
Is it not better to have a pelapa hut in paradise
Than a mansion in hell?
Could we ever get the walls,
Set the central air,
High enough?
Isn't it better to embrace than to cling?
Better to tend than to defend?

"Who is my neighbor?"
A lawyer asked a preacher.
"The one to whom you can show kindness,"
Was the only answer.
"What is my neighborhood?"
We now ask.
"Where you can show kindness"
Can be the only response.
Cain's callous, "Am I my brother's keeper?"
Can only be answered with a curse.

Set before us is the way of life and of death.
We can create deserts to water our private gardens
Or we can embrace in the rain
And meet by the riverside,
Tending common ground.
Come to the water,
Let's choose life.
Together.

The Global Century

We have become accustomed to thinking of the global system as an empire with a single core. The first century was the undisputed Roman Century, at least for the Mediterranean world. The roughly one hundred years between the defeat of Napoleon at Waterloo and the beginning of the First World War was the British Century, when the sun never set on the British Empire. Observers have tried to describe a parallel "American Century" although no one can agree on its beginning or end. The era of clear American dominance really begins with the end of World War II. While Americans cheered the victory of democracy, defeated Nazi leaders only saw the collapse of German hegemony in favor of American hegemony. They believed the United States had made a deal with the devil (Soviet Russia) in order to gain a period of unquestioned dominance of American capital. Certainly the postwar period was heavily dominated by both U.S. military and economic presence. By the endless recession of the 1970s, critics were declaring the end of the American Century (a very brief "century in retrospect). As Mark Twain had noted about himself, the news of the demise of the United States was greatly exaggerated.

In pure economic terms, the United States has worked the world's largest economy since the beginning of the twentieth century, and is by far the largest single economy entering the twenty-first century. In old terms, we are still in the American Century. Yet there is a growing realization that the old terms no longer apply. Is the United States really a "single economy" anymore, or simply some political parameters placed around a global economy? Realization that the brief period of absolute U.S. dominance is ending has led to other proposals, such as the "Pacific Century," dominated by Japan, or China perhaps, or maybe by a vigorous Pacific trade between the United States and Asia that replaces the dominance of the North American and European transatlantic trade. Yet Europe is hardly an irrelevant backwater: while no one seems sure what NATO is supposed to do, everyone wants to join it, and the Atlantic is as strategic as ever. These failed attempts at labeling seem to make only two things clear: in our ever-changing world trying to talk in terms of century-long continuities is foolish, and the emerging world does not answer to a single power center but is truly multicentric.

The sparkle of the Pacific trade has been dimmed by Asian economic problems, causing fickle pundits to look elsewhere. South Africa, after all, is no longer a boycotted pariah, encompassing one of Africa's and the world's larger economies, and certainly with one of the richest resource bases. Then there is India, long bemoaned, but at this instant looking a bit like the patient tortoise still moving ahead in contrast to East Asian "hares" now gasping after a fast start. Maybe we should plan for an "Indian Ocean Century" with a vigorous trade between Durban and Mumbai (formerly Bombay), with a 300-million-person middle class managing manufacturing in Mauritius and vacationing in the Seychelles, echoing a vibrant trade that once flourished before the coming of the Portuguese galleons.

A more sober assessment may be to accept the twenty-first century as the "Global Century" in which a multitude of cores compete, with fortunes and stock markets rising and falling in successive waves that circle the planet in great currents. Both power and opportunity have become truly global and will not be bound by territorial constraints. The Global Century will not, cannot, be dominated by a single geographic power center. The old power centers will not disappear but endure only by becoming increasingly multinational, multiracial and mulicultural themselves.

The seventy-fifth anniversary of *Time Magazine* was celebrated in grand style by the multinational Time Warner Corporation in Radio City Music Hall. As reported by a French magazine (*Paris Match*, March 19, 1998), the event included President Bill Clinton joking with actors Tom Cruise and Edward James Olmos, Microsoft CEO Bill Gates chatting with a bejeweled Raquel Welch, billionaire Donald Trump, fighter Muhammad Ali, director Steven Spielberg, former Soviet leader Mikhail Gorbachev joking with actress Sophia Loren, astronaut and senator John Glenn, German model Claudia Schiffer with magician David

Copperfield, Olympic skater Nancy Kerrigan, and U.N. Secretary-General Kofi Annan. What this assemblage could possibly have in common is only that they now share the global stage.

Whether the Global Century will be dominated by a global power elite who preside over unprecedented global pillage, or whether it will be a village democracy of many voices in a network of interwoven opportunities and responsibilities is still being decided. It is decided at global conferences, in multinational board rooms, by the two billion consumers who have discretionary income, and by the actions of transnational social movements. This is a good time to live if you love high drama, rapid scene changes, and mounting suspense.

Our interconnected world is flourishing with opportunities: cultures to explore, technology to harness, opportunities for creative and meaningful work, new possibilities for richer and more diverse relationships, fascinating new encounters between city and countryside, and a new awareness of the bounty of the natural world. It is also a world dominated by enormous concentrations of power—social, political, economic, and technical—and great numbers of excluded, exploited, displaced, and degraded people. Our task as global citizens is to use the power we have to step into the void between these extremes and build bridges of opportunity.

Somewhere amidst the bloody empire building of the ancient Middle East; amidst colossal power struggles between Egypt, Assyria, and Babylon, the mounting tyranny of lesser kings who sought to imitate the splendor of the emperors, the loss of land to absentee owners, the huge displacement of refugees and exiles, and the unending greed and turmoil that was turning the land to desert—a few voices offered an alternate vision. One such vision was recorded in the book of Isaiah:

> If you do away with the yoke of oppression,
> with the pointing finger and malicious talk,
> and if you spend yourselves in behalf of the hungry
> and satisfy the needs of the oppressed,
> then your light will rise in the darkness,
> and your night will become like the noonday.
> The Lord will guide you always;
> He will satisfy your needs in a sun-scorched land
> and will strengthen your frame.
> You will be like a well-watered garden,
> like a spring whose waters never fail.
> Your people will rebuild the ancient ruins
> and will raise up the age-old foundations;

you will be called Repairer of Broken Walls,
Restorer of Streets with Dwellings.
(Isaiah 58:9b–12, *New International Version*)

An evermore interconnected planet has brought enormous concentrations of power in the hands of a few. It has also opened up new avenues of opportunity. The same technology that brings billions to corporate giants like Microsoft and America Online is used by liberation movements to make contacts that elude government censors and to tell their story to the world. While global interconnections are by no means new, they are expanding exponentially and reaching beyond elites to everyday lives. We have seen the expanded globalization of the economy. We have also seen the globalization of culture as global media brings us in one another's homes and lives. Yet we have also seen the globalization of social movements: the beginnings of global women's networks, global environmental organizations, and global labor movements. While a few might like to buy it all, the planet has truly become common ground. Global economics have enriched some while impoverishing many others, but increased global understanding can enrich the minds and embolden the spirits of many. As people come together around common issues of concern, this new global awareness and understanding could serve to empower us all. Time is short since change is fast, but the final chapter is still ours to write.

Bibliography

Ashford, Lori S. 1995. "New Perspectives on Population: Lessons from Cairo." *Population Bulletin*. March.

Applebaum, Richard P. and William J. Chambliss. 1996. *Sociology*. New York: Longman.

Asante, Molefi Kete. 1987. *The Afrocentric Idea*. Philadelphia: Temple University Press.

Astrachan, Anthony. 1989. "Men and the New Economy." *Mr. Magazine*.

Baker, P. 1974. *Urbanization and Political Change*. Berkeley: University of California Press.

Barber, Benjamin. 1992. "Jihad Vs. McWorld." *Atlantic*. March.

———. 1995. *Jihad Vs. McWorld*. New York: Times Books.

Barnet, Richard J. and John Cavanagh. 1994. *Global Dreams: Imperial Corporations and the New World Order*. New York: Simon and Schuster.

Barth, Frederick. 1969. *Ethnic Groups and Boundaries*. Boston: Little, Brown.

Beck, Roy. 1994. "The Ordeal of Immigration in Wausau." *The Atlantic Monthly*. April.

Bell, Daniel. 1973. *The Coming of Post-Industrial Society*. New York: Basic Books.

Berger, Peter. 1974. *Pyramids of Sacrifice*. New York: Basic Books.

Bernal, Martin. 1987. *Black Athena*. New Brunswick, N.J.: Rutgers University Press.

Bernard, Jesse. 1981. "The Good Provider Role: Its Rise and Fall." *American Psychologist*. 36:1–12. January.

Bernstein, Nell. 1995. "Goin' Gangsta, Choosin' Cholita." *Utne Reader*. March/April.

Bhalla, A. S. and Frederic Lapeyre. 1999. *Poverty and Exclusion in a Global World*. London: Macmillan Press Ltd.

Blauner, Robert. 1972. *Racial Oppression in America*. New York: Harper.

Bluestone, Barry and Bennett Harrison. 1982. *The Deindustrialization of America*. New York: Basic Books.

Bolles, A. Lynn. 1992. "Common Ground of Creativity." *Cultural Survival Quarterly*. Winter.

Bonacich, Edna. 1972. "A Theory of Ethnic Antagonism: The Split Labor Market." *American Sociological Review* 37:547–59.

———. 1973. "A Theory of Middleman Minorities." *American Sociological Review* 38:583–94.

Bordewich, Fergus. 1996. *Killing the White Man's Indian*. New York: Doubleday.

Bibliography

Braudel, Fernand. 1984. *The Perspective of the World*. New York: Harper and Row.

Breeden, Stanley. 1988. "The First Australians." *National Geographic*. February.

Brown, E. M. 2000. "Learning to Love the IMF." *New York Times*. April 18.

Brown, Lester R., Nicholas Lenssen, and Hal Kane. 1995. *Vital Signs*. New York: Worldwatch Institute/Norton.

Brown, Lester R., et al. 1999. *State of the World 1999*. New York: Norton.

Budowski, Tamara. 1992. "Ecotourism Costa Rican Style." In Valerie Barzetti and Yanina Rovinski, eds., *Toward a Green Central America*. West Hartford, Conn.: Kumarian Press.

Burowoy, Michael. 1979. *Manufacturing Consent: Changes in the Labor Process Under Monopoly Capitalism*. Chicago: University of Chicago.

Cardoso, F. H. 1977. *Latin America: Styles of Development and Their Limits*. Occasional Papers Series, no. 25. New York: New York University.

——— and E. Falletto. 1979. *Dependency and Development in Latin America*. Berkeley: University of California Press.

Cassidy, John. 1997. "The Return of Karl Marx." *The New Yorker*. Oct. 20 and 27.

Chance, Norman A. 1997. "The Inupiat Eskimo and Arctic Alaska." *General Anthropology*. Spring.

Chartrand, Luc. 1991. "A New Solidarity Among Native Peoples." *World Press Review*. August.

Chase-Dunn, Christopher, Yukio Kawano, and Benjamin D. Brewer. 2000. "Trade Globalization Since 1795: Waves of Integration in the World-System." *American Sociological Review*. 65:77–95.

Clinton, Hillary Rodham. 1995. *Remarks for United Nations Fourth World Conference on Women*. New York: United Nations.

———. 1996. *It Takes a Village*. New York: Simon and Schuster.

Constable, Nicole. 1997. *Maid to Order in Hong Kong: Stories of Filipina Workers*. Ithaca, N.Y.: Cornell.

Coontz, Stephanie. 1992. *The Way We Never Were: American Families and the Nostalgia Trap*. New York: Basic Books.

Cox, Harvey. 1965. *The Secular City*. New York: Macmillan.

Dahlburg, John-Thor. 1997. "Saving the World's Children: One Little Patient At a Time." *World Vision*. June–July.

Dannen, Fredric. 1997. "Partners in Crime." *The New Republic*. July 14 and 21.

Davis, Diane E. 1994. *Urban Leviathan: Mexico City in the Twentieth Century*. Philadelphia: Temple University Press.

Denison, Edward F. 1965. "Education and Economic Productivity." In S. Harris, ed., *Education and Public Policy*. Berkeley: McCutchen.

Diamond, Jared. 1993. "Speaking with a Single Tongue." *Discover*. February.

———. 1997. *Guns, Germs, and Steel*. New York: Norton.

Duffy, Bruce. 1997. "Looking for Stinger." *Life*. September.

Early, Gerald. 1995. "Understanding Afrocentrism." *Civilization*. July/August.

Eck, Diana. 1996. "Neighboring Faiths." *Harvard Magazine*. September/October.

Edwards, Mike. 1997. "China's Gold Coast." *National Geographic*. March

Ehrenreich, Barbara and Annette Fuentes. 1981. "Life on the Global Assembly Line." *MS Magazine*. January.

Ehrlich, Paul. 1968. *The Population Bomb*. New York: Ballentine Books.

Fanon, Franz. 1961. *The Wretched of the Earth*. New York: Grove Press.

Fernandez-Kelly, Patricia. 1983. *For We Are Sold, I and My People: Women and Industry in Mexico's Frontier*. Albany, N.Y.: SUNY.

Fisher, H. T. and M. H. Fisher. 1966. *Life in Mexico: The Letters of Fanny Calderon de la Barca*. New York: Doubleday.

Fitchen, Janet. 1991. *Endangered Spaces, Enduring Places*. Boulder, Colo.: Westview Press.

Frank, Andre Gunder. 1967. *Capitalism and Development in Latin America*. New York: Monthly Review Press.

——— and Barry K. Gills. 1993. *The World System: Five Hundred Years or Five Thousand?* London: Routledge.

Frank, Robert and Philip Cook. 1995. *The Winner-Take-All Society*. New York: Free Press.

Furstenberg, Jr., Frank F. 1988. "Good Dads — Bad Dads: Two Faces of Fatherhood." In Andrew Cherlin, *The Changing American Family*. Urban Institute.

Galeano, Eduardo. 1973. *Open Veins of Latin America: Five Centuries of the Pillage of a Continent*. New York: Monthly Review Press.

Gans, Herbert J. 1962. *The Urban Villagers*. New York: Free Press.

Gardels, N. and M. Berlin Snell. 1989. "Breathing Fecal Dust in Mexico City." *Los Angeles Times Book Review*. April 23.

Garreau, Joel. 1991. *Edge City*. New York: Doubleday.

Garson, Barbara. 1988. *The Electronic Sweatshop*. New York: Simon and Schuster.

George, Susan. 1990. *Ill Fares the Land*. New York: Penguin.

Gilmore, David. 1990. "Manhood." *Natural History*. June.

Gmelch, George. 1993. "Lessons from the Field." In James P. Spradley and David W. McCurdy, eds. *Conformity and Conflict*. Boston: Allyn and Bacon.

Goertzel, Ted. 1997. "President Fernando Cardoso Reflects on Brazil and Sociology." *Footnotes*. American Sociological Association. November.

Gonzales de Casanova, Pablo. 1965. *Democracy in Mexico*. Oxford: Oxford University Press.

Gottdiener, Mark. 1994. *The New Urban Sociology*. New York: McGraw-Hill.

Gray, Lorraine. 1986. *The Global Assembly Line*. New York: New Day Films.

Grossfeld, Stan. 1997. "A River Runs Dry; a People Wither." *Boston Globe*. September 21.

Gupta, Avijit. 1988. *Ecology and Development in the Third World*. London: Routledge.

Hackel, Joyce. 1996. "Kenya School Gives Girls Hope." *Christian Science Monitor*. April 3.

Hacker, Andrew. 1992. *Two Nations*. New York: Ballantine.

Hall, David and Jonathan Scurlock. 1991. "Defending the Open Range." In Jonathan Porrit, ed., *Save the Earth*. London: Dorling Kindersley.

Harrington, Michael and Mark Levinson. 1985. "The Perils of a Dual Economy." *Dissent* 32:417–26.

Bibliography

Harris, Marvin. 1989. *Our Kind*. New York: HarperCollins.

Harrison, Bennett and Barry Bluestone. 1988. *The Great U-Turn: Corporate Restructuring and the Polarizing of America*. New York: Basic Books.

Harrison, Paul. 1984. *Inside the Third World*. New York: Penguin Books.

———. 1987. *The Greening of Africa*. Penguin Books.

Harvey, David L. 1993. *Potter Addition*. New York: de Gruyter.

Hechter, Michael. 1975. *Internal Colonialism*. Berkeley: University of California Press.

Hochschild, Arlie with Anne Machung. 1989. *The Second Shift: Working Parents and the Revolution at Home*. New York: Penguin.

Horowitz, Donald. 1975. *Ethnic Groups in Conflict*. Berkeley: University of California Press.

Hoselitz, Bert. 1957. "Economic Growth and Development: Non-Economic Factors in Economic Development." *American Economic Review* 47:28–41.

Huntington, Samuel. 1996. *The Clash of Civilizations and the Remaking of World Order*. New York: Simon and Schuster.

Inkeles, Alex and David Smith. 1974. *Becoming Modern: Individual Change in Six Developing Countries*. Cambridge: Harvard University Press.

Isbister, John. 1998. *Promises Not Kept: The Betrayal of Social Change in the Third World*. West Hartford, Conn.: Kumarian Press.

Iyer, Pico. 1997a. "Nowhere Man: Confessions of a Perpetual Foreigner." *Prospect*. February.

———. 1997b. *Tropical Classical*. New York: Knopf.

Jencks, Christopher. 1972. *Inequality*. New York: Basic Books.

Jacobs, Jane. 1970. *The Economy of Cities*. New York: Vintage.

———. 1984. *Cities and the Wealth of Nations*. New York: Random House.

Jacobson, David. 1997. "New Frontiers: Territory, Social Spaces, and the State." *Sociological Forum* 12:121–33.

John, Sue Lockett. 1997. "Soldier Boys." *World Vision*. October/November.

Jones, Christine W. and Miguel A. Kiguel. 1993. *Adjustment in Africa*. Washington, D.C.: World Bank.

Kabagarama, Daisy. 1997. *Breaking the Ice*. Boston: Allyn and Bacon.

Kane, Joe. 1995. *Savages*. New York: Knopf.

Kanter, Rosabeth Moss. 1977. *Men and Women of the Corporation*. New York: Basic Books.

Kohler, Gernot. 1978. "Global Apartheid." *World Order Models Project, Paper 7*. New York: Institute for World Order.

Koltyk, Jo Ann. 1998. *New Pioneers in the Heartland*. Boston: Allyn and Bacon.

Kotlowitz, Alex. 1991. *There Are No Children Here*. New York: Doubleday.

Kozol, Jonathan. 1991. *Savage Inequalities*. New York: Crown.

———. 1995. *Amazing Grace*. New York: Crown.

Kristof, Nicholas D. 1996. "Who Needs Love? In Japan, Many Couples Don't." *New York Times*. February 11.

Larmer, Brook. 1996. "The Barrel Children." *Newsweek*. February 19.

Lenin, V. I. 1948. *Imperialism: The Highest Stage of Capitalism*. London: Lawrence and

Wishart.

Lenski, Gerhard. 1966. *Power and Privilege: A Theory of Stratification*. New York: McGraw-Hill.

Levine, Carlisle J. "Community Museums as a Cultural and Economic Resource." *Grassroots Development* 20:10–13.

Lewis, Oscar 1961. *Children of Sanchez*. New York: Random House.

———. 1968. "The Culture of Poverty". In Daniel Patrick Moynihan, ed., *On Understanding Poverty*. New York: Basic Books.

Lipsitz, George. 1994. *Dangerous Crossroads: Popular Music, Post-modernism and the Poetics of Place*. London: Verso.

Logan, John R. and Harvey L. Molotch. 1987. *Urban Fortunes: The Political Economy of Place*. Berkeley: University of California Press.

Lomnitz, Larissa Adler. 1977. *Networks and Marginality: Life in a Mexican Shantytown*. New York: Academic Press.

Lubiano, Wahneema. 1997. *The House that Race Built*. New York: Pantheon.

Lukas, J. Anthony. 1985. *Common Ground*. New York: Knopf.

Macionis, John. 1997. *Sociology*. Sixth Edition. New Jersey: Prentice Hall.

MacLeod, Jay. 1995. *Ain't No Makin' It*. Boulder, Colo.: Westview.

Mandela, Nelson. 1995. *Long Walk to Freedom*. Boston: Little, Brown.

Marcos, Sub-Commander. 1994. "A Tourist Guide to Chiapas." *Monthly Review*. 46:8–18 (May).

Massey, Douglas and Nancy Denton. 1993. *American Apartheid*. Cambridge: Harvard University Press.

McKibben, Bill. 1995. "An Explosion of Green." *Atlantic Monthly*. April.

McLaren, Deborah. 1997. *Rethinking Tourism and Ecotravel*. West Hartford, Conn.: Kumarian Press.

McLellan, David. 1977. *Karl Marx: Selected Writings*. Oxford: Oxford Press.

McMichael, Philip. 2000. *Development and Social Change*. Thousand Oaks, Calif.: Pine Forge.

McNeill, William. 1982. *The Pursuit of Power*. Chicago: University of Chicago Press.

Medoff, Peter and Holly Sklar. 1994. *Streets of Hope: The Fall and Rise of an Urban Neighborhood*. Boston: South End Press.

Michels, Robert. 1967. *Political Parties*. Originally published 1911. New York: Free Press.

Mills, C. Wright. 1956. *The Power Elite*. New York: Oxford.

———. 1959. *The Sociological Imagination*. New York: Oxford.

Mitchell, John. G. 1993. "James Bay: Where Two Worlds Collide." *National Geographic*. November.

Mitchell, Maureen Hays. 1989. "Taking to the Streets." *Grassroots Development*. 13/1:25–30.

Mitter, Sara. S. 1991. *Dharmas Daughters*. New Brunswick, N.J.: Rutgers.

Morales, Auroa Levins. 1989. "Child of the Americas." *Getting Home Alive*. Ithaca, N.Y.: Firebrand.

Myrdal, Gunnar. 1944. *An American Dilemma*. New York: Harper.

Nee, Victor. 1996. "The Emergence of a Market Society: Changing Mechanisms of Stratification in China. *American Journal of Sociology*. 101: 908–49.

Nee, Victor, Jimy Sanders, and Scott Sernau. 1994. "Job Transitions in an Immigrant Metropolis: Ethnic Boundaries and Mixed Economy." *American Sociological Review*. 59:849–72 (December).

Nesbitt, John. 1982. *Megatrends*. New York: Warner.

Newman, Katherine S. 1988. *Falling from Grace*. New York: Free Press.

North, Douglass. 1981. *Structure and Change in Economic History*. New York: Norton.

———. 1990. *Institutions, Institutional Change and Economic Performance*. Cambridge: Cambridge University Press.

Oldenburg, Ray. 1997. *The Great Good Place*. Second Edition. New York: Marlowe.

Olson, Christine. 1992. "Where Eskimo Spirit Soars." *Parenting*. December/January.

Olzak, Susan. 1998. "Ethnic Protest in Core and Periphery States." *Ethnic and Racial Studies* 21:187–217.

Olzak, Susan and Joanne Nagel. 1986. *Competitive Ethnic Relations*. New York: Academic Press.

Palen, J, John. 1997. *The Urban World*. New York: McGraw-Hill.

Parenti, Michael. 1995. *Democracy for the Few*, Sixth Edition. New York: St Martin's.

Parfit, Michael. 1997. "A Dream Called Nunavut." *National Geographic*. September.

Parillo, Vincent N. 2000. *Strangers to These Shores*. Boston: Allyn and Bacon.

Park, Robert. 1914. "Racial Assimilation in Secondary Groups." *Publications of the American Sociological Society* 8:66–72.

——— and Ernest Burgess. 1921. *Introduction to the Science of Sociology*. Chicago: University of Chicago.

Parkin, Frank. 1979. *Marxism and Class Theory: A Bourgeois Critique*. New York: Columbia University Press.

Pena, Devon. 1997. *The Terror of the Machine*. Austin: University of Texas.

Piore, Michael and Charles Sabel. 1984. *The Second Industrial Divide*. New York: Basic Books.

Porrit, Jonathan. 1991. *Save the Earth*. London: Dorling Kindersley.

Prebisch, Raul. 1950. *The Economic Development of Latin America and Its Principle Problems*. New York: United Nations.

Reid, T. R.. 1997. "Malaysia: Rising Star." *National Geographic*. August.

Reiman, Jeffrey. 1998. *The Rich Get Richer and the Poor Get Prison*, Fifth Edition. Boston: Allyn and Bacon.

Ritzer, George. 2000. *The McDonaldization of Society*, New Century Edition. Thousand Oaks, Calif.: Pine Forge.

Robinson, Gabrielle and Mike Keen. 1997. "Café Kultur: The Coffeehouses of Vienna." *Contemporary Review*. July.

Rodgers, Adam. 1993. *The Earth Summit: A Planetary Reckoning*. Los Angeles: Global View Press.

Rodriquez, Richard. 1981. *Hunger of Memory*. Boston: Godine.

———. 1991. "La Raza Cosmica." *New Perspectives Quarterly*. Winter.

———. 1991. "Closed Doors." *Los Angeles Times*. August 15.

Roodman, David Malin. 1995. "Vital Signs: Television Continues to Spread." *World*

Watch (May–June).

Rosen, Bernard. 1982. *The Industrial Connection.* New York: Aldine.

Rostow, W. W. 1960. *The Stages of Economic Growth: A Non-Communist Manifesto.* Cambridge: Cambridge University Press.

Rourke, John. 1997. *International Politics on the World Stage.* Sixth Edition. New York: McGraw Hill.

Rubin, Beth A. 1996. *Shifts in the Social Contract.* Thousand Oaks, Calif.: Pine Forge.

Rubin, Lillian B. 1976. *Worlds of Pain.* New York: Basic Books.

———. 1994. *Families on the Fault Line.* New York: HarperCollins.

Rudolph, Susanne Hoeber and Lloyd I. Rudolph. 1993. "Modern Hate." *New Republic.* March 23.

Samater, Ibrahim M. 1984. "From Growth to Basic Needs: The Evolution of Development Theory." *Monthly Review* 36:1–13.

Sanders, Jimy and Victor Nee. 1987. "Limits of Ethnic Solidarity in the Enclave Economy." *American Sociological Review.* 52:745–73.

Scarr, Sandra, Deborah Phillips, and Kathleen McCartney. 1989. "Working Mothers and Their Families." *American Psychologist* 44; 11:1402–09.

Schanberg, Sydney H. 1996. "Six Cents an Hour." *Life.* June.

Schumacher, E. F. 1973. *Small is Beautiful: Economics As If People Mattered.* New York: Harper and Row.

Schumpeter, Joseph. 1949. *Change and the Entrepreneur.* Cambridge, Mass.: Harvard University Press.

Scott, Gavin. 1993. "I Can't Cry Anymore." *Time.* February 22.

Seiple, Robert. 1998. "Female He Created Them." *World Vision.* April-May.

Sernau, Scott. 1994. *Economies of Exclusion: Underclass Poverty and Labor Market Change in Mexico.* Westport, Conn.: Praeger.

———. 1996. "Economies of Exclusion: Economic Change and the Global Underclass." *Journal of Developing Societies* Vol. XII, 1:38–51.

———. 1997. *Critical Choices: Applying Sociological Insight.* Los Angeles: Roxbury.

Sharp, Lauriston. 1952. "Steel Axes for Stone-Age Australians." *Human Organization* 11:17–22.

Sidel, Ruth. 1996. *Keeping Women and Children Last.* New York: Penguin.

Simons, Marlise. 1990. "The Amazon's Savvy Indians." *New York Times Magazine.* February 26.

Sivard, Ruth Leger. 1997. *World Military and Social Expenditures.* Washington, D.C.: World Priorities.

Skolnick, Jerome and Arlene Skolnick. 1999. *Family in Transition.* New York: Longman.

Slater, Philip. 1970. *The Pursuit of Loneliness.* Boston: Beacon Press.

Smith, Anthony. 1981. *The Ethnic Revival in the Modern World.* Cambridge: Cambridge University Press.

Sowell, Thomas. 1993. "Middleman Minorities." *American Enterprise.* May/June.

Stack, Carol. 1974. *All Our Kin.* New York: Harper and Row.

Stark, Peter. 1997. "The Old North Trail." *Smithsonian.* July, 54–66.

Stepwick, Alex. 1998. *Pride Against Prejudice: Haitians in the United States.* Boston:

Bibliography

Allyn and Bacon.

Streeten, Paul. 1977. "The Distinctive Features of a Basic Needs Approach to Development." *International Development Review* 19:8–16.

Swartz, John and Thomas Volgy. 1992. *The Forgotten Americans*. New York: Norton.

Swerdlow, Joel. 1995. " Information Revolution." *National Geographic*. October.

Takaki, Ronald. 1993. *A Different Mirror*. Boston: Little, Brown.

Toffler, Alex. 1980. *The Third Wave*. New York: Bantam.

Toennies, Ferdinand. 1988 [1887]. *Community and Society (Gemeinschaft und Gesellschaft)*. New Brunswick, N.J.: Transaction.

United Nations. 1995. "Social Development Summit Hears Calls for New International Ethic." www.un.org/unconfs. Posted March 5.

UNHCR. 1997. *The State of the World's Refugees*. Geneva: United Nations.

Urreas, Luis Alberto. 1996. *By the Lake of Sleeping Children*. New York: Doubleday.

U.S. Bureau of the Census. 1995. *Current Population Reports*. Washington, D.C.: Government Printing Office.

Vasquez, J. M. 1983. "Mexico City—Strangling on Growth." *Los Angeles Times*. Sept. 15.

Veblen, Thorstein. 1912. *The Theory of the Leisure Class*. New York: Macmillan.

Vergara, Camilo Jose. 1995. *The New American Ghetto*. New Brunswick, N.J.: Rutgers University Press.

Waldinger, Roger D. 1986. *Through the Eye of the Needle: Immigrants and Enterprise in New York's Garment Trades*. New York: New York University Press.

Wallerstein, Immanuel. 1974. *The Modern World System*. New York: Academic Press.

Waters, Mary. 1990. *Ethnic Options*. Berkeley: University of California.

Weatherford, Jack McIver. 1988. *Indian Givers*. New York: Fawcett Columbine.

———. 1994. *Savages and Civilization*. New York: Fawcett Columbine.

Weber, Max. 1979. *Economy and Society*. Originally published 1922. 2 vols. Berkeley: University of California Press.

Weiner, Myron. 1966. *Modernization: The Dynamics of Growth*. New York: Basic Books,

West, Cornell. 1993. *Race Matters*. Boston: Beacon Press.

———. 1997. "Afterword." In Wahneema Lubiano, ed., *The House That Race Built*. New York: Pantheon.

Whyte, Jr., William H. 1956. *The Organization Man*. New York: Simon and Schuster.

Wille, Chris. 1995. "The Costa Rican Connection." *Nature Conservancy*. March/April.

Wilson, Kenneth and Alejandro Portes. 1980. "Immigrant Enclaves: An Analysis of the Labor Market Experiences of Cubans in Miami." *American Journal of Sociology* 86:295–319.

Wilson, William Julius. 1978. *The Declining Significance of Race*. Chicago: University of Chicago Press.

———. 1987. *The Truly Disadvantaged: The Inner City, the Underclass, and Public Policy*. Chicago: University of Chicago Press.

———. 1996. *When Work Disappears*. New York: Knopf.

World Bank. 1995, 1997. *World Development Report*. Oxford: Oxford University Press.

Zich, Arthur. 1997. "China's Three Gorges: Before the Flood." *National Geographic*. September.

Index

Index

Index

Index

MONICA CASTILLO

SCOTT SERNAU is associate professor of sociology at the University of Indiana South Bend. He received his doctorate in sociology with an emphasis in international development from Cornell University. He teaches courses on social inequality, family, race and ethnic relations, and urban society as well as a senior seminar on "International Inequalities and Development." He has also served as resident director of the Indiana University Summer in Mexico Program: Language, Culture and Society. His previous books include *Economies of Exclusion: Underclass Poverty and Labor Market Change in Mexico* and *Critical Choices: Applying Sociological Insight.*